The Affect Theory of Silvan Tomkins for Psychoanalysis and Psychotherapy

The Affect Theory of Silvan Tomkins for Psychoanalysis and Psychotherapy explores central issues in current clinical work, using the theories put forward by Silvan Tomkins and presenting them in detail, as well as integrating them with the most up-to-date neuroscience findings and infancy research, all based on a biopsychosocial, dynamic systems approach.

Part I describes the essentials of life, based on our evolutionary and biological heritage, namely a need for a coherent understanding of one's world and the capacity to act in that world; the infant's capacities are described in detail as embodying both. Longitudinal data is provided beginning at birth into the third year of life. Part II reviews current debates in psychoanalysis relating to motivation, and the lack of an internally consistent theory. Recent neuroscience findings are presented, which both negate drive theory, and support Tomkins' theory. His theory is then described in detail. In Part III, two case histories are presented: one is a clinical case illustrating one of Tomkins' affect-powered scripts. The second case is drawn from a longitudinal study extending from birth into early adulthood, which is made sense of with the help of Tomkins' theory. Demos concludes with a look at competing approaches to theory and responds to recent cognitive-based attempts to disprove both Tomkins' work and the latest findings from neuroscience.

The Affect Theory of Silvan Tomkins for Psychoanalysis and Psychotherapy will appeal to psychoanalysts and psychoanalytic psychotherapists, as well as psychiatrists, psychologists, social workers, and psychiatric nurses.

E. Virginia Demos is a retired member of the clinical staff at the Austen Riggs Center in Stockbridge, Massachusetts, USA, who continues to work in private practice as a clinical psychologist. She also previously taught at the Harvard Graduate School of Education. She is an authority on trauma and has also worked closely with Silvan Tomkins during her career, editing *Exploring Affect: The Selected Writings of Silvan S. Tomkins* (1995).

Relational perspectives book series

Series Editors
Lewis Aron, Adrienne Harris,
Steven Kuchuck & Eyal Rozmarin

The Relational Perspectives Book Series (RPBS) publishes books that grow out of or contribute to the relational tradition in contemporary psychoanalysis. The term *relational psychoanalysis* was first used by Greenberg and Mitchell[1] to bridge the traditions of interpersonal relations, as developed within interpersonal psychoanalysis and object relations, as developed within contemporary British theory. But, under the seminal work of the late Stephen A. Mitchell, the term *relational psychoanalysis* grew and began to accrue to itself many other influences and developments. Various tributaries—interpersonal psychoanalysis, object relations theory, self-psychology, empirical infancy research, and elements of contemporary Freudian and Kleinian thought—flow into this tradition, which understands relational configurations between self and others, both real and fantasied, as the primary subject of psychoanalytic investigation.

We refer to the relational tradition, rather than to a relational school, to highlight that we are identifying a trend, a tendency within contemporary psychoanalysis, not a more formally organized or coherent school or system of beliefs. Our use of the term *relational* signifies a dimension of theory and practice that has become salient across the wide spectrum of contemporary psychoanalysis. Now under the editorial supervision of Lewis Aron, Adrienne Harris, Steven Kuchuck, and Eyal Rozmarin, the Relational Perspectives Book Series originated in 1990 under the editorial eye of the late Stephen A. Mitchell. Mitchell was the most prolific and influential of the originators of the relational tradition. Committed to dialogue among psychoanalysts, he abhorred the authoritarianism that dictated adherence to a rigid set of beliefs or technical restrictions. He championed open discussion, comparative and integrative approaches, and promoted new voices across the generations.

Included in the Relational Perspectives Book Series are authors and works that come from within the relational tradition, extend and develop that tradition, as well as works that critique relational approaches or compare and contrast it with alternative points of view. The series includes our most distinguished senior psychoanalysts, along with younger contributors who bring fresh vision. A full list of titles in this series is available at www.routledge.com/mentalhealth/series/LEARPBS

Note

1 Greenberg, J. & Mitchell, S. (1983). *Object Relations in Psychoanalytic Theory.* Cambridge, MA: Harvard University Press.

The Affect Theory of Silvan Tomkins for Psychoanalysis and Psychotherapy

Recasting the Essentials

E. Virginia Demos

Routledge
Taylor & Francis Group
LONDON AND NEW YORK

First published 2019
by Routledge
2 Park Square, Milton Park, Abingdon, Oxon OX14 4RN

and by Routledge
52 Vanderbilt Avenue, New York, NY 10017

Routledge is an imprint of the Taylor & Francis Group, an informa business

British Library Cataloguing-in-Publication Data
A catalogue record for this book is available from the British Library

Library of Congress Cataloging-in-Publication Data
Names: Demos, E. Virginia, author.
Title: The affect theory of Silvan Tomkins for psychoanalysis and psychotherapy : recasting the essentials / E. Virginia Demos.
Description: Abingdon, Oxon ; New York,
NY : Routledge, 2019. |
Series: Relational perspectives book series |
Includes bibliographical references and index.
Identifiers: LCCN 2018045595 (print) | LCCN 2018046612 (ebook) | ISBN 9780203835913 (Master) | ISBN 9781136859809 (Adobe) | ISBN 9781136859793 (ePub) | ISBN 9781136859755 (Mobipocket) | ISBN 9780415886499 (hardback : alk. paper) | ISBN 9780415886505 (pbk. : alk. paper)
Subjects: LCSH: Tomkins, Silvan S. (Silvan Solomon), 1911- | Affect (Psychology) | Psychoanalysis. | Psychotherapy.
Classification: LCC BF531 (ebook) | LCC BF531 .D4388 2019 (print) | DDC 150.19/5–dc23
LC record available at https://lccn.loc.gov/2018045595

ISBN: 978-0-415-88649-9 (hbk)
ISBN: 978-0-415-88650-5 (pbk)
ISBN: 978-0-203-83591-3 (ebk)

Typeset in Times New Roman
by Swales & Willis, Exeter, Devon, UK

To my parents,
in memory of their deep caring and understanding.

Contents

Acknowledgments

First of all, I want to acknowledge the steady emotional support of my husband, John, throughout the years it took me to write this book. He read every word of this volume and made many useful editorial suggestions. He has always, during our fifty-five years of marriage, supported my work and valued my mind. We have shared much during all these years.

I want to thank Lewis Aron, who, after reading one of my published comments, wrote and asked me if I wanted to write a book for his series; an invitation I eagerly accepted. He has been very patient, supportive, responding to all of my questions, and enthusiastic throughout this process, including suggesting various titles for this book.

I am indebted to the Austen Riggs Hospital, first for inviting me to be an Erickson Scholar, and then allowing me to become a senior staff member, given my non-standard background in infancy work and longitudinal studies, and having received my training in psychodynamics from the self-psychologists. I was there during the directorship of Edward Shapiro who urged us all to take up our authority, which provided important support for strengthening our courage in our work with patients and with each other. I learned a great deal, both from my colleagues and my patients. In many ways my time there felt like coming home to the deepest emotional parts of myself. I have only recently retired from hospital work and I miss it terribly. There is no substitute in real life for that kind of deep work.

I would also like to acknowledge the help I received from the current librarian at Riggs, Gregory D. Farr, MLIS, CA, in locating stray references to complete my bibliography. He was always ready to help, and was often ingenious in finding the right citation. Indeed he seemed to enjoy the hunt, which made the task fun. Riggs is very fortunate to have him.

I owe an enormous debt to my various mentors. First to Erik Erikson, for whom I became a teaching assistant, in his undergraduate course offered to Harvard and Radcliffe seniors, when I was a graduate student at Harvard. He made himself very available to his TAs with weekly rotating dinners at our various apartments, and to his students, as well, with rotating visits to each of our section meetings. His deep humility, as expressed in his famous statement "I have nothing to offer but a way of looking at things" and his consistent humanity was inspiring. Over the years, when we were in the same cities, we were able to meet and talk; those conversations were never trivial. One event stands out in my memory: a meeting held at Wellfleet, sponsored by the Carnegie Council on Children, which was led by Kenneth Kenniston, and was composed of a group of academics and policy makers. After several days, the group decided that we should invite Margaret Mead to join the discussion. Since Erikson knew her better than anyone else present, he was asked to call and invite her to join us for a day. Because their relationship was somewhat difficult, this was not an easy thing for him to do. When she arrived and entered the room, she sat down in the middle of the only couch in the room, ready to hold forth. But before she could do so, Erikson walked over and sat down next to her, as if to say, "We all matter here."

I want to acknowledge Nancy Cotton, who was the director of the children's psychiatric unit at the New England Memorial Hospital in Stoneham, MA, and supervised my work there. She was very creative and generous. She had had the bathrooms painted a strong red, the color of anger, to communicate to these troubled children that they did not have to hide their anger or troubles; that we were there to listen and to help.

I owe great deal to the anthropologist Robert LeVine who hired me, sight unseen, to work in Nigeria on his study of child-rearing practices among the Yoruba. His voluminous knowledge and guidance during that year broadened my perspective enormously. Several years later, we both ended up in the Boston area, and over the years our spouses and our children have become life-long friends.

I spent a year as a postdoctoral fellow at the Boston Children's Hospital, under the directorship of Peter Wolff. He met regularly with the fellows and the discussions were always informative and lively. He also found time to sit with me as we looked at some of the videotapes I had taken of two infant girls in their homes, and told me how important he felt this work was. During that same year, I was allowed to go across the street and sit in on T. Berry Brazelton's clinic, in which mothers and infants were interviewed as part of his training of pediatricians. He made me feel welcome. He was a gifted teacher and very perceptive and sensitive pediatrician.

I would like to acknowledge the groundbreaking work in infancy of Lou Sander. He was a highly creative researcher; he designed cribs that could measure the movements of neonates in a non-intrusive way in order to study various schedules of caregiver responses and was one of the first to argue that the ego began as a state ego, not as a body ego. He was also alert to the search for order in the ever-changing development of the organism. He organized a longitudinal study, which spanned the course of development from birth through the first three years, a follow-up when the cohort entered the first grade, and then a twenty-five-year follow-up, which contains a wealth of data and represented his continuing search for order in human development. I felt honored to be part of the infancy group that was trying to match the first few years with the later outcome of these subjects. Our periodic conversations were always enlightening. Perhaps none of us knew how truly vast his knowledge of infancy was.

I want to acknowledge my debt to the late Sam Kaplan, M.D., who I got to know and value as one of the members of our infancy group, which was part of Sander's follow-up study. He also became a supervisor of my private practice. His patience, vast clinical knowledge and wisdom came through in all of our meetings. We also collaborated on writing an article that appeared in *Psychoanalysis and Contemporary Thought* (1986, no. 2, 147–221) entitled "Motivation and Affect Reconsidered: Affect Biographies of Two Infants." It was a very productive collaboration, with each of us contributing our particular expertise.

I owe a debt to Heinz Kohut, who I got to know during my two years at the Chicago Institute for Psychoanalysis, and whose clinical thinking influenced my own clinical work. He was valued greatly in Chicago, and he somehow managed to navigate the disagreements in that institute with courage, grace, and patience. He had a phenomenal memory for detail and meaning. At one of the self-psychology conferences, which went on for several days, he spoke at the end, sitting alone on the stage, and without a note, he briefly discussed every session of the conference. You could have heard a pin drop in that large room.

Finally, my deepest debt is to Silvan Tomkins. I first heard about him when my thesis advisor, Jerome Kagan, suggested that if I was interested in affect, I should read his books. I did and I was awed by the scope and power of his ideas. When my husband and I were invited to Chicago by our friend Robert LeVine, who had organized the Center for Inter-Disciplinary Study, I suggested we invite Tomkins to come and speak to our group, which included besides Levine, an anthropologist, my husband, an historian, me a developmentalist, a sociologist, and several analysts from the Chicago Psychoanalytic Institute. That meeting was the beginning of a deep friendship between Silvan and me, which included numerous phone calls, and visits back and forth over the next twenty years. Our conversations ranged over a multitude of issues; his curiosity and knowledge were vast, and he had a wonderful sense of humor. The first two volumes of his masterwork, published under the title *Affect, Imagery and Consciousness* had been published earlier. During the years I knew him he was working on the third volume, *The Negative Affects: Anger and Fear*, which was mostly about anger. He felt that I really understood his theory; so much so that in his acknowledgments in volume 3, he generously credited me with teaching him about many of its implications that he had not understood, and acknowledged what he called "my creative use of it in my work on infant affect. He also suggested to Paul Ekman that I be the editor of some of his collected papers, entitled *Exploring Affect: The Selected Writings of Silvan S. Tomkins*. This volume was part of Ekman's series on "Studies in Emotion and Social Interaction" published by Cambridge University Press. Tomkins was a grand theorist. As I wrote at the end of my preface to this volume of his works: "I knew from the beginning that this was no ordinary mind at work, and came to know that this was no ordinary human being." He was a beloved friend and mentor, and I miss him dearly.

I am indebted as well to Gary Harrington, the computer technician at Riggs. He was always available and responded to my calls for help with calm competence and creativity.

Introduction

This book is written primarily for clinicians. Psychoanalysis continues to be under pressure from managed care for shorter, more behavioral, evidence-based, or psycho-pharmacological treatments of psychological symptoms and conditions. Even though there are some recent studies validating the effectiveness of long-term psychotherapy (Shedler, 2010), and the ineffectiveness of medications for many conditions, such as severe depression (Begley, 2010), psychoanalysis is still in danger of being dismissed, both as a theory of human psychology and as a treatment modality. Non-analytic clinicians and theorists offer meaningful criticisms, stating that our theory is too anachronistic and oblivious to advances in the human sciences and that as a treatment modality it is too expensive, too long, and ineffective. Thus, there continues to be the need for an approach that makes the effort to respond to these critiques by providing a reformulation of the dynamic sources of human individuality and identifying the ways that analytic treatment is in fact tailored to address individual uniqueness. In that respect, this book seeks to reclaim, to validate, and to contribute to the further clarification of the essentials of Freud's insights.

In defending the "bedrock" of psychoanalytic theory, Schwaber (1992) states: "in its paradigmatic significance, it has changed the way we see the world" (p. 1040). This book is based on the premise that given the importance of Freud's clinical discoveries, psychoanalysis cannot continue to risk being oblivious to the major paradigmatic shifts in other human sciences, and that indeed, there is much to be gained by embracing these newer paradigms and entering into a mutually beneficial dialogue. This book will help to demonstrate these gains by providing extensive evidence and theoretical clarifications of dynamic systems theory and its impact on our understanding of the dynamics of the brain, of affect, and of infant development. It will also describe the ways in which neuroscience is validating the central motivating role of affect in all realms of psychic functioning, e.g. the role of interest in sustaining engagement with the world; the power of fear to disorganize the psyche; the way that psychotherapy works by promoting the integration of the implicit memory system with the declarative, explicit, verbal memory system; and how it broadens our understanding of the different modes of consciousness, of non-consciousness, and of the dynamic unconscious.

Put another way, this book will attempt both to validate the core of psychoanalytic understanding by recasting it, and to build bridges from that core to neighboring disciplines. It represents a consolidation, as well as an update and a more detailed presentation of my earlier efforts to suggest and demonstrate ways that the essential core of the clinical theory of psychoanalysis can be based on a more solid scientific foundation. At the heart of this effort, the reader will find a revised understanding of the human being as existing in a biopsychosocial context, which requires a deep understanding of the way our brains developed over evolutionary time, which includes a reformulation of our basic human priorities, and of the central role of affect, from the beginning of life and throughout development, in shaping the dynamics of our motivation.

Another strong argument for the value of this book is that it will present the relatively unknown affect theory of Silvan Tomkins, which continues to be the most comprehensive and internally consistent affect theory available at this time. His theory is both an example of dynamics system thinking and is in accordance with the most recent growing evidence of neuroscience. It enriches our understanding of the important distinctions between several negative affects by articulating their distinctive qualities and functions. It thereby provides a far more flexible and dynamic basis for understanding human motivation than Freud's drive theory, based on nineteenth-century neuroscience, or than other current efforts to combine drives with affects. Many clinicians have already understood that affects are the major source of motivation and of central concern to clinicians, but seem unable to let go of drive theory, perhaps because they do not have a viable alternative to the death instinct when dealing with difficult cases, or because it feels disloyal to Freud, or because they lack a systematic comprehensive way to think about affects. Tomkins' theory is complex and its articulation is embedded in his four-volume opus entitled *Affect, Imagery, and Consciousness*. Thus most clinicians are either not familiar with his ideas, or list his primary affects without fully integrating the dynamic implications of his theory that comprise his original contributions to our understanding of each distinct affect. I was fortunate to have had a twenty-year collaboration with Silvan Tomkins, and to be asked to edit his selected writings, entitled *Exploring Affect* (1995). I am therefore in a unique position to clarify his ideas and to demonstrate both their challenge to drive theory, and to current attempts to combine affects and drives, as well as to demonstrate their clinical usefulness.

Another unique aspect of this book is that it will draw on unpublished data from a remarkable longitudinal study, which began in the late 1950s, and that collected extensive data on the first three years of life. Once again, I had the good fortune to be part of this unique study, when in the 1980s, after the twenty-five-year follow-up occurred, a group of infant researchers (myself included) began to analyze the infancy data. The demands of this task required us to come to terms with two persistent, if not to say unrelenting themes, namely complexity and the search for lawfulness, or as Louis Sander, who oversaw this work, phrased it, "uniqueness and order." The longitudinal format gave us some leverage, as it is an ideal methodology for gradually separating the wheat from the chaff. From the mass of incidental or coincidental occurrences one is able, over time, to see the emergence of patterns and to test a series of hypotheses as one follows each case through time. We indeed tried to predict from each eight-month set of data to the next eight-month set, and were continually surprised. We each began with fairly strong ideas about what a young child needed in order to develop well, but we discovered that everything we thought we knew was only of limited usefulness. We had to begin to think differently about development, which led us to systems theory.

This book, then, reflects the evolution of my professional life from an initial training in human development, followed by an emersion in

Tomkins' affect theory, training in psychoanalytic theory, then the extraordinary and humbling experience of organizing the extensive early data from the longitudinal study, interspersed with over forty years of clinical work in both child and adult psychiatric hospitals and in private practice.

The book is organized in three parts. Part I will focus on development, which will be an integration and further elaboration of some of my earlier published work, presenting a dynamic systems view of development, the contributions of neuroscience in understanding consciousness and affect, locating the infant in a biopsychosocial context, demonstrating the competence of the neonate, the central role of affect in organizing the psyche, and arguing for a reformulation of basic human priorities, based on our biological heritage. This section will end with longitudinal data on infants and young children, illustrating the usefulness of this approach in understanding the early development of the psyche.

Part II will draw on the ideas presented in Part I, with a focus on the current search in psychoanalysis for a more viable theory of motivation that can replace drive theory, based on nineteenth-century neuroscience, and accept the central role of affect. It will start with a brief review of the tangle of ideas and unresolved issues put forth by Freud on the relation of affects to drives and to psychopathology, then follow with a review of the contributions of Lictenberg and Kernberg, and others who have attempted to acknowledge the central role of affects in motivation while retaining aspects of a drive or instinct theory. I will then discuss the limitations of these and other current attempts to provide an internally consistent understanding of human motivation, as a prelude to presenting recent contributions of neuroscience in defining and clarifying the nature of affects and their central role in motivation, and to pose the question of what it would mean to adopt such an approach to human motivation.

Silvan Tomkins' comprehensive affect theory will then be presented, which systematically differentiates the functions of drives and affects. His theory is based on his discovery of the distinctive, biologically determined, facial expressions and the autonomic patterns related to them. I will describe the function and qualitative characteristics of each of the primary affects as he has articulated them. This will be followed by a description of Tomkins' polarity theory, which is based on the differences in the socialization of each affect, and that will include items from his polarity scale and research findings using this scale. I will then describe the usefulness of Tomkins' distinction between the temporary amplification of affects and the process of affect magnification, a process that binds affects over time into families of scenes that leads to the formation of affect-powered scripts. The process of script formation and the nature of each of these affect-powered scripts will then be described. Scripts represent a formulation of the development of personality over time that incorporates affects as the primary motivational factor and that articulates the dynamics of both continuity and change, which emphasizes the idiosyncratic processes involved.

Part III will present clinical case material demonstrating the usefulness of Tomkins' script theory in differentiating the affect script dealing with disgust, which emerges from the defensive dynamics involved in the repetition compulsion, from the affect script dealing with terror and rage, which results from the defensive dynamics involved in trauma. The implications for clinical work drawn from developmental issues discussed in Part I will then be discussed, as well as a summary of the main implications of the evidence and theoretical advances presented in the book for psychoanalytic theory and practice.

Part I

Early beginnings

Basic essentials, neonatal capacities, and longitudinal data on two infant girls into their third year of life

Chapter 1

New developmental paradigms

This chapter will begin by discussing the limitations of stage theories of development. It will then present the basic assumptions of a dynamic systems approach to development that requires locating the infant in a biopsychosocial context. The discussion will focus on our biological givens, brain organization, distinctions between conscious, non-conscious, and unconscious, the infant's capacity for psychological experience, infant perceptual capacities, infant intentionality, and infant social capacities. It will argue that we inherit general capacities, not content, such as a preformed image of the human face, or a preformed attachment system. The chapter ends with concluding implications of this approach and what new capacities emerge over time.

The most general definition of development, taken from the *Oxford Universal Dictionary* (1955) is "a gradual unfolding: a fuller working out of the details of anything." If we take the human psyche as our subject and consider its development over time, our focus will be on specifying what it is that unfolds, namely what psychic components and capacities does the infant begin life with, and what are the rules and constraints that regulate the details of their unfolding. Before we can introduce the new paradigms that change the previous rules regulating development, we first need to review briefly what the old rules were.

Stage theories

One of the most prevalent conceptual frameworks for thinking about development has been a stage theory model, which has taken a variety of forms, e.g. Werner (1957), Piaget (1967), Klein (1952/1975), Mahler, Pine, & Bergman (1975). There are several assumptions embedded in any stage thinking. First, it requires the existence of a necessary invariant order that is governed by a master plan laid down somewhere in our genes, or in our nervous system, which is directed toward a predetermined or desired end goal. Progression is then defined by stages, which are assumed to be more or less homogeneous across a wide range of functioning and contexts. And finally, it is assumed that we start out with capacities that are global, undifferentiated, primitive, un-integrated, and therefore lacking in volitional coherence, organization, and effectiveness. It follows, therefore, that development, which proceeds by stages, is the process of getting better, or closer to some optimal functional goal of organization, control, and effectiveness. Thus, for example, Piaget (1967) described the period from ages 2 to 6 as the pre-symbolic stage of cognitive development, defining this stage in terms of deficits, namely, the seeming inability of these young children to reason symbolically when given standard tasks. In stage theories, functioning at all ages is compared against a yardstick of optimal adult functioning, so by definition, earlier stages are deficient. For many years, this pejorative lens prevented theorists and researchers from exploring what infants and young children were actually doing, since, if the theory says the capacities are not there, then no one bothers to look.

The value of a stage theory approach and its general appeal has been that it has organized vast amounts of data into a few general categories. But it did so by overvaluing homogeneity and treating individual differences as noise, and by overvaluing the end product as represented by optimal performance on defined tasks. By so doing it ignored the competence of the organism at each age and the processes by which the organism defines relevant tasks at all ages. Both of these stances also obscured the importance of context, and the dynamic nature of the match occurring in the transactions between the organism and the context. Finally, it has always been difficult for stage theories to account for the emergence of new behaviors and the process of change, namely what causes one to go from one homogeneous stage to the next, without recourse to vague notions of maturation or to changes in the brain.

All stage theories have been under attack for the last several decades due to a variety of factors, e.g. advances in video technology allowing for the slow motion exploration of infant behaviors, new statistical tools, extensive reexamination of Piaget's tasks and his choice of materials, and changing concepts of dynamic processes in other sciences. Piaget's theory has received the most thorough exploration and has been challenged on all fronts. As more and more data have accumulated, the claim for homogeneous functioning across cognitive tasks has not held up (e.g. Fisher & Pipp, 1984). And as tasks were redesigned to approximate young children's actual experience with the world, using materials and situations relevant to the lives of 2- to 5-year-olds, their early logical reasoning abilities became evident (see Donaldson, 1977) thus the claim of reasoning deficits during this time period has not held up. And Baillargeon (1990) has demonstrated that by 3½ months of age infants already understand that objects continue to exist when hidden, that they cannot move through the space occupied by other objects, and that they cannot appear at point A and then at point B without traveling from point A to point B, thereby seriously challenging Piaget's timetable regarding the infant's understanding of object permanence. As more data has accumulated on infant capacities over the last three decades (which I will come back to), the assumptions of incompetence in Piaget's and in Mahler's theories, or of super competence in Klein's theory have not held up. But perhaps the most compelling and comprehensive challenge to stage theory in understanding development and psychic organization has come from non-linear, dynamic systems theory. It represents a *radical shift* in our understanding of these phenomena.

Dynamic systems theory

A major requirement of any developmental theory is to provide an account of both change and continuity over time. Thus one of the major sources of dynamic systems theory came from the work of embryologists. Studies of the roundworm were reported in the journal *Science* several years ago. The roundworm was used because of the small number of cells it contained (959 to be exact), each of which could be traced from its embryonic form, through a series of transformations until it took its place in the corpus of the mature roundworm. But it was discovered that *no set of cells ever followed the same pattern of transformations. There seemed to be an infinite number of routes taken, yet the end product was always the same.* Other embryologists such as Von Bertalanffy (1952) had argued that all living systems begin with highly complex organization plus something he called "primary activity," which he saw as an impetus arising endogenously, from within the organism, that governs *initiation or action* and function. Such systems are equipped to regulate simultaneously internal changes and exchanges with the external environment, and are therefore *self-regulating*. Adaptation was not simply a matter of cause and effect, or stimulus and response, but was often observed to involve the emergence of novel organization, not predictable from, or deducible from, or reducible to prior lower-level conditions, for example, a small change, sometimes called the tipping point, led to a *novel non-linear shift in organization*. In this approach adaptation is conceived as being complexly governed by the active engagement of a self-organizing biological entity with its specific environment. The emergence of new organizations and forms result from the dynamic processes of assimilation and accommodation engendered by these transactions (Piaget had also recognized these processes, but embedded them in stages). This approach is also called complexity theory (see Goodwin, 1994) (I will return to the notion of a self-organizing biological entity later). The conceptualization of self-organizing systems has also been elaborated in the neurosciences (see Edelman, 1987, 1998; Kelso, 1995; Panksepp, 1999a, 1999b), and has led to mathematical modeling, as well as being modeled in studies of artificial intelligence (see Goldstein, 2007 for a review).

In developmental psychology, the work of Esther Thelen and her colleagues, in studies of infant physical development have led the way (Thelen, 1984, 1986; Thelen & Smith, 1994; Thelen, Ulrich, & Niles, 1987). In a series of ingenious experiments exploring the emergence of walking in infants, Thelen demonstrated the dynamics of non-linear shifts in organization. A stepping pattern is present at birth, but had earlier been conceptualized as a reflex, organized at a sub-cortical level, which was thought to disappear as the cortex slowly became more dominate. Its later reappearance, although influenced by learning, was thought to be governed by a predetermined genetic timetable and controlled at the cortical level. Thelen showed that walking behaviors do not disappear. When the young infant's lower body is submerged in water, and the upper torso is supported, the walking pattern is fully evident. She further demonstrated in a series of ingenious experiments with treadmills, that the walking pattern continues to be present, and that the onset of bipedal locomotion occurs only when the infant's muscular strength has increased sufficiently to allow the infant to support his or her body weight on one leg. She argued that the manifestation of walking is controlled by the changing ratio of body fat to muscle strength. She reasoned that since humans are not born with a layer of insulating fur or hair, the need to regulate body temperature takes precedence over the need to move around, thus, in human infants, body fat accumulates faster than muscle strength increases, and suppresses walking behaviors. But as soon as an infant is strong enough to support his/her weight on one leg, the ability to walk emerges. One would therefore expect there to be an enormous variability both in the timing of the emergence of this behavior and in the pre-walking motor patterns. And indeed this is so. The normal range in age for the onset of walking is anywhere from 8 months to 2 years and the pre-walking motor patterns propelling the infant forward encompass a range of idiosyncratic solutions of crawling and of scooting. This is an example of how in a self-organizing dynamic system, a local change in the ratio between two continuous variables, as in this case muscle strength and body fat, can shift the system into the emergence of a new organization, in this case the emergence of the ability to walk upright. There is, therefore, no need to postulate a genetic timetable or plan.

All such dynamic systems operate within certain constraints or initial conditions, or biases, or values (see Edelman, 1987, 1992). Thus we all become bipedal walkers, constrained by our evolutionary history, which shapes our skeletal, muscular, and metabolic capacities. But even here, it is assumed that dynamic forces, many of which we do not yet understand, were operating in evolutionary time to determine the nature of those constraints. These initial conditions function in a general way, providing the setting within which dynamic transactions can occur, transactions that are responsive to and governed by the specifics of local variations both within the organism and in the environment. When these variations are within the parameters of the self-organizing system to recognize and assimilate, then only minor or no changes occur, and the system remains stable. But all self-organizing systems have to be capable of adapting to new situations by changing, thus there have to be parts of the organizational system that are neither too orderly nor too random. These areas have been conceptualized variously as *windows of opportunity* (Langton, 1996) or *edges of chaos* (Kauffman, 1995).

There is some consensus that there is an optimal degree of mismatch or size of variation encountered by any self-organizing system that would allow for the propagation of emergent phenomena to take hold within the organism. When these optimal conditions exist, then what Goldstein (2007) calls the activity of "*self-transcending constructions*" (STC) can occur (p. 127, italics mine). He goes on to say that the emergence of novel changes in complex systems "is a radically creative process that must entail both a following of previous patterns and a simultaneous negation of these same patterns in order for a truly original outcome to be possible" (p. 127). But if the variation or mismatch is too large it can overwhelm the system and lead to disorganization and dysfunction. Therefore, the emergence of any new behavior is conceptualized as the result of a *good enough match* that can occur in a dynamic exchange between the specific organizational characteristics of the organism, which includes the organism's intention to do something, and the specific characteristics of the task or context. It follows then, that *lived experience is as powerful a determinant in shaping developmental outcomes, as are genetic factors*.

It also follows that *individual variation and idiosyncratic adaptations are the rule*. Thelen's work is once again relevant here. Her work on infant reaching behaviors illustrates both the methodological and theoretical importance of this rule. Piaget argued that reaching and grasping behaviors in early infancy were dependent on the infant having obtained a certain level of cognitive organization, namely the coordination of a visual schema with a tactile schema in order to form a schema of a reachable, graspable object. However, with the aid of slow-motion film, infant researchers (e.g. Bower, 1977) have been able to demonstrate that what seem to be random swiping motions of very young infants are in reality quite well-organized reaching and grasping motions directed at objects. The infant's hand moves through a perfectly executed grasping pattern that reaches its apex just as the hand comes closest to the object. *The effort fails not because of the lack of knowledge or of cognitive organization, but because the very young infant does yet have sufficient muscular strength to support and guide his/her own arm in a accurate path to the object.* Mandler (1988) has argued that a conceptual form of representation is apparent at birth and develops simultaneously and in parallel with the sensorimotor system, with neither system being derivative from the other, *thus infants are thinking and creating nonverbal concepts right from the beginning of life.* Given that infants begin life with relatively weak musculatures and thus are not able to "do" very much, and given that in Piaget's system, knowledge could only be built up slowly, step by step through acting on the environment, muscle weakness became synonymous with a lack of an accessible cognitive, organizing function.

Thelen (Thelen et al., 1993) studied the onset of reaching behaviors longitudinally in four young infants. The age of the first reach ranged from 12 to 22 weeks, and each infant used a different strategy, involving the coordination of different muscle groups, e.g. the two more active infants had to learn how to damp down their movements, while the two quieter infants had to learn to increase the speed and energy of their movements. Successful reaching emerges when the infant could intentionally adjust the force and direction of the arm. Thelen and her co-workers concluded:

> These results suggest that the infant central nervous system does not contain programs that detail hand trajectory, joint coordination, and muscle activation patterns. Rather, these patterns are the consequences of the natural dynamics of the system and the active exploration of the match between these dynamics and the task.
>
> (p. 1058)

In summary, a non-linear, dynamic systems approach focuses our attention on specifying the initial constraints or biases of the system; on the basic capacities of the organism, e.g. motor, perceptual, affective, cognitive, memory, and drive mechanism; on the self-organizing capacities of any biological entity; on the specifics of the fit between that organism and its environment; on the complex dynamic processes involved in all transactions with that environment; and on the activity of the organism in both maintaining its stability and in creating novel organizations or adaptations as may be required by changes in internal or external conditions. This approach requires us to give up previous notions about predetermined goals or outcomes, or set stages of progression. It emphasizes that *idiosyncratic variations are the rule*, and therefore, that longitudinal case studies of the emergence of new behaviors and organizations become the preferred methodology.

Adopting a biopsychosocial perspective to development

I have focused on the emergence of these familiar motor patterns to illustrate some of the principles of a dynamic system's approach to development because they are easier to comprehend than the more abstract models of dynamic systems found in physics and mathematics, but primarily because they deal with living human organisms, which raises all the issues of the role of motivation, consciousness, and choice, as well as the organization of the human mind and nervous system. If we return now to the development of the human psyche, and approach it from a dynamic systems perspective, we must locate the infant within a *biopsychosocial context.* I will, therefore, be trying to integrate this dynamic perspective with current knowledge of the neurosciences, and to establish a biological foundation of infant capacities for psychological experience, for affect, and for relational transactions. I will also be drawing on my own formulations based on my participation in longitudinal case studies of infants and caregivers observed in their homes and in a variety of settings.

My view differs from other available conceptualizations of these processes in several ways, namely: (1) in my emphasis on neonatal competence that is continually elaborated over time in lawful and systematic, yet highly idiosyncratic ways; (2) in articulating the central role of affect in organizing early experience; and (3) in arguing against predetermined agendas or stage-like sequences in development. In my view, the infant psyche is neither buffeted by impervious instinctual energies of the id, nor guided by a predetermined attachment agenda, nor essentially created or activated by the ministrations of a caregiver, but rather is guided by what, I am arguing, are the two most basic, biological human goals, namely *protecting psychic coherence and organization*, in which the vicissitudes of affects play a central role, and *maintaining a sense of agency* (I will discuss these goals in more detail in Chapter 2 and provide illustrative longitudinal data in Chapter 3). Here I am arguing that the infant arrives in the world possessing complex psychological functions, guided by these two basic goals, operating at a general abstract level, with a set of uniquely human biases and organizational capacities and is ready to engage in dynamic transactions with the animate and inanimate world. *It follows that the infant's psychic development will be determined by the dynamics of these intrinsic, biologically based characteristics, by opportunities for* ***matches*** *between intrinsic dynamics and external conditions and situations, and by the specific dynamics of these transactions with caregivers and with the world.*

Biological givens: the human brain neurons

Let me begin with the biological givens of the infant, which includes constraints as well as initial capabilities, particularly for psychic experience and organization. First we need to understand the nature of the human brain. Current neurosciences have provided us with a framework for understanding the origin of the mind, e.g. category formation, consciousness, memory, and affects. To look to the brain sciences for our baseline is neither to equate mental life with nor to reduce it to biology, but rather to insist that mental life is the result of and is constrained by evolutionary processes that have shaped the principles governing the anatomy and functional characteristics of neurons.

The adult human brain contains about 30 billion neurons, which are densely overlapping, branching and interconnected, producing a hyper-astronomical number of synapses: 10 followed by at least a million zeros (Edelman, 1998). And these synapses are themselves regulated by chemical and electrical processes that operate in variable and complex ways, further magnifying the complexity of connective possibilities and of dynamics. Edelman (1998) claims "that the human brain is special both as an object and as a system – its connectivity, dynamics, mode of functioning, and relation to the body and the world is like nothing else science has yet encountered" (p. 37) (scientists are just beginning to track the interconnections of the 959 neurons of the roundworm mentioned earlier). We, therefore, have to be prepared to accept new concepts and explanatory models to account for the dynamic psychic phenomena observed by developmentalists and clinicians alike.

At birth, the distribution of neurons is complete. There are very few places in the brain where new neurons develop; therefore, development in the brain is the result of lived experience, which leads to the proliferation of dendrites, axons, and increasingly complex neural networks. Unused neurons die off. The functional unit of mental activity is not located in the activity of a single neuron, but rather is constituted by the integration of a network of interconnecting neurons all activated at the same moment, as a response to changes in local conditions both within and outside the organism, which result in a thought, a memory, a perception, a feeling state, etc. All information is represented in the brain by temporal configurations of interconnected neurons. The brain operates like a complex dynamic system.

The nineteenth-century model of physical energy utilized by Freud in the *Project for a Scientific Psychology* (1895/2001) led him to conceptualize the nervous system as designed to keep quantities of excitation from building up, or failing that, to rid itself of excitations, through mechanisms such as neuronal contact barriers, screens, and dampeners, and direct neuronal connections that facilitated discharge through motor pathways. By contrast, current neuroscience formulations describe the nervous system as *intrinsically active*, and focus their efforts on understanding the complex organization and dynamics of this system. There is continual activity at all levels of the system, from the micro-anatomical level of the nerve cell and the synapse, to the synchronized networks level of neuronal action, to the conscious experience of a perception, thought, or feeling. The nervous system is connected through multiple synapses via electrical signals and the release of neural transmitters (chemical signals) all of which contain *"information" not psychical energy*. These signals are designed to create within milliseconds a complex configuration or pattern of neuronal activity that "re-presents" a simulation of a sensory or motor event. The brain is designed to function as a reality simulator, not as a tension reliever as in Freud's model. It does not apprehend the world directly and thus requires ongoing sensory input in order to do its job of creating a simulation of the world. Sensory input modifies ongoing neuronal activity, resulting in momentary temporal patterns of neuronal activity that can be "recognized" or "matched" when they recur, and the more they recur, the stronger the neural connections become, thereby allowing the organism to learn from experience, to adapt to and predict change, so as to live in and act on the world as effectively as possible.

Brain organization

Given our evolutionary history, our brain is organized hierarchically beginning from the bottom, and moving up from the brainstem, mid-brain, limbic, and subcortex to the neocortex, and, in some respects, it develops neural networks in this same order. Thus at birth, although the distribution of neurons is complete, the density of dendrites and synapses is more prevalent in the first four regions of the brain than in the neocortex. But these are relative differences, for the right hemisphere of the neocortex quickly begins to develop dense connections in the first year of life, while the left hemisphere of the neocortex is slower to do so. Since the brain depends on lived experience to develop its neural networks, one of the constraints operating is the need to achieve a balance between circuit permanence and circuit plasticity, or to state this need in psychological terms, a balance between relying on past experience and remaining open to new possibilities. One consequence of this balance seems to be that the subcortical, limbic, emotional circuits that develop in infancy tend to have relatively less plasticity, while the neocortex continues to develop new dendrites and synapses throughout life. Therefore early emotional learning can have long-lasting effects on psychological functioning, but these effects can be modulated and regulated by continued developments in the neocortex.

Another important consequence of the hierarchical organization of the brain is the difference between implicit and explicit processing of experience, which effects the way learning is represented in memory. Damasio (1994), based on his work with brain damaged patients, has argued that learning derived from these two different modes of processing is stored in separate parts of the brain. All early learning occurring in the neonate and infant is processed through the limbic, subcortical, and right-hemisphere regions of the brain, and is called implicit or procedural knowledge. Panksepp (2012) emphasizes both that these regions of the brain are part of our shared evolutionary history with all other mammals and *that the early experiences processed in these brain regions are conscious*. Such experiences involve how to do things, as well as non-verbal concepts of sensory-motor, and emotional-relational patterns of behaving and interacting that occur implicitly through sensing, preverbal thinking, feeling, and doing. Thus early, non-verbal, emotionally patterned communications between infants and caregivers are stored in implicit, procedural memory. Implicit, procedural learning continues throughout life, but by the middle of the second year of life, language and the capacity for symbolic thought emerge as a result of increased neural activity in the left hemisphere, the hippocampus, and the corpus callosum, which dynamically "tips" or shifts the organism into a new organization called explicit, declarative learning. It involves integrating sensory and emotional information with spatial and temporal sequential information, over longer time spans and with semantic associations or images, producing narratives, characteristic of linguistic representations. These two memory systems can remain separate or through conscious efforts to label and articulate experience, as in self-reflection (a capacity that emerges in the second year of life), or through exploring feelings in psychotherapy, implicit knowledge can become explicit, but there is no predetermined necessity or plan for either outcome. This is a capacity that must be encouraged and learned and can occur at any time; without such learning much implicit experience can remain un-mentalized throughout life (see Fonagy & Target, 2000 on the importance of mentalizing experience).

Conscious–non-conscious–unconscious

The understanding of consciousness and non-consciousness that is emerging in neuroscience is more developed and more complicated than in either developmental psychology or in psychoanalysis. There are at least three different phenomena specified in neuroscience, namely, conscious, non-conscious, and a defensive, dynamic unconscious. There is also a distinction between primary consciousness, involving an awareness and experiential registration of the current, continual stream of perceptual, emotional, cognitive, and motor events, and self-reflective consciousness, involving an ability to reflect on mental processes in a symbolic, re-representational mode, creating a virtual reality that can be altered.

The capacity for primary consciousness is present at birth, and perhaps earlier (see DeCasper, 1990 for a description of learning that occurs in utero). In states of wakefulness, the neonate is experiencing events in primary consciousness, including emotional states, all of which are processed cognitively in implicit, procedural learning and memory. The capacity for self-reflective consciousness emerges some time in the middle of the second year, and is correlated with explicit, declarative learning and memory.

These varieties of consciousness may be unique in humans, but, as we continue to learn more about animal behaviors, the capacity for primary consciousness is present in many other species as well. Tomkins (1962) argues that consciousness evolved as a necessary evolutionary adaptation when organisms began to move about freely in space, and thus needed to be capable of learning and making voluntary choices. Such capabilities require an internal context in which the organism can become aware of new surroundings, actively compare these to previous situations, construct meanings, devise action strategies, and monitor responses (I will argue later that the neonate is capable of all of these activities). The state of consciousness is such a context. In Tompkins' formulation, consciousness is a distinctive kind of knowing that cannot be defined precisely. It shares some characteristics with wakefulness and awareness but is not synonymous with them. We can be asleep and be conscious of our dreams and remember them the next morning. Nor is it exactly the same as awareness because we can be conscious of things that we only later become aware of. Thus the focus of our awareness at any given moment is not the totality of our consciousness. And, as stated earlier, primary consciousness and thinking does not require self-awareness or language.

Tomkins argued that all new learning has to occur in a conscious state, registered in subjective experience. *There is no other entry to the mind.* Sensations or events arising from internal or external sources must be subjectively registered in consciousness if they are to become meaningful to the organism. Only there can they be processed, given meaning, compared to past, present, or future meanings, and become elements in plans and goals. Such goals may include defensive efforts designed to exclude them in the future from consciousness, thereby becoming unconscious for defensive reasons. But this is not the unconscious of

Freud, filled with libidinal and aggressive instinctual energies and aims, or content inherited from the history of the human species. This unconscious is comprised of experiences that were once conscious but could not be subjectively tolerated and thus cannot now be allowed to recur. They are dynamic potentialities that could be reassembled and reactivated in certain situations, or under certain conditions. But if they remain intolerable, and threaten psychic cohesion, defensive activity becomes necessary and is designed to prevent such a reassembly and reactivation.

Consciousness seems to function as a control center for the organism, operating as a dynamic system seeking organizational coherence, therefore its channel capacity is limited. As information theory has determined, that limit is around seven bits of information. Its capacity would quickly become swamped if it had to be conscious of everything that was going on inside the organism. Many neurological, chemical, and homeostatic processes, as well as many perceptual, cognitive, and motor processes are designed to function outside of consciousness, and we can never become conscious of these processes, even though they clearly support and effect this realm and are in turn effected by it. These activities are non-conscious. But all those phenomena that are in the realm of conscious mental functioning must compete for entrance into the limited channel capacity of consciousness.

What are the rules governing this selective process? Freud taught us long ago that the motivated wish not to know about painful affects is a major dynamic criterion for excluding entry into consciousness, yet even here there were exceptions, such as traumatic memories that force their way into consciousness against the individual's wish to know, as in flashbacks. *But not all negative affects are intolerable*. Tomkins has argued that the amplifying function of affects is designed to gain our attention, in this competition for consciousness, while simultaneously containing qualitative information, thereby both motivating and shaping our responses (I will present his affect theory in more detail in the second part of this book). There are undoubtedly several factors operating in the competition for the limited channel capacity of consciousness, some motivated and some simply not urgent enough to win out in the competition, and thus would be non-conscious, but could become conscious at any time when there is less competition.

Infant capacity for psychological experience

So far we have reviewed the characteristics of the neonate's brain and nervous system derived from the contributions of neuroscience. What have we learned from other researchers about the neonate's capacities for psychological experience? Neuroscience's formulations about primary consciousness correlate very nicely with the work of several infant researchers influenced by psychoanalytic ideas, and interested in finding constructs that would shed light on the complex connections between the biological level and the psychological level. Both Sander (1969) and Wolff (1973, 1987) articulated the centrality of state and state organization in early infancy as such a construct. They conceptualized state as any well-defined organizational coherence within the infant, which can be recognized by the infant when it recurs and that determines how the infant will respond. Thus, they saw state as the psychological manifestation of an integration of multiple physiological subsystems within the infant. Most attention was paid to the cyclical states along the sleep–wake continuum, which were given descriptive labels such as regular sleep, irregular sleep, drowsiness, alert inactivity, waking activity, alert activity, and crying. Sander (1982) argued from his data that the infant's experiences of her own recurrent states represent the focal points around which the infant's inner awareness or consciousness consolidates. He later went on to say that:

> [A] capacity for inner experience exists at the outset of postnatal life – as an initial level in the organization of consciousness. This initial root of the sense of self does not await the organization of a body image or depend on production effects, or on visual or tactile experience, or the double-tactile experience that through touch begins the differentiation of self and other. The ego begins as a "state ego, rather than a body ego."
>
> (Sander, 1985, p. 20)

And, further in that same article, he stated that "*the organization of state governs the quality of inner experience*" (p. 26, italics mine).

What is the quality and content of the neonate's conscious states? Contrary to earlier psychoanalytic descriptions of the infant alternating between sleep and overwhelming states of tension with no organizing ego (see Mahler et al., 1975; Noy, 1969; Winnicott, 1965), I have argued and presented evidence elsewhere (Demos, 1986, 1988, 1989) that these organized waking states of the neonate are distinctive affect states. Thus for example, the alert states are states of interest, and the crying state is the affect distress or the affect anger, depending on the intensity and pattern of crying. This claim is based on Silvan Tomkins' (1962, 1963a) theory of affect (which I will describe in detail in Part II of this book) and on the available evidence on infant affect expressions and behaviors. Tomkins' theory and the facial affect coding manual derived from it (Ekman & Frieson, 1978) provide a considerable gain in precision, allowing researchers to examine the correlated sets of facial, vocal, bodily, and autonomic responses of young infants and conceptualize them as discrete affects. The following patterns have been observed. The interested baby will widen and focus its eyes intently on a stimulus, with brows raised or knitted, cheeks raised, and mouth relaxed, holding its limbs relatively quiet, and will tend to scan the stimulus for novelty (Langsdorf, Izard, Rayias, & Hembree, 1983; Oster, 1978; Wolff, 1965). Wolff (1973) reported that during the first month of life, this state accounts for 50 percent of waking time. The joyful baby will smile and tend to produce relaxed, relatively smooth movements of its limbs, savoring the familiar (Brazelton, Koslowski, & Main, 1974). The angry baby will square its mouth, lower and pull its brows together, cry intensely, holding the cry for a long time, then pause for a long inspiration, its face will redden with increased blood flow, and it will tend to kick and thrash its limbs forcefully or arch its back (Demos, 1986, 1988). By contrast, a distressed baby will produce a rhythmical cry, with the corners of the mouth pulled down and the inner corners of the brows drawn up and will tend to move its limbs and head around restlessly (Demos, 1986, 1988; Wolff, 1969). A surprised infant will open its eyes and mouth wide and stop its activity (Sander, 1995).

These facial, vocal, and motor affect responses are not random. They are clearly patterned and coordinated with each other. *They are also not learned.* Every healthy neonate knows how to gaze with interest, smile with enjoyment, and cry in distress or in anger. *Nor do they operate in a reflex like manner.* They are exquisitely responsive to subtle changes in the internal and external environment. We still do not have a complete picture of the full innate affect program for these affects or of the other innate affects as described by Tomkins, but the data we do have are in agreement with the patterns he has detailed. They are also in agreement with the latest neurological findings reported by Panksepp (1999a, 1999b). I will discuss his work in more detail in Chapter 4.

The quality and content of the young infant's psychic experience therefore is partly determined by the frequency and intensity of each of these affect states. In the normal, full-term infant these states are recognizable both to the infant and to the caregiver when they recur. However, there are individual variations in infants in the clarity or organizational coherence of their states. This is particularly true of premature infants, and of the more recent phenomenon of crack-addicted babies. These babies have a more difficult time achieving well-organized, coherent states of sleep and wakefulness. Sander's earlier statement, "the organization of state governs the quality of inner experience" (1985, p. 26) is relevant here. The organism needs to be able to achieve a basic level of organizational regularity and stability that can provide the background against which changes in coherent unities can be perceived and recognized. In a well-functioning neonate with a responsive caregiver, this can be achieved in the first week of life (Sander, 1975). Both the baby and the caregiver make contributions to the ease or difficulty of achieving this regularity, which has been conceptualized as a process of reciprocal transactions requiring mutual regulations and adaptations from both partners.

Other determinants of the quality and content of the young infant's psychic experiences have to do with the kind of stimuli provided by the external environment. In a normal, full-term baby the duration of an alert awake state (which usually occurs after a period of sleep and after a feeding) increases steadily from 5 to 20 minutes in the first few days of life, to 30 to 60 minutes by the first month of life. Thus this alert awake state is likely to recur three to five times a day. At such times the infant is looking at, listening to, touching, smelling, and tasting the world around him or her. Our understanding of the infant's perceptual and cognitive capabilities has radically changed over the last several decades, which has grown out of Gibson's (1969) and Mandler's (1988) theoretical ideas, and the experimental work of many researchers, such as Bower (1977, 1982) and Spelke (1976, 1979), to mention only a few.

Infant perceptual capacities

The current consensus argues that infants begin life with a highly complex and unified perceptual system that is designed to detect abstract invariants in stimulation, such as intensities, rates of movement, contours, mass, etc., and that operates across modalities. For example, infants can visually recognize the shape of an object that they have previously only explored with their mouth or tongue (Melzoff & Borton, 1979), and they can match the intensity of a sound with the intensity of a light (Lewkowicz & Turkewitz, 1980). They can recognize the common temporal structure present in auditory and visual events, and will match a soundtrack to the appropriate film on the basis of temporal synchrony. They can also make categorical judgments about color, musical tones, and phonemes similar to those made by adults. Bower (1982) argued that the newborn lives in a world as close to pure perception as is possible, perceiving the general, abstract stimulus qualities of objects and that over time the infant fills in the details and begins to detect specific features of objects. There are some limitations or constraints as well. As a species we can only hear sounds within certain frequencies, we can only see color within certain wavelengths, we can only perceive movement at certain rates, we can only smell orders in certain ranges, etc. One needs only to take a walk with a dog, to realize how their sense of smell is far more developed than our own.

Infant intentionality

Much of this evidence suggests that during waking hours, the neonate is actively exploring the world, an activity that implies a capacity for intentionality. DeCasper and Carstens (1981) have demonstrated in an amazing experiment (which I will describe in detail in Chapter 2) that the neonate is exquisitely sensitive to contingences, which involves making distinctions between voluntary events and involuntary events. This finding, and other evidence to be discussed later, puts us right in the middle of a controversial issue, namely whether the infant lives in an undifferentiated world, or is capable of differentiating its psychological experience and existence from that of another. If the infant can distinguish voluntary from involuntary events, it is only a short step further for the infant to realize that voluntary events emanate from the inside and that most involuntary events emanate from the outside.

Stern (1983) made a similar argument. Because infants possess predesigned perceptual and cognitive operations (many of which I have just described), they are able to perceive the organizational unity of individuals in terms of their spatial locations and temporal intensity synchronies, and they can maintain these perceptions in the face of interfering stimuli and changing configurations. Infants are also able to discriminate different schedules of reinforcement and are thus in a position to determine effects that are self-caused and separate them from those that are caused by others. Thus, given an expectable human environment, infants will inevitably construct schemata of at least two separate organizational entities, namely, that of their own functioning and that of the behaviors of the other. These schemata are not innate but have a high probability of emerging from the integrated functioning of the inherited capacities of the human infant. The remaining question for Stern (1983) was "how does the infant 'know' that his organization of behaviors is the one that belongs to him?" (p. 65). It is at this point that Stern stressed the importance of the experience of an *intention* or *motive* that accompanies the infant's own behaviors but not those of the other, and the importance of proprioceptive internal sensations that always and only accompany the infant's own behaviors.

I would add to this discussion an explicit acknowledgment of the role of affective experience in enabling the infant to differentiate his or her own experience from the sensations and behaviors emanating from the other, namely the amplifying function of affect in producing the experience of the affect interest, involved in motivating intentionality. Affect is a powerful source of proprioceptive sensations that occur in distinctive, qualitative patterns. What evidence do we have that infants can discriminate their own affect from the affect of another? Martin and Clark (1982) reported that calm newborns (18 hours old) will cry and that crying newborns will continue to cry when they hear the tape-recorded crying of other newborns. This finding demonstrates the contagious nature of affect. However, in the next condition of this experiment, calm newborns do not respond vocally and crying newborns stop crying when they hear their own tape-recorded crying, *a highly unique event*. Also, calm newborns do not respond to the cries of a chimpanzee or an older child, thus they are not simply responding to an aversive sound when responding to the cries of other neonates. The authors conclude that neonates are able to discriminate between the cries of others and their own cries, and so do not cry to the recording of their own cries. But they do not offer any explanation for how or why this might occur.

I would suggest that the infant is making this distinction on the basis of the presence or absence of the perceived internal autonomic and motor sensations that usually precede and accompany the infant's own crying, combined with the infant's capacity to perceive and recognize the distinctive temporal and vocal pattern of its own versus the other's crying. Thus the infant cries when it hears another infant cry because of the general amplifying function of affect. Because of this amplifying function, all affect is to some extent contagious, and perhaps more so for neonates who have fewer resources for breaking into an escalating positive feedback loop. This phenomenon makes the infant vulnerable to intense affects emanating from the caregiver, which can swamp the infant's capacities to differentiate the source of the affect. But in this experiment, when the calm infant hears a recording of its own cry, the infant can recognize the temporal and vocal pattern as its own cry, but now it is neither preceded by nor accompanied by the usual proprioceptive stimuli. *Thus hearing it represents a highly discrepant stimulus*, namely, a recognizable sound and temporal pattern, without any of the perceived internal proprioceptive, autonomic, and motor sensations that normally go it with it, and so the calm infant does not cry. The crying infant, who also recognizes the recording as its own cry, may stop crying because the temporal and vocal patterns of the recorded cry are not an exact match of its own ongoing crying, which again makes no sense, and so it too stops crying. The researchers do not report what these 18-hour-old infants did, but I would suggest that they became very attentive, experiencing intense interest, if not something akin to confusion or surprise as they tried to understand this highly unique, out of context, mismatched event.

Infant social capacities

All of these data converge on a picture of a highly competent newborn with complex psychological capacities for consciously processing cognitive, perceptual, and affective experiences. What are the newborn's social capacities? Other investigators have demonstrated the neonate's responsiveness to human stimuli. The Brazelton Neonatal Behavioral Assessment Scale (NBAS; Brazelton, 1973) was the first scale to focus on the neonate's responsiveness and orientation to the human voice and face, and to demonstrate the neonate's readiness and capacity to interact with a human caregiver. Examiners trained in the administration of the NBAS report being able to elicit smiles from well-organized, alert neonates held in the *en face* position (Modansky, personal communication, March 1981). Wolff (1963) reported that the human voice, which is a distal cue, is the single most effective elicitor of neonatal responses, but that the face and the voice together are also highly effective. And Field, Woodson, Greenberg, and Cohen (1982) have demonstrated that neonates are capable of discriminating and imitating three facial expressions (happy, sad, and surprised) modeled by a live adult. This finding illustrates not only the infant's responsiveness to human stimuli, but also the infant's cross-modal capacities discussed earlier, specifically the infant's capacity to match a visual image with a proprioceptive image based on the feedback from its own facial muscles. We also know that infants prefer light–dark contrasts and contours, hear voices best in the higher frequencies, and focus their vision best at a distance that is roughly the distance between the mother's face and the infant's eyes when held in the mother's arms in a nursing position, and tend to focus on the mother's eyes. The human face contains all the elements that would interest an infant. When the caregiver props the feeding bottle and leaves the infant alone, the infant looses the opportunity to explore familiar human faces and as well the opportunity for shared eye-to-eye contact.

Since many of these perceptual biases comprise stimulus characteristics that are routinely produced by other humans, there is no need to postulate the existence of a pre-formed idea of a human face or of a pre-formed attachment agenda. *We inherit general capacities, not pre-formed content.* In a dynamic systems model, given the match between the dynamics of the infant's perceptual biases, and responsive capacities, and the availability and dynamics of existing adult faces and voices, and given an expectable and receptive environment, it is inevitable that the infant will be drawn to other humans, and as a result of those transactions will quickly construct a representation of the voices and faces seen and heard most frequently. Without such experiences, an infant cannot develop an attachment

Concluding implications

This picture of a highly competent newborn and young infant may seem amazing and unbelievable to many, even to infant researchers. Blass concludes his article entitled "The Ontogeny of the Human Face" (2010) by stating "all of these findings in 1- to 3-month-old infants were unexpected. I have been impressed by the precision, persistence, apparent goal-directedness and regular time of onset of these ontogenetic changes" (p. 60). Such findings of the infant's capacities for thinking, acting, and feeling may cause others (perhaps mostly mothers) to wonder at how long it has taken us to appreciate and explore systematically the neonate's capabilities. Thus we need to pause a moment to stop and ponder the full implications of evolution theory. As Bower reminded us, earlier formulations arguing for an incompetent infant ignored a basic evolutionary rule, namely, that *the more capable a species is in adulthood, the more capable is the newborn of the species*. We could not possibly learn everything we are capable of as a species if we had to start from scratch. But let us be clear about the implications of these data. They do *not* support the notion of preformed images (e.g. the human face), concepts, experiences of past lives, or attachment agendas. What they do strongly indicate is the existence of pre-adapted *general capacities* for feeling, thinking, perceiving, remembering, and some motor patterns, e.g. head movements, ocular focusing, sucking, and stepping. The human infant therefore starts out with a uniquely human brain, nervous system, and body, which in some respects will limit and constrict the range of possible experience, but in the main, provides the infant with an enormous head start in adapting to the human and inanimate world. The infant's self-organizing and self-regulating capacities will be manifested in ever new initiatives and behaviors that will require the caregiving environment to recognize and adapt to this new active agent in the family.

What new capacities emerge over time? Or to put it another way, if the infant already has what it needs to make sense of the world, and to explore its agency, what is the experience of dynamic transactions with caregivers and the world contributing? I would suggest there are at least four major kinds of changes going on: (a) these general capacities of the infant are becoming elaborated and shaped in unique and specific ways; (b) the infant's experience of being in control of and making sense of internal and external events and thus its motivational organization is being shaped and determined by interactions with the caregiving environment; (c) the infant's motor strength is increasing and thus its instrumental competence is increasing, which will require new adaptations with caregivers; and (d) in the second year of life the child is gradually learning to decontextualize its knowledge of the world and of its place in the world, which will lead to the beginning of a process of self-recognition as reflected by the feedback from others.

Throughout all of these changes, the degree of matched specificity between the infant and the caregiver will determine the ongoing stability in the infant of the coherence of a sense of inner sameness, and the ability of the infant to use inner cues to guide behavior.

These new capacities represent more or less gradual, continuous changes that interact and influence each other. The outcome of this last change is more discontinuous, in that it involves the emergence of symbolic capacities in the second year of life, ushering in the capacity for language and self-reflection. Other discontinuous changes are the adrenal changes in middle childhood (roughly around age 7) that affect brain development, and the hormonal changes that occur in adolescence, ushering in reproductive capacities. Each of the changes will become intertwined with and contribute new elements to the more continuous changes. I will describe some of these changes in more detail in the chapters to follow.

In this chapter, I have presented evidence from a variety of fields to demonstrate how our knowledge of the infant and young child's development and organization has been greatly enhanced by the advances in these various fields. Since we are all dealing with same organism, and each approach explores some part of the terrain, ideally we can benefit from an open dialogue. These advances, therefore, offer a challenge to our efforts to construct viable theories that are in accordance with new knowledge representing current scientific consensus about human origins and functioning.

Chapter 2

Basic human priorities

This chapter builds on the material presented in Chapter 1 and represents a further elaboration and integration of those efforts to continue an open dialogue in order to deepen our understanding and clarify the basics. Thus this chapter will discuss the two basic psychological priorities derived from our biological heritage. These two priorities are (1) the need to maintain psychic coherence and (2) the need to be an active agent in bringing about desired goals. Each priority will be discussed in detail with supporting evidence. This approach may challenge many existing beliefs and theories, but it is in accordance with the more recent findings of neuroscience.

I am motivated by the belief, which has only grown stronger through my intensive work with residential patients at the Austen Riggs Center, that we have much to learn if we are to help our patients overcome the powerful defensive and potentially lethal psychic solutions to non-optimal and/or abusive experiences that have occurred earlier in their lives. The risk of rigidifying our theories and thinking, as Galatzer-Levy (2004) has suggested, is that phenomena that cannot be incorporated in a theory become effectively invisible. We cannot afford to be blind, as were those proverbial men examining the elephant. Our best chance to enrich and preserve our psycho-dynamic approach to patients requires us to embrace fully an informed understanding of human origins and functioning that is in concordance with the most current scientific consensus. Freud strove to do no less, but he was constrained by the limitations of the science of his day.

Initial conditions of psychic development

As we continue to locate human development within a biopsychosocial context, we are now required to try to articulate the relevant initial conditions of psychic development that are contained in our biological history. Following the embryologist Von Bertalanffy (1952) and his characterization of *all living matter as possessing primary activity and a highly complex organization*, it becomes necessary to grant the human infant the designation of a self-organizing, active biological entity. As such, I would argue that the infant psyche is highly likely to be guided by the following two biologically based human preferences or biases, which function by differentially weighing experience so that they are felt to be of the highest priority. These two most basic human biases are: (1) a preference for psychic coherence and organization, in which meaning and the vicissitudes of affect play a central role; and (2) a preference for being an active agent in effecting the desired course of both internal and external events. Other psychoanalytic thinkers, such as Ghent (2002) and Greenberg (1991) have also speculated that these two biases may exist in early life, and that they then may dynamically generate other motivational systems such as attachment. That attachment is conceptualized in a non-linear, dynamic systems model as an emergent motivational system, as opposed to being a pre-organized biological given, may be jarring to many readers; I will return to this issue later. But first we need to look at supporting evidence for these biopsychosocial propositions.

Psychic coherence

In regard to coherence, Ghent (2002) states: "I think a value or bias of this nature must underlie the tendency of neural networks to categorize and re-categorize successive experience along the lines suggested by Edelman" (p. 779). Here Ghent is looking to neuroscience for support for our need to continually create meaning, so as to adapt as we encounter ever new experiences. I quoted Edelman (1998) in Chapter 1, as describing the complexity of the human brain, as "like nothing else science has yet encountered" (p. 37). Thus we must be prepared to accept new findings that may help us account for the dynamic psychic phenomena observed by developmental researchers, described in the previous chapter, and clinicians alike.

We are still in the early phases of understanding the full psychological implications of how the brain works, but as stated in Chapter 1, there is a consensus that the brain functions as a complex non-linear, dynamic system, continually re-presenting a simulation of internal and external events. We are indeed meaning-making organisms. As these momentary temporal patterns or coherences of neural activity repeat over time, they can be recognized or matched, and the more they recur, the stronger the neural connections become. *It is through recurring coherences that the organism is able to learn from experience, and to adapt to and/or create new meanings and responses.*

One of the most important kinds of coherence is *mental state*. In the first chapter I cited the work of Wolff and Sander as articulating the coherent states of the infant along a biorhythmicity that involves 4–6 awakenings in the 24-hour sleep–wake continuum and I also quoted Sander's important statement that the ego begins as a state ego. I then argued that the waking states they described were discrete affect states. I have based my understanding of affects and their function on the work of Silvan Tomkins (1962) who argued that the human organism evolved as a "multi-mechanism system" comprised of the affect mechanism as distinct from the sensory, motor, memory, cognitive, and drive mechanisms, and that each mechanism is capable of acting independently, dependently, and interdependently with any or all of them. He theorized that affect functions as an *analog amplifier*, and is comprised of a correlated set of bodily responses, which include facial muscles, vocal, respiratory, blood-flow changes, heightened skin receptor sensitivity, and other autonomic responses that create an *analog* of the rate and intensity of stimulation impinging on the organism, from either internal or external sources This correlated set of responses has evolved to combine urgency, abstractness, and generality (e.g. a sense of "too much" or "too fast," or "just right"), and is experienced as a qualitative affect state, able to both capture consciousness, thereby causing the organism to care about what is happening and with its qualitative valence, informing the organism so as to shape and facilitate a response.

Neuroscience has supported many aspects of Tomkins' formulation. Panksepp (1999a) for example states that affects are generated by "extensively ramifying sub-cortical command circuits that generate and synchronize various emotional behaviors and accompanying bodily changes" (p. 25). He also speculates that they "*inform us of fundamental evolutionary values* that are not only the harbingers of intended actions, but also the processes that allow social creatures like mammals ... to communicate efficiently and urgently their needs, desires, and intentions to others" (1999b, p. 75, italics mine). He emphasized that affects are not learned, but, "*emerge directly from the evolutionary epistemology of the brain*" (p. 25, italics mine). At another point he states "in early childhood there is no sustained line of thought without a sustained line of affect" (p. 17), and that affects have more than a transitory effect, but "surely have longer-term regulatory effects on future behavioral outputs" (p. 30). He differentiates affect dynamics from cognitive processes in the following way: "In fact to really understand emotions and moods we may need to cultivate conceptions that deal with primitive global state variables, which are far more embodied and fundamentally *analog*, than is easy to envision in traditional information-theoretic terms" (Panksepp, 1999b, p. 80, italics mine). Throughout, Panksepp stresses the complexities of the ways affect is represented in the brain, including integrating primitive sub-limbic systems with limbic and higher-order systems, as well as hormonal parameters that modulate circuit sensitivities and forms of neuropeptidergic coding. He laments that neuroscience is only beginning to deal with such global states in the brain, but so far there is evidence for some emotional entities, such as fear, rage, pain, distress, eagerness, or seeking (in Tomkins' theory this would be the affect interest) and joy. Tomkins would not classify pain as an emotion, but the other five coherent organizations Panksepp names are basic affects according to Tomkins' work derived from facial expressions, published in the 1960s. This concurrence of findings between facial expressions and deeper brain functions is highly compelling.

Psychic organization

So far, we have an active infant existing in a human environment, who with the help of a responsive caregiver, can achieve within the first week of life coherent states, which, when awake, are states of primary affects. According to Sander's (1975) data the 24-hour-cycle in the first week of life consists of a biorhythmicity that involves four to six awakenings. What do we know about the infant's capacity to organize these states, by which I mean the infant's capacity to recognize and compare them to previous states, and to use them to make sense of events and to guide actions? I have often described the remarkable experiment reported by DeCasper and Carstens (1981) as an example of *the neonate's capacity to coordinate affective, perceptual, cognitive, memory and motor functions in order to bring about a desired event.* In this experiment, *3-day-old* infants quickly learned to lengthen the pauses between their bursts of sucking in order to turn on a recording of a female voice singing. To be able to succeed in this task, the newborn had to coordinate perception (detecting the contingency), emotion (interest in the stimulus and the contingency) cognition (generating a plan to repeat this interesting event), motor patterns (voluntarily lengthening the pause between sucking bursts), and memory (remembering the plan and comparing the outcome to the goal). Some 24 hours later, these same infants became upset when they were placed in the non-contingent phase of the experiment, in which they discovered that hearing the singing voice was no longer contingent on the length of their pauses. A second control group of infants were placed in the non-contingent phase first, during which the length of their pauses had no effect on the occurrence of the female voice singing, and thus they did not change their sucking pattern during this time; later, when this group was put in the contingent situation, they had already learned that their sucking and pausing had no effect on the onset of the singing voice and so *they did not attend* to the timing of that onset and thus did not detect the contingent relationship between their longer pauses and the onset of the singing voice.

Blass, Ganchrow, and Steiner (1984), in an equally remarkable experiment demonstrated that *in the first day* of life neonates could be conditioned to orient their heads in one direction in order for their foreheads to be gently stroked, which they had *learned* was associated with getting a small solution of sucrose. In the extinction period these same infants cried when the sucrose was no longer associated with forehead stroking.

My description above of the infant's self-organizing capacities includes the assertion that 1- to 3-day-old infants in these experiments were "making sense" of events, and learning, namely, they were thinking as well as feeling and perceiving. Mandler (1988) also argues that from the beginning the neonate is capable of some kind of perceptual analysis or comparison that leads to primitive and perhaps global categories, which are stored in an accessible form, and are continually refined and elaborated over time (see Bower, 1982 for a similar view). Mandler (1988) also states that given "the language saturated character of adult concepts" (p. 127), it is extremely difficult to describe the characteristics of neonatal concepts. In arguing against Piaget's model, which put perception first, as the building blocks that led to the creation of concepts, Mandler argues that based on existing evidence one has to conclude that *conceptual analysis and perception co-exist from the beginning and are interconnected*: "The perceptual system provides the information that gets interpreted conceptually, and the conceptual system often determines what gets perceptually processed" (p. 132). This last assertion that from the beginning concepts determine what is perceived was demonstrated in the DeCasper and Carstens (1981) experiment above by the control group of infants, whose previous learning resulted in their lack of attention to the timing of their pauses and the onset of the singing voice in the contingent condition.

These experiments demonstrate several things about the capacities of the neonate, including the preference for being an active agent, which I will elaborate on shortly. But for now I want to emphasize both the remarkable activity and the self-organizing capacities demonstrated by the group of neonates in these ingenious experiments. In both of these experiments the efforts of the infants resulted in a coherent understanding of the situation that led to an effective adaptation and action that produced the desired result. But when the situation changed, these neonates could no longer "make sense" of the situation, and they could not adapt, leading to a distressed state. An upset also occurred in the Blass conditioning experiment when during the extinction phase, the stroking of the forehead was no longer followed with sucrose. These results highlight a particular kind of challenge to the goal of maintaining coherence, namely the role of a *violation of expectations* in trying to understand the meaning of events (I will return to this threat to coherence when discussing the effects of trauma on the psyche in the last section of this book). In these experiments, the meaning was contained in the contingent relationship between the infant's actions and the external stimulus, and when the possibility for that contingent relationship was removed, thereby violating the infant's expectation, the situation went beyond the infant's capacity to understand, and it then evoked the negative affect of distress. In the first experiment, to the infant the situation appeared to be the same 24 hours later, namely, sucking on a nipple, lengthening their pauses, and expecting to hear a female voice singing, but something inexplicably had changed. In the second experiment described, facilitating the stroking of the forehead by turning in that direction had always led to the sucrose, but then something inexplicably changed.

In many other cases, the threat to coherence comes directly from the inability of the infant to regulate exposure to all kinds of stimuli, including affect states generated by others. We are now moving from the biological and psychological capacities of the infant, into the social realm and the role of the caregiver. Sander (1982) maintains that "the infant's own states, where coherent, recurrent, desired, or essential to key regulatory coordinations that become established with the caregiver, become the primary target or goals for behavior" (p. 16).

Stimuli and affect regulation

Although infants possess many capacities as demonstrated above, they have only modest abilities to regulate exposure to stimuli, such as by shutting their eyes, turning their heads away, arching their backs, spitting out or up bad tasting food, or falling asleep. They cannot rid themselves of excessive auditory or tactile stimuli, nor can they use cognitive strategies to deal with information overload, as evidenced in the experiments above. Caregivers are essential in regulating stimulus variables such as pacing, intensity, duration, clarity, and the optimal mix of redundancy and novelty, all geared to their infant's individual needs. Indeed mothers all over the world, emerging out of their desire to communicate with their infants, seem to have creatively invented "motherese," which is a slow, redundant, exaggerated, affectively positive, modulated universal language. Thus it represents a "goodness of fit" or a match between the capacities the infant brings and the adaptability that the environment can provide, and thereby helps the infant to remain in an optimal state of attentive coherence, fueled by the affects interest/excitement and enjoyment/joy, for processing stimuli.

The caregiver's role in modulating stimuli and achieving an optimal level is perhaps even more important in the realm of helping the infant and young child regulate negative affect states. The data from infant research (Demos, 1992, 1993) and from neuroscience (Gunner, 1992; Porges, 1992), indicate that infants are capable of self-regulation when arousal levels are low to moderate and that this emotional arousal is both necessary, in order to mobilize attention and information processing, and manageable. Infants vary in their vigor and intensity of expression, but in general, they have a very limited repertoire of responses for managing higher levels of distress or anger. They can suck on their fingers or hands, or look at an interesting object to distract themselves, but as the negative affect increases, they do not possess the instrumental capacities, the experience, or the knowledge to modulate it, and without a caregiver's help it can escalate in a positive feedback loop, cycling up into higher and higher densities moving from distress to anger, to fear, and disorganization resulting in a potentially traumatic experience, which can set in motion massive defensive efforts.

When Provence and Lipton (1962) wrote about the infants they had studied, who were cared for in institutions, and who were fed, and changed every four hours, and otherwise were not responded to, they commented that these infants *never* cried. I would argue that these infants had cried initially, since in the early months of life infants need food every two to three hours, and hunger is an innate activator of the distress cry, and that their cries were not responded to. Thus, they must have experienced the escalation of negative affect in a positive feedback cycle described above until they must have fallen asleep, exhausted. This is a very traumatic and disorganizing sequence; therefore, I believe these infants had to learn to stop crying at the earliest sign of distress. This level of negative affect is clearly an example of deregulated affect, which represents a real threat to the infant's ability to organize their experience and maintain psychic coherence, and requires the infant to marshal a massive defensive effort to prevent such a recurrence. Not all negative affect is intolerable, or deregulated, thus this kind of escalation is to be distinguished from modulated, optimal densities of negative affect that allow the infant to remain organized and focused on trying to do something about the situation.

It is difficult to specify this optimal level, since it will vary from infant to infant, from moment to moment and from context to context. It therefore requires judgment from the caregiver and the ability to "read" their infant's states. It also requires the capacity of the caregiver to allow for an empathic engagement with their infant. The ease or difficulty that a particular infant–mother pair experiences in trying to regulate the infant's negative affective states at optimal levels is influenced both by the infant's characteristics (e.g. vigor, threshold for stimulation, capacity to achieve smooth transitions between states), and by the mother's history of distress (e.g. her tolerance for crying) and her other characteristics (e.g. calmness, soothing skills, ability to dose the quantity of stimulation, beliefs about infant crying, etc.). But aside from these general characteristics of the individuals involved, this regulatory process is also influenced by affect dynamics, namely, by affect contagion, so that a crying infant tends to evoke an emotional response in the caregiver. A number of studies using rating scales and/or physiological measures have shown that adults experience infant crying as arousing, distressing, aversive, grating, irritating, etc. in varying degrees depending on the type of cry and on several adult variables (see Lester & Zeskind, 1982 for an excellent review of these studies). These studies validate Tomkins' proposition that affect functions as an analogue amplifier, thereby evoking more of the same affect in a positive feedback loop, both within the person experiencing the affect and in the observer.

The degree of distress evoked in the observer depends on a number of factors, such as other competing affects, the context and meaning for the observer of the infant's distress, the degree of responsibility felt by the observer for doing something about the infant's distress, and the degree of defensiveness of the observer with regard to distress. For example, Wiesenfeld, Malatesta, and DeLoach (1981) report that mothers show more autonomic responsitivity to their own infants' distress cries than fathers do, and more than they do to an unfamiliar infant's distress cry; Frodi and Lamb (1980) report that abusive mothers show greater autonomic arousal and produce more negative emotional ratings than controls to infant cries; and Boukydis (1979) reports that primiparous parents showed their highest levels of arousal to average cries, whereas multiparous parents and non-parents show their highest levels of arousal to difficult cries and lowest levels to easy cries. Hence there is no simple, direct relationship between the intensity and kind of affect expressed by the infant and the intensity and kind of affect evoked in the observer. Nevertheless, because of the amplifying function of affect, and the relatively higher intensity and density of affect expressed by infants, it is highly likely that a caregiver who is engaged with a crying infant will experience a variant of the affect expressed by the infant.

When the infant's distress and/or anger evokes distress and/or anger in the caregiver, then the caregiver's ability to soothe and help the infant will depend on the caregiver's response to her (or his) own affect experience at that particular moment. This response may vary in characterological ways, according to a learned tolerance for distress, or to defense mechanisms or learned affective sequences (such as distress followed by anger, or vice versa). It may vary from situation to situation; for instance what is acceptable in private may not be acceptable in public, or in front of particular people (e.g. a critical mother-in-law). It may vary from affect to affect, in that distress may be acceptable, but not anger, or vice versa. It may vary from moment to moment, or day to day, depending on mood, fatigue level, cumulative factors, or other competing concerns. This phenomenon of affective contagion and responsiveness thus activates the caregiver's unique personal history of learning, relevant to the evoked affect, and both informs and complicates the caregiver's task of perceiving and understanding the infant's experience and needs and of providing a helpful intervention. Empathy is an information gathering process that requires the caregiver to be able to differentiate their own response from their infant's experience and to then be in a position to produce a response that is appropriate to the infant's needs, namely providing feeding, comfort, encouragement, or at later ages, support in completing a task, or dealing with the cause of the distress.

The caregiver's role thus entails two functions: (1) protecting the infant from affect deregulation that can lead to disorganization in the infant and threaten the infant's psychic coherence by calming the infant; and (2) providing support to the infant through optimal densities of negative affect, thereby enhancing the infant's capacity to endure, tolerate, and persist in the face of "trouble" in order to develop instrumental coping skills. Taken together, these two aspects of the caregiver's modulating function lead to a *sense of trust within the infant* – a trust in the reliability and manageability of the infant's own inner experience.

Here we are in the realm of learned affect meaning for the infant. With inner trust, the onset of distress or anger does not mean an escalation and the need to retreat, and thus does not evoke dread or shame, but rather it reflects the learned expectation that these states can be tolerated, that their causes can be resolved, that they have a beginning, a middle, and an end, and that one can return to a more positive state. Such an infant is also likely to learn that others are helpful and reliable and perhaps that the world is trustworthy. Taken together this learning provides a baseline of perseverance and optimism in the psyche, and a recognizable experience of inner cohesion and sameness. I believe that the caregiver's role in facilitating inner trust is what Erikson (1950) may have meant when he proposed trust vs. mistrust as the first stage of psycho-social development. But the salient task of organizing one's experiences in order to enhance psychic coherence is an ongoing, dynamic process, and thus, as the infant's world continues to expand, it must continue to be supported by the child's human environment.

The involvement of a caregiver is also essential in helping the infant to sustain and elaborate the positive affects of interest and enjoyment, which are needed to sustain any ongoing effort. These positive states do not thrive, simply in the absence of negative affects. Infants and young children have limited capacities to develop new ideas and strategies on their own. In the longitudinal data to be presented in the next chapter, the more that children received support in expanding, sustaining, and communicating their states of interest and enjoyment, the more they were able to experience themselves as the source of interesting ideas and events, to sustain their interests when alone, to invest in their interests readily and easily, and to find a wide range of objects and activities interesting and enjoyable. By contrast, the less the caregiver was a facilitating presence, or became frustrated with the child, the more these infants and children constricted their interests, experienced boredom, were unable to engage others, or to sustain their interests when alone, and did not derive enjoyment or excitement from their activities.

The positive affect dynamics involved caregivers allowing their interest and enjoyment to be evoked by the child, and offering just the right amount of support when the child's interest led to frustration, so that the child could persist and once again experience interest, thereby creating a positive–negative–positive affect sequence. This "scaffolding" activity by caregivers can create in the child an optimistic attitude of "I can do things!" or "my interests matter," or a general optimistic attitude. By contrast, when the caregiver's interests were not engaged, or when they became frustrated, thereby amplifying the child's frustration and then left the child alone, the child experienced a positive–negative–negative emotional sequence, and often gave up on the task. When this sequence became a chronic experience for the child, it tended to create an attitude of "nothing works" or "I can't do anything, so why try," or "my interests are not important."

Papousek, Papousek, and Koester (1986) come to a similar conclusion based on their experimental work with young infants:

> [I]nfants appear to be just as attracted to the expectation of a pleasurable outcome that accompanies success as they are motivated to avoid the negative affect experienced with too much incongruency, dissonance, or the inability to discover the contingencies and adjust their own behavior accordingly.
>
> (p. 99)

Tomkins (1962) has also argued that the positive affects of interest/excitement and enjoyment/joy are experienced as inherently rewarding states and, as such they can become goals in and of themselves. In this realm of positive affects, it seems that the rich get richer, and the poor get poorer as early patterns spontaneously build on themselves (see Demos, 1986, 1988, 1989, 1992, 1993 for more extended discussions of these issues).

Programs such as Head Start and attending school can potentially counter such unfavorable trends by providing a more responsive environment, thereby giving children a better foundation for developing their capacities. While this positive–negative–negative sequence does not represent a direct threat to the maintenance of coherence, learning cannot be sustained without being amplified by the positive affects of interest/excitement and enjoyment/joy. This is a specific explication of Panksepp's (1999b) statement, quoted earlier, namely: "in early childhood there is no sustained line of thought without a sustained line of affect" (p. 17). Thus this sequence can markedly restrict the child's conceptual world, limiting the range and growth of their potential competence to create adequate and flexible new meanings of their experience. It can also severely compromise the child's potential for actualization, of their abilities, thereby inhibiting their agency, to which we will now turn.

Agency

The evidence for a biological bias and preference for being an active agent in making things happen in ones life comes from a variety of sources, including research from animal studies in the 1950s (e.g. see Harlow, 1953; Hill 1956; Leuba, 1955). More recently, Grigsby and Osuch (2007) have reviewed several studies on rats, in which electrodes were implanted into the ventral tegmenetal area (or VTA) of the brainstems, an area involved in reward and behavioral reinforcement. They summarize the results as follows: "when rats could stimulate the VTA themselves by self-initiated behavior, the outcome was desirable, but the same stimulation became aversive when it was administered by the experimenters and not preceded by self-initiated, goal-directed behavior" (p. 72). The authors go on to say: "*the act of engaging in self-initiated effort toward a goal is fundamentally different and activates more brain regions than non-self-initiated stimulation of even highly rewarding brain regions*" (p. 72, italics mine).

Other evidence for the primary importance of agency comes from the research on human infants. The DeCasper and Carstens (1981) experiment described earlier, in which the neonates, who had learned to control the onset of a female voice singing, became upset when put in the non-contingent phase of the experiment, and they could no longer actively control onset of the stimulus, and in the Blass et al. (1984) experiment in which neonates turned their heads to facilitate the stroking, and then cried when the sucrose did not appear in the extinction phase. These experiments revealed both the neonate's remarkable sensitivity to and preference for being an active agent, namely that events are contingent on the infant's behavior, and that the issue of agency is highly pertinent from the beginning of life, influencing learning and attention, and is continually being shaped by transactions with the environment. Grigsby and Osuch (2007) describe agency: "*as containing the components of foresight, choice, and self-initiated behavior and involving the cognitive functions of planning, organizing, self-monitoring and the autonomous regulation of behavior*" (p. 67, italics mine). *All are functions that are present in the neonate's repertoire of capacities and manifest in both the DeCasper and Carstens and Blass experiments*.

The neonate's ability to imitate facial expressions experienced passively (Field, Woodson, Greenberg, & Cohen, 1982), and to replace reflex sucking with voluntary sucking (Bruner & Bruner, 1968) are other examples of the neonate's preference and intention to do voluntarily what has been experienced involuntarily. Such an intention involves generating the idea that this would be something to do. It is *as if* the infant thinks "this is nice, but I'd rather do it myself." Of course the infant does not think in words, but their actions indicate they do think and demonstrate a strong preference for being the agent that brings about a desired result. This was demonstrated in the Blass experiment, in which 1-day-old infants learned the connection between forehead strokes and sucrose, and then actively began to turn their heads in order to facilitate the stroking. Where does such a preference come from? Tomkins (1978) in discussing these very early phenomena, gave the following answer, which derives from his dynamic systems perspective:

> It represents an extraordinary creative invention conjointly powered by primitive perceptual and cognitive capacities amplified by excitement in the possibility of improving a good actual scene by doing something oneself. These are real phenomena and they appear to be highly probable emergents from the interaction of several basic human capacities. This is why I have argued that we have evolved to be born as a human being who will, with a very high probability, very early attempt and succeed in becoming a person.
>
> (p. 215)

In their work with rats Grigsby and Osuch (2007) conclude their discussion of agency with the following comments:

> From this discussion of agency, it is evident that the capacity for this complex psychological-physiological process is critically important to proper mental functioning. It is a functional system that transcends psychiatric diagnoses and may, in fact, be a common element of the dysfunction that occurs in most psychiatric illness.
>
> (p. 74)

In his recent book, David Shapiro (2000) has presented compelling clinical data to support just such a claim, namely, that "*abridgements of volition are at the heart of all mental illness*" (p. 47, italics mine).

What environmental conditions are necessary to support this basic and vital human goal? Sander (1982) has suggested that when a family can facilitate the infant's own efforts at goal realization and provide opportunities for the infant to initiate goal-organized behaviors, it will provide "the conditions which establish not only the capacity for self-awareness, but conditions which insure the use of such inner awareness by the infant as a frame of reference in organizing his own adaptive behavior" (p. 17). He goes on to say in the same paragraph that, "*the valence of this inner experience under these conditions of self-initiated goal realization will be felt as the infant's own*" (p. 17, italics mine). In other words, the family has to make room for a new self-organizing agent within its midst, and negotiate this issue of initiatives, for it will involve inevitable clashes of agendas between the infant's goals and the goals of other family members.

Several other researchers (Dunn, 1977; Provence & Lipton, 1962; Watson, 1966) have pointed out that when a caregiver's behaviors are contingent upon the affective and behavioral cues coming from the infant, rather than geared to a schedule or to the caregiver's convenience, then the baby gradually develops a *sense of effectance, an expectation that his or her own actions make a difference*. Once again, individual variation is the rule, thus there are many possible scenarios (see Demos, 1986, 1988, 1989) that involve the timing, content, intensity, and coherence of the caregiver's responses, combined with many infant variables that together result in complex dynamic transactions that gradually shape the infant's efforts to preserve and exercise agency.

AIM and affective sequences

I will explore the timing and content of the caregiver's responses to demonstrate some of the complexities involved. Imagine a mildly distressed infant, whimpering and stirring, who slowly works up to a rhythmical cry and more restlessness and begins to look around. In this sequence the infant will become aware of a distressed affective state (A), will experience an intention to end or decrease it (I), and will begin to mobilize efforts to achieve that goal (M). I refer to this psychic process as AIM. It represents the dynamic coming together, within the infant's psyche, of an optimal level of *affective arousal*, with whatever past experience has accrued from connecting the antecedents and consequences of previous similar states of coherency, which results in the emergence of an *intention* or a goal and the beginning of *mobilizing an action* to achieve that goal. When the caregiver intervenes at that moment, and is able to *match the specificity* of the infant's goal, the infant will experience a *recognition of and validation of his/her own initiative*, as well as a realization of the goal. And echoing Sander, *this entire transactional event will enhance the infant's use of internal cues and self-generated goals as a frame of reference for future plans and actions.*

When the caregiver intervenes too early, before the psychological processes of AIM emerge, the infant receives a remedy before experiencing any affective awareness of a problem and of an intention and the need to mobilize a response, thereby resulting in a passive experience for the infant. The caregiver's response is then experienced as coming out of nowhere or as unrelated to the infant's signals, or agenda. Alternatively, when the caregiver intervenes too late, as in the example letting the infant's cry build up to a high intensity, the processes of AIM will be disrupted by the non-optimal level of negative affect. Thus the infant's inner experience of being able to achieve and recognize a coherent, organized internal affect state, a desire to respond and mobilize an action, resulting in a feeling of effectance will not occur. *Meeting the infant, during the moment the infant is most aware and ready to receive help, and matching the specificity of the infant's goal is crucial in fostering the infant's experience of agency.* There are obvious parallels here to the timing and specificity of interventions in the therapeutic process.

Caregivers' abilities to respond in this optimal way involve many variables. First, they need to be able to perceive their infant as an autonomous agent versus as a completely helpless being and thus not intervene too soon, anticipating the infant's every need. Second, they have to value their infant's specific initiatives, without perceiving them as silly or perceiving this new agent as a threat to their authority and turn interactions into battles of who is boss. At the same time this recognition of the infant's capacity for agency has to be balanced by a realistic perception of the infant's self-regulatory limitations so as not to overestimate those capabilities, and abandon the infant in overwhelming states. This involves being able to judge their infant's optimal frustration level that will be experienced as a doable challenge; as well as being able to tolerate the infant's bumbling or awkward efforts at mastery, without becoming intrusive, angry, or contemptuous, and thereby evoking undue fear, rage, or shame in the infant. In other words, for optimal outcomes, caregivers have to get to know their infants and adapt their own skills, patience, self-awareness, judgment, containment, and empathy to the particularities of that unique little being.

The content of the caregiver's responses are also important. Imagine an infant gazing at and reaching toward a nearby object – a manifestation of AIM – the affect of interest, the intention to explore the object, and the mobilization of a reaching action. But the infant cannot fully execute the plan and begins to express mild frustration. The content of the caregiver's response at these moments can take on a positive or negative meaning for the infant. Facilitating the infant's efforts will likely enhance the infant's interest and persistence. Becoming irritated, or punitive, or ignoring the infant's fussing will likely lead to the infant becoming more frustrated and/or distressed and giving up the goal. I am suggesting that the infant experiences these moments as *affective sequences* – the first example is a positive–negative–positive sequence (interest/frustration at not being able to explore ones interest and receiving help in still trying) and the second is a positive–negative–negative sequence (interest/frustration receiving increased frustration or distress). Thus the caregiver's response can determine the motivational meaning of the whole sequence for the infant, namely what to expect when one experiences a particular affective state in a context and tries to carry out ones intentions and actions mobilized in that context. Clearly the positive–negative–positive affective sequence enhances the infant's experience of agency and effectiveness.

In the positive–negative–negative sequence, several aspects of the infant's engagement are at play simultaneously, and their meanings are unclear to the infant, with the lack of caregiver support. Is my interest or my frustration wrong? Is my reaching wrong? Is the object wrong in some way? Without guidance, the infant tends to place a negative meaning on all three aspects of AIM. Thus a steady diet of this sequence will gradually undermine the infant's sense of agency and efficacy.

For example, in a study of the development of self-esteem, I reported on two toddlers, who I had videotaped over a period of six months, presenting a detailed analysis of a three-minute segment of videoed transactions obtained in home visits, as well as data from the entire thirty minutes, which contained typical interactions of these two pairs. This segment compared the involved, mutual transactions of pair C with the relatively uninvolved or incompatible transactions of pair D. I used a measure representing the child's tendency to try things at the limits of his ability, and his persistence when things got difficult, qualities related to skills needed in school. I found that child C tried many more activities and produced a ratio of 10:6 victories versus non-victories, while child D rarely tried, and his activities produced a ratio of only 2:0 (Demos, 1983).

I want to be clear about the affect dynamics involved over time in this positive–negative–negative affective sequence. Positive affects are minimized, negative affects are compounded and intensified, and the infant/child is often either berated and/or left alone to cope with the consequences (these observations come from the longitudinal studies cited above). In motivational terms, the infant/child learns that his/her affect states and agency, namely his/hers wishes, plans and actions related to these affect states, are not acceptable, or important, or valuable to caregivers, or cannot be shared and elaborated with caregivers. Thus the inclination to use one's inner awareness of the affects, goals, and efforts as a frame of reference for organizing future behavior is not supported. In terms of agency the infant/child learns that when alone, he or she cannot persist and develop skills and solve problems (see above example of child D) or endure or modulate negative affect, nor can he or she reestablish positive affect. At such times the infant/child experiences the self as devalued, ineffective and helpless. Such a state, heightens the need for parents, and leads the infant/child to shift away from a focus on inner states and goals as reliable guides for developing agency, and to focus on the goal of obtaining and sustaining a parent's involvement. While this strategy can help the infant/child retain some semblance of agency, it substantially *constricts the degrees of freedom open to the infant/child by closing off internal sources of vitality, affective information and self-initiative*. One is reminded of Winnicott's (1965) notion of the false self, or of Kohut's (1991) notion of the enfeebled self. Here I am articulating the affective dynamics that may lead to such outcomes.

The interplay between coherence and agency

In all non-linear dynamic systems, one of the best sources to explore the interplay between variables is in longitudinal case studies. Thus, given our focus on human psychic development, it follows that the use of longitudinal case studies of infants/children in their family contexts are of primary importance. I had the good fortune to become involved in the twenty-five-year follow-up phase of the Boston–Denver longitudinal study that began initially in the 1950s, and produced the most thorough, in-depth, exhaustive data set, yet available, on thirty families, through the pregnancy, birth, and subsequent development over a three-year period of their first child. Based on this data, Lou Sander (1975) has articulated an epigenetic series of issues that were continually negotiated over time in these families as their infants developed increasingly complex, new organizations and initiatives, thereby making new demands on the family system, representing a progressive expansion of the scope of self-regulation of the infants vis-à-vis the control of situations in the environment.

> The regulation of infant functions, based on behaviors that have become harmoniously coordinated between mother and infant, will become perturbed with the advent of each new, and usually more specifically focused and intentionally initiated, activity of the infant. Thus adaptation or mutual modification on a new level is required.
>
> (p. 135)

What follows is a brief description of this epigenetic series of issues. From birth to roughly 3 months of age the central issue being negotiated is the initial regulation of coherent states of sleeping, waking, eating, elimination, and so on. As the infant's awake states become longer, and more predictable (roughly from 4 to 6 months) the infant is more available for "reciprocal exchanges" of smiling behavior, vocal and motor responses. If the caregiver responds, affectively spontaneous back-and-forth sequences, for the sheer joy of them can then occur. Throughout this phase the infant gradually becomes more active in initiating exchanges, which ushers in the next phase called simply "initiative" (roughly from 7 to 9 months). During this phase the infant becomes more intentional and goal directed, and is becoming more mobile, such as crawling, presenting altogether new challenges to the caregiver. As the infant becomes able to move away from the caregiver, a new behavior, which Sander calls "focalization" emerges (roughly from 10 to 13 months). The infant now needs to determine how available the caregiver will be when the infant makes a bid for attention, and until this issue is resolved, the infant becomes intensely focused on the caregiver's whereabouts, presenting a different, and often difficult challenge to the caregiver. This is the period of separation anxiety and stranger anxiety. As the infant becomes increasingly mobile and walking (roughly from 14 to 20 months), he/she becomes more self-assertive about goals, which are now asserted intentionally, and at times against the caregiver's wishes, again, requiring a new adjustment between caregiver and infant. Sander calls this phase "self-assertion." Others often call it "the terrible twos." During the period of 18 months to 36 months two issues emerge and are being negotiated between the child and the caregiver. With the advent of language and secondary processing, the child becomes more aware of his inner intentions, state, and fantasies, and can now experience that another is aware of what he is aware of within himself. This makes possible a more self-reflective experience of "recognition" by another and of self-recognition. The second issue that emerges in this same period is the need to disrupt and then restore mutual coordination with the caregiver through intentional, aggressive disruptive and repair behaviors, so as to experience, and to test the limits of "continuity" of a separate self and in relation to the other.

Throughout this series of seven issues, whatever pattern of coherence within the infant and coordination with the caregiver is obtained, it is then disrupted, and re-worked as more focused and directed levels of agency and initiative progressively emerge in the infant. There are many ways these negotiations can occur, and again, idiosyncratic variations are the rule. When things go well, the infant continues throughout to develop a strong inner-directed agency, with coherent and stable inner states. But at each of these moments, in which new behaviors emerge in the infant that require establishing a new fitting together, things can go wrong, and there will be a failure to achieve a new inner coherence and mutuality. Some of these possibilities have been described above, in which the infant or child's coherence and/or agency can be impaired. In the next chapter I will present two longitudinal case studies that illustrate how the development of coherence and agency are manifested in these issues as they evolve over time, and will also include a wider range of examples from this larger longitudinal study.

Where does attachment fit in?

Bowlby (1969) argued that the child's tie to the mother is governed by an attachment behavioral system, developed over our evolutionary history as a protection against predators, *pre-organized in our brains and automatically triggered by separation from the caregiver.* Bowlby's stated goal was to provide a different, biologically based instinct theory, which would replace Freud's drive theory. He looked to animal studies that formulated control theory models that specified the conditions that initiated and terminated any set of behaviors. He seemed to make an implicit assumption that there exists an immediate, unmediated perception of separation, which equals danger and automatically triggers attachment behaviors. Thus at times his model can appear to be a simple stimulus–response, black-box model of human functioning. There have been many challenges to this formulation (see Demos, 2001 for a more detailed discussion of these issues), but I would like to focus here on his claim for a "pre-organized" attachment behavioral system.

If the brain is a self-organizing, dynamic system, then the functions available to the infant cannot be so specialized and already dedicated to such a specific goal. Panksepp (2001) laments the lack of data on human bonding, but based on his knowledge of how the brain works, argues that the processes involved in bonding are generalized and operate throughout life. "The underlying neurobiological processes that mediate bonding surely fluctuate greatly as a function of development, with considerable specie-typical, gender-typical, as well as individual variation in the underlying processes" (p. 162). Thus he emphasizes *generality and variation*, which are characteristics of dynamic systems. Given the infant's human brain, we know it possesses some biases that predispose the infant to attend to human stimuli, but they operate in a general way. As stated earlier, the infant hears all high-frequency sounds better, therefore female voices are heard more easily. The infant prefers light–dark contrasts, and focuses on contours, and movement, all characteristics found in human faces, as well as in other objects, and can see best at short visual distances that favors seeing a face and eye-to-eye contact while nursing. Yet *there is no evidence for a preformed image of a human face.* In the beginning the infant is a generalist and will smile at any human face and voice, and differentiate phonemes from any language. Only with exposure to a consistent face, voice, and language, will the infant, over time, become a specialist, and smile only at familiar faces and voices and recognize only the language of the particular culture he/she was born into.

The same can be said for the basic emotions. According to Tomkins (1962) the distress cry is evoked by *any non-optimal stimulus* that continues, for example hunger, noise, fatigue, and so on. Initially the infant does not know that anything can be done to make things better. It takes experience with a responsive, reliable other to create the conditions that will allow the infant to begin to develop, through the processes of AIM described earlier, an expectation that the other will be helpful. In my longitudinal, videotaped data (Demos, 1986) the empathically responded-to infant began to use the distress cry as communication at around 3 months of age. Thus, the distress cry *can only be called a separation cry, if the infant is already positively bonded to a caregiver.* The experiences of relief related to decreases in ones own distress cues that have been aided by another and the experiences of the pleasure of engaging in positive, reciprocal exchanges (see Beebe, Lachmann, & Jaffe, 1997) are the mediating variables that are necessary to create a bond between an infant and a caretaker (see Schaffer & Emerson, 1964 for a similar view). The work of Provence and Lipton (1962), cited earlier, documented what can happen when infants are not responded to in relation to their cues, and are not provided with rewarding human interactions. These infants, living in institutions, had stopped crying, and when adopted into families later, they showed deficits in the capacity to bond, although their cognitive functioning was developing adequately. *Thus the general potentialities for attaching to other humans within the infant can only emerge as an organized system if they meet and are facilitated by a responsive human environment.*

It seems that human beings, born into dire or less than optimal environments can live without becoming bonded or attached to other people. It is these extreme examples that clarify the essentials, namely, that the most basic human priorities are about protecting psychic coherence and optimizing ones ability for initiative and agency. Those infants raised in institutions had to learn to protect their affective coherence, at the cost of relating, in order to develop any agency. We know from clinical work that some adults (such as sociopaths) show no evidence of having ever bonded to other humans. I would argue also, that the delusions of a paranoid schizophrenic are created to preserve psychic coherence and some semblance of agency or control, often at the expense of human relationships and a shared reality.

Fonagy (1999) rejects Bowlby's notion that the evolutionary function of attachment is protection from predators, arguing that it is not a good evolutionary strategy, given the high cortisol levels involved in fight–flight responses. He argues instead that the goal of attachment and proximity is to enhance the creation of a particular inter-subjective environment that provides psychic containment and the opportunity to develop a coherent and symbolizing self, which he has called the reflective function. I would add to this formulation, the *explicit* function of providing emotional modulation and containment, thereby enhancing psychic coherence, as well as the function of nurturing the infant's own efforts at achieving self-generated goals.

There are many possibilities that lie between the extreme examples cited above and psychically healthy outcomes – many more than can be encompassed by the four types of attachment described in the literature. In a dynamic systems approach, one becomes aware of the astonishing idiosyncratic variations that emerge. In order for life to feel livable, each person has to find their own way to make coherent sense of their experiences and to feel they have some control over what happens to them. Optimally, this will include rewarding relationships with others. But under extreme conditions, even when relationships exist, if the world no longer makes sense, as seems to be true for some returning veterans of war, and/or if one feels there are no viable actions available, the last act of initiative may be suicide.

In conclusion, I have described the advantages of a dynamic systems approach to development that focuses our attention on the specifics of the fit between a self-organizing and active infant and the human and inanimate environment, and on the complex dynamic processes involved in all transactions with those environments. Thus the infant exists in a biopsychosocial context that emphasizes the basic biological priorities of maintaining psychic coherence and agency, as the infant creates novel organizations and adaptations as my be motivated by changes in internal or external conditions. This approach requires us to give up previous notions about predetermined goals, stages, or outcomes and emphasizes that idiosyncratic variations are the rule, and thus longitudinal case studies of the emergence of new behaviors and organizations become the preferred methodology.

I have presented data that demonstrate that infants arrive in the world with general pre-adapted capacities for feeling, thinking, perceiving, remembering, and acting, and with the organizational ability for coordinating these capacities in primary consciousness to produce voluntary acts. They are exquisitely sensitive to contingencies and to certain general qualities manifested by humans, e.g. motion, light–dark contrasts, etc. But infants do not come equipped with a preformed image of a face or a pre-organized attachment agenda. Thus, contrary to Winnicott's (1965) statement that "there is no such thing as a baby" (p. 84), there is indeed a baby with a functioning set of unique social, experiential, and organizational capabilities, guided by the basic biological priorities of maintaining coherence and agency, and there is a mother with her unique history, capacities for nurturance, affective tolerances and the idiosyncratic meanings she attaches to her infant. The infant clearly needs a caregiver, but that role in a dynamic systems approach is seen an enhancing, supporting, interfering with, discouraging, impairing, or ignoring the infant's ongoing processes and efforts, as manifested in AIM. The mother has considerable influence, *but this influence does not amount to creating de novo organization and basic capacities within the infant.* How and whether bonding emerges between the infant and the caregiver, given the idiosyncratic characteristics of both partners, will depend on the specifics of the ways they each learn to live together.

Chapter 3

Longitudinal studies

In this chapter, I will primarily be presenting the data on two infant girls, videotaped over a two-year period in their family settings, illustrating the ongoing negotiations that the infant's changing capacities for coherence, namely affect regulation, and agency required from their families, as outlined by Sander in the last chapter. To provide a wider range of possibilities, I will also include brief examples drawn from the data from two other sources – my own video-taped series on infants and toddlers, at three different age levels, followed over a six-month period, and examples from the data of the first two years collected in the 1950s and 1960s consisting of interviews, testing, and written observations of home visits and play sessions drawn from the twenty-five-year Boston–Denver longitudinal study mentioned earlier.

Let me begin with the two infant girls. Before the birth of each child, the parents had agreed to participate in a pilot study of normal infant development, observed in their family environments. We used this video-taped data to help us develop categories for dealing with the infancy data from the twenty-five-year follow-up study mentioned above. Soon after the birth of each baby our regular home visits began at a frequency of every two weeks during the first year, and every three weeks during the second year, at various times of day. A half-hour videotape of life as usual was collected, with the camera always focused on the infant. This method highlights both the ongoing state shifts and activities of the infant, as well as the specific cues that draw the caregiver into more direct transactions with the infant. Interview data were also collected at each visit. Every attempt was made to put the families at ease. In previous presentations of this data, I have used the names Cathy and Donna for these two infant girls.

Cathy was the second born, first daughter of upper middle-class parents. When we first met her at 10 days of age, she was an easy-going, alert, sociable baby. The mother was relaxed and delighted with her daughter, feeling that she had fulfilled her dream of producing first a son and then a daughter. Donna was the third born, second daughter, also of upper middle-class parents. At 9 days of age she was alert and somewhat sober (her father had already nicknamed her "sourpuss"). The mother was very competent and tender in her handling of Donna, but expressed some surprise, and perhaps mild disappointment, that Donna did not look like her first daughter. Although in that first visit Donna was less "smiley" than Cathy, and produced moderately intense responses, temperamentally both babies clearly fell into the "easy baby" category as defined by Thomas and Chess (1977). Both babies were healthy and neurologically intact and both had the good fortune to be born into families who had looked forward to their coming and were ready to nurture them.

Initial regulation: birth to 3 months

I will begin with Cathy and her family and describe the first three months of her development, during which the first of Sander's issues is being negotiated, namely the initial regulation of coherent states of sleeping and waking. At our first visit (at 10 days of age) the mother's transactions with her baby were tender, gentle, affectionate, and competent, unbothered by the baby's spitting up or hiccupping. After a nursing and a diaper change, Cathy was alert, interested, and looking around. Her mother then turned on a musical mobile, which Cathy looked at with interest, but after a while, her mother began to engage Cathy in social interaction that lasted for a relatively prolonged period of several minutes, during which she was able to elicit several smiles from Cathy by using a combination of visual (her own face), vocal, and tactile stimulation. It is important to notice that satisfying the hunger drive did not lead to quiescence. To the contrary, undisturbed by drive needs, Cathy was free to attend to other matters, during which the relatively well-organized affect states of interest and enjoyment, evoked by auditory and visual stimuli, were the primary motivators throughout the remainder of this visit.

The sustained face-to-face exchanges observed during this first visit, however, were not to become characteristic for this pair. By our second visit, at 3½ weeks of age, the mother began to exhibit several behaviors that would become a regular part of her interactive style throughout the first year. Whenever Cathy would gaze with intent interest at her mother's face, without smiling, the mother would interpret her quiet, focused interest as boredom. This inference that Cathy was bored was frequently verbalized by the mother. She would then pull back her own face, out of Cathy's visual range, and jiggle a toy in front of Cathy's eyes. This sequence was observed many times over the next several weeks. During this same early time period, another pattern began to emerge that involved the way this mother distributed her attention between her infant daughter and her son (aged 4). Whenever her son was around, the mother would turn away from Cathy and focus her attention on him, even though this often meant interrupting or foreshortening an interaction with Cathy. Each time the mother turned away, either to substitute a toy or interact with her son, the animated interest on Cathy's face would fade as she looked at a toy with only mild interest or as she looked away with a somewhat blank expression.

As described in Chapter 1, infant studies clearly indicate that the human face contains all of the perceptual elements that most engage the infant's attention, and therefore is the stimulus, par excellence, to evoke and sustain the infant's interest, particularly when combined with the human voice. Toys cannot function as effective substitutes at this age. Infant studies also demonstrate that from birth on infants are "making sense of" their experiences, and since these early moderately intense states of interest were coherent and focused, they would be recognizable to Cathy whenever they recurred. So what was Cathy learning about her states of interest in these sequences when her mother did not allow her to gaze at her face for prolonged periods, until she was ready to stop? I would suggest she was learning the following: (1) my states of interest and enjoyment do not last long; (2) interesting objects, namely mother's face, disappear at random; (3) my behaviors and wishes can't keep mother's face here; and (4) I am not a source of interest and joy to my mother. Thereby Cathy did not experience that her interests and enjoyments mattered to her mother, or experience herself as an effective agent in prolonging her states of interest and enjoyment, in exchanges with her mother.

By 2½ months, Cathy began to make her own contribution to the evolving pattern. Having learned to expect that these exchanges would be brief, she would often initiate the turning away in face-to-face exchanges with her mother. While this may have preserved some remnant of agency for Cathy, the turning away mainly represents her assessment of these face-to-face exchanges as not providing a contingency relationship for her. When this new piece of Cathy's behavior was added to the mother's characteristic pattern, in a reverberating circuit, it increased the likelihood that their social exchanges would be brief and relatively low in intensity.

During this same period, Cathy was enjoying animated social exchanges with her father in the evenings and on weekends, and to a lesser extent with her brother, whose style was somewhat rough and intrusive. And she was socially responsive to our overtures. Yet, she spent the largest portion of her waking time with her mother, and we began to observe a gradual dampening of affective intensity in Cathy, as well as a growing passivity.

We need to turn now to a description of Cathy's experiences of the negative affect states of distress, anger, and fear, and her self-regulation of the sleep–wake cycle in the first three months. From the very beginning, Cathy was not allowed to build up to even a mild level of distress. At the first sign of Cathy's restlessness or mild vocal fussing, the mother would pick her up and nurse her. Indeed during the first six and a half months of our observations of this family, we never saw or heard Cathy cry. This absence of observed crying was not merely an artifact of our visits. At a visit when Cathy was 2½ months, when the mother joined us in watching Cathy sleep, she expressed surprise in seeing Cathy wake with mild fussing, look around, and eventually fall back asleep. She commented then, that perhaps she had never given Cathy an opportunity to engage in this kind of self-regulation. This moment of self-reflection on the mother's part offers a plausible summary of her basic attitude toward her baby. We noticed repeatedly that the essence of the mother's responses seemed to function to provide a soothing, quieting, and minimally challenging surround for her baby. This stance was encapsulated by her comment: "Up to 3 months, I'll do everything I can to comfort her; I'll carry her around, nurse her, and do everything I can to keep her contented."

From Cathy's point of view, there were very few experiences of even moderate distress because of her mother's premature interventions. We did observe at roughly 5½ weeks, one instance of self-regulation during a waking state. When Cathy was left alone briefly, and began to fuss in a mild way, she began to move her head from side to side, visually scanning the environment, and found an object to focus on with interest, and quieted briefly (an experience of AIM). Soon, the fussiness began again, and she returned her gaze to this object, becoming focused, interested, and quiet again, until the mild fussiness came back and by then her mother returned and picked her up. Here we see an example of how the more organized state of focused interest can be used to override a low level state of distress, a method caregivers have often use to calm their infants, and in this instance, a method that Cathy discovered on her own. In the main, however, she was not allowed to experience AIM, namely, the awareness of the discrete affect of distress, the intention to want to lessen it, and the effort of mobilizing a response. Often, before she could develop an intention and mobilize a response, her mother intervened. Thus one important source of motivating information, namely that coming from internal affective signals was being short-circuited. This left Cathy with little incentive and few opportunities to make a connection between a felt need and the remedy offered, resulting in only a few opportunities to experience herself as the active agent in developing her own capacity to self-regulate, either in order to either prolong a positive state of interest or enjoyment or to decrease a state of distress.

In this first three-month period, then, Cathy's experience of both the positive affects and the negative affects was interrupted prematurely by the mother's characteristic interventions. Thus, by and large, Cathy was prevented from experiencing the emergence of the psychological processes of AIM and the experience of being actively engaged in influencing events. At the same time her capacities for self-regulation, crucial for sustaining coherence of affective states, were not being facilitated by her mother's premature interventions.

We now must shift our focus to Donna and her experiences during her first three months of life. As described earlier, although she was not a particularly "smiley" baby, she was alert and displayed an early capacity for long periods of focused, intent gazing at her mother's face. Her mother consistently facilitated this display of interest as she maintained and sustained *en face* interactions by providing Donna with an ever-changing array of facial, vocal and cutaneous stimulation. Her two older siblings (aged 3 and 5) quickly tuned into their mother's style and became another source of interesting stimulation for Donna. The mother was remarkably skillful in supporting their nurturing and playful interchanges with Donna, so that this baby was offered a rich social world.

By roughly 5½ weeks, we observed the same self-regulatory capacity in Donna that we described for Cathy, namely, when alone, and mildly distressed Donna could focus on an interesting object and calm herself down. By 10 weeks of age we already see Donna developing a capacity to remain interested and to maintain a state of alert, active equilibrium for prolonged periods of time. The mother's capacity to sustain *en face* interactions, and to respond to the baby's cues, allowed Donna to influence the duration and intensity of these exchanges. Thus Donna seems to have learned: (1) my states of interest and enjoyment can be prolonged and intensified; (2) interesting objects, namely mother's face, are likely to appear and to remain available; (3) my behaviors influence the beginning, the duration, the intensity, and the end of these experiences; and (4) I am a source of interest and enjoyment to my mother.

When we look at Donna's experience of the negative affects of distress, anger, and fear, we witnessed the same process of mutual accommodation between Donna and her mother. The tone and style are conveyed during our first visit, when Donna was 9 days old. Donna was hungry, but the mother, in an effort to stretch out the interval between feedings, decided to bathe her first. As she held Donna, who was crying intermittently and trying to mouth her hands, she turned to us and said: "I think you'll get at least ten minutes of crying." Indeed, Donna did cry intensely during her bath, but was easily comforted afterward. The crying looked and sounded like intense distress alternating with anger (see a description of these affects states in Chapter 2) evoked by the combination of the level of her hunger, the massive increase in stimulation resulting from being naked and wet, and the immaturity of her 9-day-old nervous system, which did not yet allow her to manage such a high level of continuous, non-optimal stimulation, nor yet to draw on her memory of past experiences of having been comforted or bathed. Thus, even though the mother remained calm and soothing throughout Donna's alternating states of distress and anger, her actions were not effective in significantly reducing the density of negative affect experienced by Donna on this occasion.

Nevertheless, it is important to note that the mother demonstrated several qualities during this first visit that were characteristic of her throughout our observations: (1) her ability to remain calm and unflustered in stressful situations; (2) her ability to accurately perceive her infant's states, although in this instance, she chose not to act on her perception, e.g. she did not feed the baby before the bath (see Demos, 1984 and Schwaber, 1981 for a discussion of empathy as a data-gathering process, distinct from how one decides to use the data so gathered); and (3) her continued support of her infant, and her confidence and expectation that stressful situations can be managed, endured, and that solutions can be found. Donna also demonstrated some characteristic qualities: (1) her ability to emit clear signals; (2) her ability to recover quickly from intense distress and anger; and (3) her ability to modulate her less intense states, i.e. before and after the bath when she was dealing only with her hunger.

We also saw the mother helping Donna to modulate these states by employing a common technique for quieting a fussy baby, namely the evocation of the competing affect of interest. Thus after the bath the mother held Donna in an *en face* position, gently rocking her up and down, talking softly and gazing at her face. Donna responded by looking at her mother, whimpering, then quieting and continuing to gaze, with interest, for several minutes. This is a good example of how one affect can not only mask or override another affect, but can also mask and override a drive-affect complex. In this particular instance, Donna's interest in her mother's face and voice competed with and overrode her hunger-related distress. However, later, when again the mother tried to stretch out the interval since the last feeding, and tried to use a toy, it failed to evoke sufficient interest, and Donna's hunger-related distress returned, at which point the mother nursed Donna.

Over the next several months, Donna was allowed to experience a range of intensities of distress, going from mild fussiness to moderately intense crying, and occasionally even to intense angry crying. The mother's tolerance and calmness allowed her to respond with an appropriate remedy to each situation, as she assessed what her daughter could tolerate and manage. For example, if Donna was fussing during a transition between sleep and wakefulness, the mother would tend not to intervene, thereby giving Donna the opportunity to regulate these transitions on her own. Thus, Donna could experience AIM and developed her own capacity to successfully manage these moderate challenges with relative ease. However, when Donna cried because she was tired or in one position too long, tired of looking at the same thing for so long, or was hungry, etc., the mother would respond quickly and appropriately, by changing her position, providing her with a more interesting environment, or nursing her. And when she could not respond quickly with a solution, either because she was temporarily busy, or wanted to stretch the feeding intervals out a little, she would offer a variety of supports and/or distractions to help Donna tolerate the delay. In general the mother's interventions tended to provide the optimal responsivity needed to help Donna achieve and maintain an organized state and to support Donna's own efforts to self-regulate.

Donna's experience of negative affects were of sufficient intensity and duration so that the processes of AIM could emerge, namely, she became aware of the distinctive quality of the affect, experienced an intention to decrease it, and mobilized a response. But these experiences were not so intense and long lasting that she felt overwhelmed or disorganized by them. Indeed, these distinct experiences of distress and anger almost always resulted in Donna's own successful modulation of the negative experience, or in bringing the mother, who successfully helped Donna to modulate the experience, by providing just the right amount of assistance. Thus, Donna's capacity both to maintain psychological coherence and to exercise her agency was being continually fostered.

We began to see evidence that she expected her mother to respond to her expressions of distress and anger at 3 months of age. Her mother placed her in an infant seat on the table while she prepared dinner for the family, and Donna began to cry in response to her hunger and no longer being held in her mother's arms. However she repeatedly alternated this basic distress cry with a brief, angry, more intense "protest" cry, which was combined with a turn towards and a direct look at her mother, followed by a brief pause, as if waiting for a response, before she turned away and resumed the basic distress cry. This cycle was repeated several times. Her mother spoke to her throughout. We interpreted this more intense, focused cry both as an expression of Donna's impatience, and a communication to her mother to "hurry up," with the expectation that her mother would respond quickly and appropriately. As such it represents an important advance in affective competence, for it requires that the infant be able to modulate the distress cry and produce a more intense, brief, *intentional signal cry.*

In this first three-month period then, Donna's capacity to prolong her experiences of positive affects and to tolerate and modulate her experiences of distress and anger was continually expanding with ongoing support from her mother, siblings, and father, thereby enhancing her experiences of psychological coherence and of being an effective agent in making things happen.

Reciprocal exchanges: 4 to 6 months

During this period of more extended wakefulness, the infant is available for longer periods of face-to-face exchanges of social play, which can result in affectively positive spontaneous back-and-forth sequences for the sheer joy of them. Several infant researchers, capitalizing on this extended wakefulness, have provided models of the dynamics of the face-to-face engagement between mother and infant by videotaping infants and mothers in the research laboratory (e.g. see Cohn & Tronick, 1988; Fogel, 1977; Stern, 1977). But the work of Beebe, Lachmann, and Jaffe (1997) provides the most sophisticated statistical approach and theoretical clarification of the complex processes involved, revealing the young infant's extraordinary capacities for social interaction with an available other. Using a time-series regression statistical model, they were able first to analyze the predictability of each partner's own behavior (auto-correlation), which is then removed from each partner, allowing for a test for any further variation due to the influence of the other. This method can provide separate assessments of the mother's influence on the infant, and the infant's influence on the mother. They have demonstrated a robust mutual influence process that operates with split-second timing of responses that are almost simultaneous, and much too fast to be based on a stimulus-response model. Such responses entail a continuous anticipatory processing, which creates a continuous temporal and spatial prediction of a sequence. Thus the infant responds to each event not only as a discrete event, but also as an element of a predictive series. Beebe et al. (1997) argue that time, space, affect, and arousal are all critical elements in creating a temporal-spatial-affect schema, which they call a "*mini plot*" (p. 159, italics mine) that is a representation of the coordination of the two partners' behaviors.

They go on to argue that facial-visual affect, with its high degree of subtle modulation, carries unique information, forming the foundation for intimacy throughout life.

> To the degree that facial mirroring interactions are positively correlated, so that the partners are changing in the same affective direction, the baby represents the expectation of matching and being matched ... These matching experiences contribute to feeling known, attuned to, on the same wave length ... this matching provides each with a behavioral basis for entering into the other's feeling state.
>
> (p. 160)

Tomkins (1968) has stated that, "the shared eye-to-eye interaction is the most intimate relationship possible between human beings." He goes on to say:

> There are universal taboos on looking directly into the eyes of the other because of the likelihood of affect contagion, as well as escalation, because of the unwillingness to express affect promiscuously, and because of concern lest others achieve control through knowledge of one's otherwise private feelings. In our culture only lovers and parents and infants are permitted to gaze into each other's eyes uninterruptedly.
>
> (pp. 327–328)

The time series regression statistical method utilized by Beebe et al. (1997) was also able to demonstrate a turn-taking structure, in which both partners were tracking and influencing the durations of each other's vocalizations, pauses, and switch pauses, a capacity that is already in evidence at 4 months of age, and that is remarkably similar to adult–adult speech patterns.

Other patterns of interacting have been described in the literature, such as the disruption–repair pattern, or the chase and dodge pattern. Several psychoanalytic theorists have argued that disruption is necessary to provide the motivation for the infant to create representations of events (see most recently Blatt's 2004 review). Others, including myself, would argue that ongoing coordination, namely the experience of "being with" is equally, if not more, important, in supporting the basic capacity to sustain an initial engagement, which can then be disrupted and re-established, and that all forms of interactions are being represented internally. The disruption–repair pattern provides the experience of coping with disjunction and successfully returning to a more coordinated pattern, which is an example of a positive–negative–positive affective sequence I described in the previous chapter, which can lead to persistence and optimism in the face of difficulty. When a repair cannot occur, as happens with depressed mothers (see Field, Goldstein, & Guthertz, 1990; Tronick, 1989), the infant is left to rely on his or her own self-regulatory capacities, without the support of the mother, and is unlikely to return to a positive state. Thus, this failure can become a source of psychopathology in the first year of life. The chase and dodge pattern often represents a failure of flexibility in the mother, manifested in a need to try too hard to engage the infant, without regard to the infant's cues, namely the infant's turning away as a signal of "this is too much." The baby is left only with a veto power to disengage, thus, when combined with the mother's vigilance or her giving up, the experience of "being with" is rarely achieved.

An extreme pattern of avoidance, not reported in the literature, occurred in the Boston–Denver longitudinal study mentioned earlier. One of the mothers, during this highly social period of her infant, placed her baby outside in a carriage, for much of the day, so she would not be tempted to interact and thereby risk being "controlled" by her baby (see Tomkins' (1968) quote above). In another family in this study, the shared characteristics of the parents and the infant worked against the infant's optimal development. The infant manifested an unusual degree of inactivity, which matched the parents' slowness and cognitive limitations, thus these parents were very pleased and comfortable with their baby's characteristics, and saw no reason to intervene, and so left their baby alone for long periods of time during this phase of development, thereby compounding the infant's initial deficits. Later on, this infant showed marked developmental delays.

Let us return now to our two infants, beginning again with Cathy. During this period the interactive pattern described in the first three months continued, resulting in brief face-to-face exchanges between Cathy and her mother. Cathy displayed a readiness to respond socially to her father, to visitors, and to her mother's brief availability, but she rarely initiated such exchanges and did not protest their cessation, as if she did not expect to have any effect on others. This somewhat passive stance toward others was at times actively modeled by the mother, who would manifest a palms-up, shoulder shrug – a "what can you do?" response, or would verbalize her own feeling, "we've been left again," when Cathy's brother or father would leave the room. Cathy appeared to be somewhat self-contained, with little overt distress, but with little overt joy either. She was often in the role of an observer, showing brief moments of joy interspersed with longer periods of staring into space. Her play with toys at this age was characteristically languid, suggesting only mild to moderate interest, and her explorations were dominated by sucking, with little elaboration of other exploratory behaviors. The prominence of sucking was viewed not as a response to a heightened oral drive, but rather as a failure of the infant–mother system to facilitate both the acquisition of a repertoire of exploratory behaviors, and Cathy's inability to sustain her interest in people and toys.

In Cathy's passivity we can see the continuing impact of the "lesson" learned in the first three months, namely, that she does not experience herself either as the active agent in initiating and prolonging interesting and enjoyable social exchanges, and thus she rarely initiates exchanges, and that she is not the source of interest and enjoyment for others, thus she accepts their disruptions with little protest. She seems to require the active, vigorous stimulation provided by father, brother, or visitors as the necessary prelude to the mobilization of her interest and enjoyment. Thus the enhancing experience of "being with" and of feeling intimately known or attuned to through mutually regulated, face-to-face positive exchanges prolonged over several minutes seems extremely rare for Cathy.

In terms of negative affects, the pattern we described earlier of Cathy's mother intervening very early to head off any experience of distress, thereby preventing Cathy from experiencing AIM, and developing self-regulating capacities continued during this period. By 3½ months of age, Cathy had not yet developed the ability to sleep through the night; her mother continued to nurse her in the middle of the night. By the fifth month, her mother reported that Cathy could not sleep for more than four hours at a stretch, and upon reflection said:

> I don't really think it is Cathy who can't give this up; it's me. These are the loveliest moments we have together. I just adore it when we are in bed together and I am nursing her ... it is idyllic. The pediatrician is starting her on soft foods and it makes me feel awful to think of all those substances going into her body.

It was during nursing that this mother felt most attuned with her infant and most confident of her own care-giving abilities. She characteristically used nursing as a first or a quick second response to nearly all of Cathy's mild fussy states. In Cathy's experience, when she and her mother are most attuned, she is in a passive, recipient role, so that whatever capacities she has for becoming an active social partner, developing reciprocal interactive skills, or for developing self-regulated, negative affective states, as well as developing a repertoire of instrumental behaviors and coping strategies for managing distress are not being supported and enhanced. Whatever the cause of her mild distress, being nursed, sooner or later, was nearly always the consequence. This lack of differentiation in the mother's response, combined with being put in a passive role when most attuned, foreclosed many learning opportunities for Cathy during this phase of development.

Throughout this same period, Donna and her mother had developed a variety of ways of being together. By 3½ months Donna was already laughing and cooing and trying to vocalize during prolonged face-to-face social exchanges with her mother, which over time included the expression of a range of intensities of the affects of interest and enjoyment, with reciprocal vocalizations, and well-practiced routines.

In these exchanges she was clearly experiencing being intimately matched, attuned to, and being known by the other, and constructing "mini plots" of positive interactions with another. Donna was also enjoying roughhouse play with her father in the evenings, as well as a variety of positive social interactions with her two older siblings.

Her mother also facilitated Donna's engagement with toys by participating in the play, elaborating the possibilities inherent in the toys, and by contributing her own enthusiasm to these activities. With this support, Donna's play with toys was characterized by sustained, intense interest, and enjoyment, and by a variety of actions, e.g. banging, moving back and forth, dropping, and shaking. She was observed to struggle to reach toys when left on her tummy on the floor, and to protest if unduly frustrated or if left too long with one thing. She was able to remain focused, involved, and organized in the face of what often seemed to us, as observers, an excessive amount of stimulation coming from her siblings. By the time she was 6 months old, Donna was able to sustain an intense, active interest in toys for relatively long periods, with only brief contact with her mother or her siblings. She vocalized almost continuously, revealing a rich repertoire of growls, laughs, squeals, and raspberries. She could watch, as well as be actively involved in her own activities, and was observed to imitate her siblings. Donna also displayed at this time a remarkable ability to persist in her own goal-directed plans, in spite of delays, frustrations, and interruptions, manifesting both an intense involvement in whatever she was doing, e.g. practicing her skills with zest and enjoyment, as well as self-reliance, as she tried actively to meet challenges on her own. Her approach to her world conveyed the strong impression that she expected to succeed, as she so often did.

Donna's active response to the people and objects in her life reflects both the ongoing, well-tuned support of her environment, as well as a continuation of the "lessons" she had learned in the first three months, namely, that good things last, that she can be the source of good things, and that she can be the active agent in bringing them about and prolonging them. We witnessed an explosion of riches in a positive feedback loop as Donna's manifest ability to succeed at a variety of tasks served to maintain her interest and enjoyment at a high level of intensity and to provide her with the significant message that she can make things happen, allowing her to increasingly take the initiative in doing just that. It is noteworthy that during this same period, in contrast to Cathy, Donna showed a paucity of sucking and mouthing behaviors.

Donna's expression of negative affects during this period were mostly around her protests when her repeated efforts failed, or when tired, bored, uncomfortable, or hungry, and were usually in the form of the distress cry or brief, communicative protest cries, that evoked an appropriate and relatively quick response from her mother or her siblings. By this time, Donna had also discovered that she could get her thumb into her mouth voluntarily. This represented a gain in Donna's control over her own states of fussiness and distress. These two aspects of Donna's affect competence, namely her ability to modulate her distress and anger and produce a brief, protest, communicative signal, or to soothe herself continued to be characteristic of her throughout her first year. There were, of course, occasions, such as illness, when her physical discomfort increased the level of non-optimal stimulation with which she had to cope, overwhelming her usual adaptive capacities. At such times she could experience more intense, prolonged distress and anger, to which her mother always responded with calmness and support. At 5 months old, she displayed the first sign of startle/surprise or fear, when an unfamiliar aunt swooped down and picked her up. Up until that time, she had been friendly, in a variety of situations, which included strangers. She had a regular daytime babysitter, a collection of evening babysitters, and was exposed to family friends, relatives, and our regular visits. Her response at 5 months of age seemed to involve the element of surprise, as did other events during this same period, e.g. she was surprised and cried, when her mother momentarily disappeared from sight, bending over to pick up a towel, or some other object. These negative experiences were very brief and quickly resolved.

Initiative: 7 to 9 months

During this phase the infant is more intentional and goal directed and is becoming more mobile, thereby presenting new challenges to the caregiver. Given the infant's growing emotional investment in his or her own plans and initiatives, which results in caring a great deal about what happens, the issue of clashing agendas can begin to come into sharper focus. In the Boston–Denver longitudinal study there was great variation in the manner in which these situations were handled, which I will describe below, but each provides an important source of learning for the infant. The parent's response conveys information about whether or not the infant's initiatives and the internal emotional investments are valued and respected, about whether disagreements or different agendas can be resolved and negotiated, and about the style of such negotiations and the range of possible solutions or compromises that become established.

Because the frequency of these moments of clashing agendas is slowly increasing in the daily lives of these families, the power of the learning that occurs is increased by the redundancy inherent in the process of generalizing from one situation to another. I have described elsewhere (Demos, 1984) the three components comprising AIM, namely the stimulus or event that triggers an affective experience, the intention to respond in some way, and the mobilization of a response, which involves the recruitment in memory of past experiences, as well as motor responses and plans, and how the caregiver's response affects all three components. Imagine that an infant sees a pair of scissors, which evokes interest in this novel object, and a wish to touch and explore it, and begins to reach for or move toward the object to explore it further. All three of these components can be inferred from the infant's behavior. Clearly some intervention is necessary to protect the infant. Because all three of these components are present simultaneously in the infant's experience, whatever the caregiver's response, it will provide information about all three components. If the caregiver merely says "no" and removes the object, the infant is left with the question: no to what? Is the caregiver saying no to the object, no to the state of interest and wishing, or no to reaching or crawling toward the scissors; the no will put a stop to all three components. If instead, the caregiver removes the scissors and replaces them with a safer object, the infant can then sustain the state of interest and the intention and the actions to explore such objects. In the latter response, all components of AIM, the infant's state of interest, wish, and actions to explore are not only perceived, but are valued and facilitated.

Let us return to Cathy, and pick up her development during this next phase. An advance in her gross motor capabilities occurred in her eighth and ninth months, and it had a moderately invigorating impact on her experience of herself as an active agent who could now pursue her interests in the world around her. Thus, she began to take more initiative in seeking out toys that interested her and "problems" to solve. These new behaviors engaged her mother's interest and responsivity. Now, the mother's propensity to depend on toys when interacting with Cathy fit nicely with Cathy's readiness to explore a variety of objects within her crawling range. There is, then, for a period of several months, a better match between Cathy's focus and her mother's preference to focus on toys.

Her mother became visibly enthusiastic about Cathy as she told us happily during our visit at 8 months: "She is very cute lately; she's crawling all over the place." During this period, the mother showed her most sustained efforts to engage Cathy, and there were some wonderful, albeit brief, moments of responsivity on the baby's part. However, the mother's interactive style was to adopt either a didactic role or an observer role, resulting, once again, in relatively little sustained, reciprocal interaction. Also, Cathy was now more absorbed in her toys, which had become more interesting to her, as they provided more contingent and predictable responses than did people. Thus it seemed as if the mother was now trying hard, but Cathy was relatively unavailable. The observer, who engaged with her, commented as follows:

> When I was playing with her, the reciprocal interaction went from her to me to her and then stopped, she would then turn away. She always cut it off, i.e. would not imitate a sound or play back to me, and seemed therefore to be self-contained.

Her dyadic activities then tended to be a series of still shots, fleeting and short-lived, rather than a sustained, reciprocal sequence. Cathy's turning away from an available play partner, whether mother or visitor, seemed to reflect her expectation that people are not likely to remain available and be interested and responsive to her initiatives and desires. But this learned strategy was now depriving her of ongoing support in elaborating her play, which researchers have called a scaffolding function of the adult. So, although Cathy was now more engaged with objects and could experience herself as the controlling agent, her play continued to be somewhat repetitive and uncreative, with no one there to help her to see new potentials and possibilities, thus her level of interest was in the moderate range, without peaks of excitement and joy.

Cathy's inability to sustain positive social interactions or to imagine she could use the other to develop new ideas and instrumental skills reflects the failure during the previous phase of reciprocal interaction of her family system to develop sustained, face-to-face interactions during which both partners are actively engaged in co-creating enjoyable sequences, and experiencing a range of intensities of shared emotional states. It also represents a failure to provide differentiated responses to Cathy's behaviors. In this mother–infant pair, sustained attunement occurred only during nursing, initiated by the mother, and placing Cathy in a passive, recipient role. During this same period Cathy was observed to laugh whenever the adults laughed, which seemed to be her effort to feel included in the fun, even though she was an observer, and the jokes were well beyond her comprehension.

This passivity is also reflected in Cathy's rare experiences of negative affect. The first time we observed Cathy crying occurred when she was 6½ months, when her mother disappeared briefly into another room. Her crying in that instance had the characteristics of early expressive crying, namely, a manifestation of distress without the expectation of relief, and without the intention to communicate (e.g. there was no protest in it). Her mother reported at this time, that when Cathy was left with a babysitter, she cried all afternoon and refused a bottle. Here we see the limitations of her mother's strategy to soothe her infant by intervening prematurely to prevent any real upset, and thereby preventing opportunities for Cathy to develop self-soothing capacities, or the capacity to ask for help. When this strategy is combined with the lack of differentiation in the mother's response, namely, her use of nursing as the solution to all problems, her infant was rendered helpless when left with a babysitter.

Cathy had not had the support or opportunity to learn any self-soothing behaviors or instrumental behaviors, nor did the mother facilitate Cathy's learning how to turn to others for help or how to relate socially to another person. Without being near her mother or being nursed, she had no way to cope with a babysitter. Tomkins (1966) has described the development of an all-one pattern of coping with negative affect, as a pre-addictive pattern, namely, that whatever the source of trouble, there is only one remedy, e.g. in adulthood, using a cigarette, drink, or drug for every difficulty. It may not be such a large inference to imagine that Cathy is developing an "addictive" pattern to her mother, without whom, she feels helpless, and overwhelmed, and as with any addiction, no instrumental behaviors are being facilitated or learned.

During our visits, by 8 months of age Cathy was shy and uneasy in our presence, but could remain in the room with us in her mother's absence. But by 9 months, the distress and fear in our presence had increased considerably; she actively turned away from us, crawling rapidly to be near her mother. Also, the sleeping problem we mentioned earlier had persisted, but by 8 months, Cathy was no longer able to fall asleep without being nursed. This sleep issue persisted throughout the entire time of our thirty-one months of observations, representing a failure in this family system to successfully resolve the first issue, of facilitating the self-regulation of coherent states of sleeping and waking.

By contrast, Donna's investment in her initiatives had already begun to increase near the end of the previous phase, and during this same period, her investment in her growing initiatives and plans continued to flourish, as she expanded her repertoire of instrumental capabilities and her range of interests. Her efforts were fairly consistently met by her mother's enthusiastic participation, as well as by her siblings' intermittent, but growing interest in her activities. Her capacity to sustain coherent states of interest and persist in the face of frustrations continued to be characteristic of her, and her efforts often led to success or to the helpful intervention of her mother or siblings. Thus many objects and events had become interesting and enjoyable for Donna, as she experienced prolonged states of interest, excitement, and enjoyment with a range of intensities, and as her world slowly expanded.

At the same time, her mother reported that Donna had shown distress and fear reactions to particular experiences with strangers, e.g. when a woman at the swimming pool picked her up to calm her, or when her mother handed her to the teacher as part of a swimming exercise. The mother summarized Donna's response to strangers as follows: "She's friendly to other people as long as they don't hold her." However, by 9 months, the mother reported that Donna had become clingier when separated from her. We witnessed this reaction during this same time, when one of the observers was a stranger (a male) to Donna, a change that seemed to represent a surprise in our usual visits. She was initially wary but interested as she emptied a basket of toys, but when the visitor tried to engage her more actively, she began to whimper, looked down and away from him, and quickly went to her mother. She was then able to resume her interested play with her toys. But, when her mother left the room, her activity stopped abruptly. She then stared at the stranger, whimpered, tried valiantly to contain her response, but dropped her toys and looked increasingly tense. When her mother returned, her mood shifted suddenly and she relaxed immediately. Throughout, her mother, when present was talking to her about the stranger, and trying to facilitate an inclusive and friendly atmosphere. In summary, Donna was able to stay in the fear-inducing setting, although visibly tense and inhibited, and was immediately reassured and reactivated by her mother's return.

The Boston–Denver longitudinal study provides even more variations in dealing with this particular phase of development and the challenges it presents to the families. In an extreme case, as soon as the infant began to display initiative in a persistent manner, the parents perceived life as a battle and stated, "The baby will fight, but we will win!" They presented this infant with a trio of insurmountable forces: a united front, hypervigilance, which included a relentless interference with the infant's plans, and the use of shaming and humiliation to obtain compliance. All three components of this infant's experience of AIM were interfered with. Following an illness at around 15 months, this infant seemed to give up an active struggle, and became listless, wan, and an irregular sleeper and eater. Another family, who were also relatively inflexible, and adopted negative techniques to obtain compliance, namely, spanking, angry commands, isolation, and threats of abandonment and banishment, seemed to allow this infant only the choice to surrender and comply. But, unlike the previous family's vigilance, this infant was left alone for long periods of time, and was, when alone, over time able to carry out its own plans, as well as to act out defiant fantasies and conflicts around obedience.

In some cases, the parents and infant both shared characteristics, but even here there were variations. In the family mentioned earlier, where both the infant and the parents shared passivity and cognitive limitations, during this phase of development, when the infant was unusually inactive, the parents were pleased and saw no reason to intervene, thereby continuing to compound the infant's initial deficits, resulting in marked developmental delays. In another case the mother and infant were matched in vigor, activity level, and exuberance, and they were able to engage in many highly stimulating interactions that included chortling and laughter. However, this infant was also capable of quieter, dreamier states, which this mother found difficult to accept, and at such times she would try to provoke her child into activity. This mother could also become intolerant of certain behaviors and set quick and harsh limits, and at such times the infant would comply, but this mother always repaired any rift between them.

In cases where mother and infant were not well matched, again variation was the rule. In one family the mother made extraordinary efforts to compensate for her infant's initial deficits and provided more stimulation and activity than would normally be necessary, which were of enormous benefit to her child. In another case the baby was active, vigorous, and persistent but was paired with a cautious, fearful mother, who tried to inhibit her infant's activities. This infant could outlast the mother and withstand her prohibitions, but winning these battles rarely led to the gratification of shared play and an elaboration of strategies and skills, as the mother would withdraw. Without the mother's facilitation and support, this infant's vigor and persistence gradually took on a driven, scattered quality, seeking novelty by changing objects often, rather than through elaboration, resulting in a repetitive sameness with little flexibility and resiliency. In several families, the range of acceptable infant initiatives was narrow and limited. These infants' initiatives became guided primarily by external stimuli, namely by gaining the approval of the caregiver, rather than by internal motivations and cues, and it is here in this phase of development where the development of a "false self" (see Winnicott, 1971) can take on larger meaning, which, over time entails the gradual devaluing and lack of attention to internal cues.

Some families manifested a marked ambivalence toward their infant's initiatives, which cut across a wide range of situations and activities. In one family it was ambivalence around closeness and dependency. The mother could allow it for only so long and then would withdraw, but would become angry if the infant turned to another adult for comfort or for interaction. In another family it focused on enjoyment. This mother would encourage or permit the infant's activity, but in the middle of the infant's excitement and enjoyment, she would suddenly interfere and prohibit the activity – a veritable killjoy. In another family, the mother would initially offer support, but would then begin to tease and frustrate the infant, in an attempt to make the child tough and strong. If the infant dissolved into tears, she would once again become comforting and supportive. In each of these families this ambivalence was repeated often, thus each infant was faced with an uncontainable and insolvable problem, and each child gradually imposed idiosyncratic constrictions and solutions. In the first example that involved dependency, this child gradually became defiant, turning away from proffered help, and insisting on doing things alone. In the killjoy example, this child gradually became oversensitive to intrusions, narrowed his interests, and defended them with stubborn persistence. And in the example of teasing and toughing, this child gradually took on the mother's teasing, aggressive style, insisting on being in control of interactions, while pursuing goals with a grim tenseness.

Finally, two families in this sample displayed minimal involvement with the infant. In one case the mother would hover anxiously over the infant's physical functions, e.g. eating, sleeping, and bowel movements, but otherwise offered no support, protection, or facilitation of the infant's initiatives, and could become exasperated with the infant's actions, labeling them as bad. In this atmosphere, this infant began to restrict activities, with a decline in skills. In another family, with young parents, the mother felt trapped and depressed by parental responsibilities, and developed a breezy, permissive, inattentive, almost negligent style of parenting, both parents expecting the infant to be independent and to work out its initiatives and plans alone. This child gradually developed a precocious independence, leading to plans becoming more limited, less ambitious, and a turning away from people and relationships.

All of these examples illustrate the important learning that is occurring during this phase of development regarding the infant's growing investment in his or her own initiatives and plans, and the powerful effects of the caregiver's responses in either facilitating or interfering with or ignoring this new challenge.

Focalization: 10 to 13 months

As the infant becomes more mobile, and can now move away from the mother, it now becomes important for the infant to determine how available the caregiver will be when the infant makes a bid for attention. Until this issue is resolved, the infant becomes intensely focused on the caregiver in the effort to monitor the mother's movements as well as its own. This presents a different and often difficult challenge to the caregiver, as the infant's focused need to be able to see and/or to know both where the mother is, and how quickly she can be reached if needed, can often feel intrusive and claustrophobic to the mother. This is the phase of increased separation anxiety and stranger anxiety. We saw the beginnings of this focus in both Cathy and Donna in the last phase.

At 10 months old, Cathy still showed distress in our presence, but if she was near her mother, she could get absorbed in her toys. But by 11½ months, her mother's presence was not sufficiently reassuring, and Cathy was restricted and inhibited when we were in the room. A month later she cried as soon as we arrived, and her play was repetitive and monotonous. When the male visitor gently made overtures, trying to help her achieve some degree of comfort in his presence, she did not allow him to enter into her play, turning her back on him, as she tried to maintain her poise with monotonous, repetitive play. Here again, we see the enduring effects of not having developed a repertoire of positive, face-to-face, reciprocal exchanges earlier, during which representations of the experience of jointly creating "mini plots" of being in tune with, known by, and accepted by the other seem not to have occurred for Cathy. Thus without the mother's actual presence, she has no access to a representation of a positive, cooperative, mutually enjoyed outcome.

There was no sign of a decrease in Cathy's distress in our presence over this period, and her mother offered her very little support or facilitation in helping her to befriend us, often talking to us about her in her presence, but not including her in our interactions. This inability to be inclusive seemed to mirror her stance toward her two children throughout our observations, namely interacting with each one separately, but failing to facilitate a three-way interaction. Indeed both parents had this difficulty, and reported problems when all four of them were together. Thus they cherished time when they could both be with one child, or when each was alone with one child.

We observed Cathy's anger for the first time during this period. Her passivity in the past seemed to mute her affects so that prior to this period she had never worked up to an angry protest or response. At 10½ months, Cathy, her mother, her brother, and ourselves were all in the kitchen, as the mother tried to prepare dinner with one hand, while holding Cathy in the other arm. Cathy was shy and clingy in our presence, but did not cry. The mother commented, "Wait until I put her in the highchair, then you'll hear her scream." And indeed, a moment later, when the mother tried to put her in the highchair, Cathy began to scream even before her feet touched the chair. The mother relented, and continued to hold her, and in response to our interest, said this reaction had to do with Cathy's current problem with not eating well lately. Eventually, the mother put Cathy in a walker-chair on the floor, and Cathy produced intense angry crying, that included an initial period of breath holding. Her brother gave the walker a shove from behind, causing a toy to fall off the tray, in response to which the mother briefly laughed and said, "Oh well," as Cathy continued to cry intensely. The mother then talked to Cathy's brother, ignoring Cathy's angry crying, while continuing to prepare the food. Finally, the mother brought the food over, sat on the floor, and began to feed Cathy, who quieted and ate eagerly, gradually trying to feed herself.

How do we understand Cathy's intense anger? Her eating behavior, plus her weight do not fit with mother's explanation that Cathy's crying was due to an eating problem. But the mother's prediction of the crying indicated that Cathy had reacted like this before. One possibility is that it was a combination of her hunger, the loss of physical contact with her mother, and the absence of any other efforts by her mother to help her deal with the delay in feeding, culminating in a high intensity of non-optimal stimulation both from internal and external sources, which in Tomkins' theory (1962) is a trigger for anger. The mother's "oh well" comment seemed to capture her predicament of having no strategies that fell between holding Cathy to keep her quiet, feeding her, or ignoring her. The nature of Cathy's angry cry, namely, a basic expressive cry, without modulation, suggests that Cathy has not had the opportunity to develop a communicative, protest cry, *based on the expectation of a helpful response*. Thus, this basic angry crying represents another result of the mother's inability to help Cathy in the past to develop self-regulating capacities to modulate affect and in the present to offer her any support. Her angry crying in this instance, therefore, continually escalated in a positive feedback loop.

It is also possible that the lack of opportunities for learning how to cope with anger could have been due to the rarity of Cathy's experience of anger. We had seen earlier how Cathy did not protest the cessation of interesting and enjoyable activities, and how on several occasions, when her brother treated her rather roughly, she did not respond with an angry protest, but with a whimper, and had seemed only moderately invested in her activities, looking languid, or seeming content to be an observer. Thus it is possible that only after the previous phase when Cathy had developed the cognitive and motor capacities to carry out her own initiatives and plans with toys, did she experience a sufficient intensity of investment in her wishes to become angry when they were delayed or frustrated as in this episode.

Shifting now to Donna, we learned at a 10-month visit, which occurred shortly after the family's return from a vacation, and again, two weeks later at our 10½-month visit that Donna had experienced several episodes of breath-holding and turning blue since their return home. One episode happened when a relative picked up Donna as the mother was leaving, and the mother returned quickly to soothe and calm Donna. In another episode, the parents were going out, the babysitter had arrived, and the mother decided to nurse Donna before leaving to help calm her. She held Donna in one arm and tried to undo her dress with the other. Failing in this effort, she laid Donna down on the floor to free both her hands, and Donna immediately screamed, held her breath, and began to turn blue. The mother quickly picked her up, calmed her, and then nursed her. These incidents seemed to have in common the threat of mother's leaving, during this heightened period of focalization, as well as a sudden violation of expectation, e.g. being picked up by a stranger, and before the mother leaves, being laid on the floor when expecting to be nursed, which was an added stress.

At our 11-month visit, there are no further reports of Donna turning blue. She did demonstrate a build-up of tension when her mother left the room, but she was able to respond to our offer of distracting toys, and became interested in the proffered play opportunities. Three weeks later, Donna was once again full of joy, vigor, and enthusiasm. At this visit, with her mother present, she made overtures to us and even climbed into the arms of one of us. And, with only one exception, she remained comfortable in the room with us when her mother left, and continued her interested play with her toys. She showed a range of interests in a variety of toys, and there was no hint of inhibition during her mother's absences. Her affect was well modulated, and she was capable of an exuberant flinging of toys, interspersed with a deliberate, quiet, prolonged interest in particular objects.

Throughout this phase, the mother remained consistently available as she actively promoted and facilitated Donna's efforts both to cope with the distress, fear, and anger evoked by strangers, and to develop adaptive ways of being with newcomers. This pair, then, represents a successful resolution of this new challenge manifested by the infant's increased focalization on the mother's availability, as Donna appeared to have developed the expectation and confidence that her mother would be available when needed. In the Boston–Denver longitudinal study, we noticed a marked increase in the number of mothers who chose to go to work during this "claustrophobic" phase of their infant's development, which resulted in a number of cases that failed to resolve this issue. Such a lack of resolution can set in motion an enduring anxiety around separation and dependency needs and around the reliability of others. This anxiety might be manifested in an ongoing clinginess, fretfulness, precocious independence, or a deep ambivalence around dependency. By this period the individual variations and complexities are multiplying as each new phase in the infant builds on the successes or failures of the previous phases, and as each family demonstrates their own idiosyncratic capacities for flexibly adapting to the infant's changing needs or for the repetition of old patterns in response to each new challenge.

Self-assertion: 14 to 20 months

In this phase, the infant has become increasingly mobile and in most cases is walking, and has become more self-assertive about goals, which are now asserted intentionally, and at times, against the caregiver's wishes, thereby, once again presenting a new adjustment for the family. Some have called this period "the terrible twos." If clashing agendas have not yet become a central issue, they are highly likely to become so now, as children at this age are likely to force the issue, by getting hold of something that is either dangerous or breakable, or demanding something they cannot have, or insisting on doing something at an inopportune time, or in their own way or that is beyond their capabilities. The parents are faced with the need to set some kind of limit, and run the risk of either over controlling or under controlling their child's developing assertions.

As Cathy moved into her second year, her skills in walking increased, and by 16 months her growing language skills began to play an important role in her efforts to establish a dialogue with her parents. She became more assertive and persistent in making demands, expressing them clearly and loudly, which at times included temper tantrums. But as we saw earlier, the mother's responses to Cathy's initiatives and assertions still fell within the limited range of teacher or observer, so although she was more likely to become engaged in Cathy's cognitive advances, e.g. when Cathy showed mastery of a toy, it did not lead to an experience of mutuality and an expansion of Cathy's initiatives. When Cathy was unsuccessful in engaging her parents and was left essentially to her own resources, her play was repetitive, limited, and sometimes even aimless, and her demeanor was subdued and half-hearted. Thus we see the continuation of the effects of her earlier experiences with interest and enjoyment, namely the rarity of "being with" experiences. She has rarely experienced herself either as being "met" in her initiations, which could lead to sustaining give-and-take transactions, or as a valued source of these positive affect states. It is also a continuation of the effects of her mother's stance of prioritizing physical comforting over fostering self-regulatory capacities, or a repertoire of reciprocal social exchanges, and instrumental coping skills in her daughter.

Cathy could become animated and more expansive in her play only when her mother or father joined her. But the exchanges with her parents were characterized by only brief moments in which Cathy could experience herself as sustaining a communication with the other, or as pursuing her own initiatives, or elaborating her own plans. The parents, although different, with the father being the more active partner, both tended to use language that was beyond Cathy's comprehension, and to move in quickly to structure the play or to override Cathy's initiatives. They might begin by staying within Cathy's frame of reference, and then seemed to accentuate the distance between the adult and the child by producing sardonic comments, which might be humorous for adults, but clearly left Cathy way behind. For example, in a play sequence with several dolls, each of which were missing a leg, the father commented

"Oh yeah, that baby's in the same medical study that this one is in. That baby also has a lost leg. Are you doing a critical survey of babies with lost legs?" He then laughed.

From roughly 16 months until our observations ended at 31 months, Cathy's isolated play was dominated by the theme of people or objects disappearing and reappearing, e.g. she would cover up babies and uncover them, or hide small figures and then find them again. She repeated these actions over and over again, on many occasions, with no further elaboration beyond this basic theme. Thus she seemed to be stuck in trying to resolve the issue from the previous period of focalization, namely the availability of her mother when needed. Throughout this same period, she also continued to need to be nursed to sleep at night and back to sleep in the middle of the night, when she often awoke and cried.

By contrast, Donna's persistence and assertion began earlier, than 14 months. By 11 months she was already pursuing her goal of getting at her sister's crayons despite numerous prohibitions and injunctions by her mother and her sister. Early in her second year, Donna was very persistent in wanting to climb a ladder chair that her sister refused to relinquish. She fussed, vocalized her protest, distracted herself briefly with other toys, but eventually crawled back to the ladder chair, when her sister left, only to find her sister quickly running back to reclaim possession. The mother intervened at this point telling the sister that Donna wanted to climb. Donna tried to mount the stairs, but was simply unable to master the task. Her mother helped her, and Donna looked triumphant when she reached the top. She climbed back down, with mother's help, and the mother, in an effort to make the task easier, then put the chair on its side. Donna protested immediately and vigorously, and her mother, respecting Donna's goal and assertion, returned the chair to its original position. Donna then worked very hard and successfully to get up the first step. She vocalized happily as she then continued her climb to the top. This process was repeated over and over again, and each time she reached the top, she sang a song of victory. She was completely absorbed in the climbing, as her mother retreated into the background, remaining available if needed, but not intruding. Donna's interest remained high as she learned to manage her legs and become an adept climber, and she gradually introduced variations as she ascended from the opposite side. Her joy at her success was palpable, and was manifested by her happy smiles and her singing.

Donna's singing at the top of the ladder was striking. We called it a song of victory because it occurred at the apex of her effort, but it is perhaps more accurately described as a song of joy. There was no exhibitionistic quality in it, no "look what I've done folks" quality in her behavior or posture. She did not look around at her mother or at the cameraperson for acknowledgment or approval. She appeared to be totally absorbed in her own activity and experience, as after each ascent, she would pause and sing in order to prolong and magnify the success and joy of it all. Tomkins has referred to this phenomenon as "a celebration of positive affect" (personal communication) a phrase that aptly captures the spirit of Donna's singing.

As Donna's physical skills increased, and her language abilities emerged, her play soon involved elaborate dramatizations of internal sequences and fantasies. The themes of her play varied and included such things as cooperating with her mother, as well as saying no to her mother, taking on baby roles and big-girl roles, or experimenting with new ways to do familiar things. Her mother continued to be an active participant in Donna's play and was very skilled at entering Donna's world and facilitating her plans. Their exchanges were characterized by smooth alternations between mother following Donna's lead and Donna following her mother's lead, providing a truly collaborative experience for Donna. This spirit of facilitation and cooperation was evident throughout the family, so that even Donna's siblings were observed at times to help each other.

In the Boston–Denver longitudinal study, we saw a wider range of responses to the increase in the developing infant's assertiveness. In some families the infant's persistence and saying no were experienced as a threat to parental authority, which was dealt with punitively, leading to spankings, harsh verbal corrections, or to isolation. Depending on the degree of the positive strength of the infant's felt bond with the parents, the result of such parental responses could either lead to compliance out of fear, or to defiance, which could lead to more punishment. In other families some of the infant's assertions were acceptable but others were definitely not, and again could be dealt with harshly. There were also patterns of inconsistency that would vary according to the parent's mood or energy level, or that would involve misinterpreting the infant's intent as aggressive if the result of the infant's actions led to too much noise, or to some kind of difficulty. At such times the infant's actions would be labeled as bad. In such instances of mislabeling the child's intent, the distinction between healthy assertion and intentional aggression is blurred and may create confusion in the child or lead to the beginnings of a sense of an assertive self as bad, unacceptable, unlovable, and devalued, etc.

Recognition and continuity: 18 to 36 months

The experience of recognition by the other and by the self becomes possible with the advent of language and secondary processing. Only now is the child capable of self-reflection and is therefore more aware of his inner intentions, states, and fantasies and can now experience that another is aware of what he is aware of within himself. The second issue that emerges in this same period is the need to disrupt and then restore mutual coordination with the caregiver through intentional, aggressive disruptive and repair behaviors, so as to experience, and to test the limits of "continuity in the self and in relation to the other."

The shift that occurs at around 18 months ushering in the capacity for self-reflection has been documented in several research studies. Lewis and Brooks-Gunn (1979) demonstrated that before this age, when rouge is put on a child's forehead and he looks in a mirror, he touches the forehead of the image in the mirror, but by 18 months, the child touches his own forehead. Kagan (1981) described how younger children, when instructed to copy the adult's block structure, were content with their own, more limited structures, but by 18 months, when children compared their limited structures to the adult's block structure, they burst into tears. While both studies demonstrate the increased self-awareness of this period, Kagan's study illustrates the child's acute sensitivity in recognizing that now he or she can see and be seen by others as smaller, and less competent than others, eliciting distress and shame. This emotional aspect is more explicit in the second stage of Erikson's (1950) epigenetic sequence of crises namely autonomy versus shame and doubt, during which decisive encounters occur to determine the balance between autonomy and coercion. This new sense of self-awareness, in

Sander's (1965) terms, "makes possible the child's comparison of himself and his activities with the direction and order of those activities going on about him" (p. 11), and is related to the child's felt need to disrupt and then repair transactions by insisting on and/or feeling frustrated by trying to do things one's own way, perhaps in an effort to shore up a sense of uncertain competence, and coming up against the perception of one's own real smallness and limitations.

In Sander's epigenetic sequence, the young infant, prior to this phase has moved through several periods in which inner wishes, initiatives, and plans were expressed directly through actions and expression, and became more persistent or conflicted, as the prior adaptations that have occurred between the infant and the care-giving system will now influence how this issue will be experienced. This period is described as a "phase of optimal awareness," in which the child's capacity for consciously "owning" his own experience and using it to organize and guide behavior, thereby influencing future adjustments is now possible, thus the communications between child and caregivers are now more highly pertinent, in a self-conscious way. When the child's intentions are misinterpreted, or his cues are misread, it can lead to confusion in his inner perception of himself. But when the child's intentions are accurately understood and accepted, the transactions between the caregiver and the child are then reciprocally coordinated, resulting in a specific matching of the communications by the caregiver to the cues expressed by the child. The child can then experience the other's accurate recognition of one's own inner experiences and perceptions, as an external validation of one's own self-representation, and this recognition will foster one's self-awareness.

This capacity to be self-aware of one's own feeling states, imagery, intentions, and anticipations, which can then be used as guides for behavior, is related to the more recent formulations of Fonagy and Bateman (2008) of the capacity for mentalization. But Sander's work helps us to formulate and understand the epigenetic, developmental, and psychological underpinnings of this capacity, as well as the process during this phase of development of *consolidating a self-concept through the achievement and stabilization of reciprocal interactions of recognition, defined by reciprocal experiences of a shared awareness on the level of inner perception, with its aim and intention, which is expressed and confirmed by another's response.*

Our observations of Cathy ended at roughly 31 months of age, and with Donna at 33 months, and given the enormous amount of data produced by the Boston–Denver longitudinal data, which did continue into the third year, our analysis of that data ended at the two-year boundary. Thus, we have relatively less data illustrating these last two issues from that study.

Cathy appeared not to have entered into these two issues by the time we ended our visits with her family. We have described her mother's limited repertoire of responses that alternated between nursing, and/or holding Cathy, or leaving her pretty much on her own, with only minimal supports for Cathy's initiatives. This stance by her mother failed to provide sufficient facilitation of Cathy's innate potential to develop cooperative social experiences or to expand her interests and instrumental behaviors, or to enable her to modulate or cope with her negative affect states, or to use her internal cues to guide her behavior. As a consequence, Cathy's experiences have, by and large, alternated between successfully obtaining safety in her mother's arms, or assuming a passive, observer stance, or feeling relatively helpless in the face of escalating distress (not being able to fall asleep on her own, or when left with a babysitter), or anger (with a delay in feeding).

She appeared to still be struggling with the issue of her mother's availability in her repetitive play, and with the issue of engaging in reciprocal interactions, having accepted the passive role of an observer, e.g. laughing when others laugh without fully understanding the content, or being unable to deal with strangers.

In terms of Cathy's interactive skills, we described earlier this family's inability to develop sustained, eye-to-eye, positive interactions in which both partners actively engage, in creating experiences of attunement and feeling known, during which the infant constructs "mini plots" of "being with" the other. The most intimate moments Cathy and her mother experienced were and continued to be in the context of nursing, during which Cathy is in a passive position. We have also described how later, the style of her parents' interactions in play sequences with Cathy was didactic, e.g. over-structuring, or using language beyond her comprehension, which again seemed to perpetuate the pattern of Cathy being the recipient of whatever the other offered, which was often miss-attuned to

Cathy's internal experience, and offering little support for her to develop, explore, and elaborate her own interests, plans, and skills.

In one of our later visits, we observed the following play sequence with her father, which illustrates some of the above characteristics of Cathy's situation, particularly her passivity, in the context of a lack of parental attunement. Cathy was looking at toys and her father asked, "Ok, what shall we play with now?" Before Cathy could respond, he said, "Do you think this baby should have a nap?" Cathy picked up a doll and said, "play." Her father then said, "Oh, they're going to play now?" and he quickly suggested how they would play. "Raggedy Ann's going to dance now," and he made his doll dance. Cathy imitated with her doll. Father then said, "Mine's dancing faster!" Cathy said, "faster." The father said, "Mine's dancing very fast!" Cathy repeated, "very fast." The father said, "Mine's dancing slow." Cathy repeated, "slow." The father said, "Mine's sitting." Cathy said, "Mine's sitting." The father repeated, "Mine's sitting." And Cathy also repeated, "Mine's sitting." The father then paused, looking somewhat dismayed. Cathy moved her doll. He then asked, "What's yours doing now?" Cathy repeated, "now." He then said, "Yeah, what's yours doing now?" She repeated, "doing now." And so the exchange continued.

In this sequence, although Cathy's initial focus on dolls was accepted, as well as her rejection of the idea of dolls napping with her word "play," yet before she could generate a play theme, the father quickly took over, and just as quickly Cathy slipped into the role of imitator, as if she did not really expect to be the source of novelty and fun. We can see how her ongoing passivity and lack of initiative in transactions with others may now serve to invite the other to move in and supply a direction, in a self-fulfilling cycle, but the father too contributed by the quickness of his taking over, and only later on, did he think to try to enlist from her a contribution, by asking, "What's yours doing?" She was not yet testing the limits of continuity, and it is difficult to ascertain how self-aware she had become by this time. In this exchange she did not act as if she was aware either of her own intentions, states, and fantasies, or that the other could be aware of her inner life. Certainly, whatever was happening within her mind was not consistently cued into, explored, or validated. She seems to have learned not to expect that the other will respond to her initiatives. Thus there is little indication that

Cathy has been able to develop a sufficient autonomous self, which could be manifested in a state of self-awareness, which could then result in an ownership of her initiatives, assertions and feeling states in relation to another.

During this same period, Donna's use of language had expanded to express a variety of internal experiences and feelings. When leaving the beach one evening, the mother reported that Donna had paused and said, "Nighttime is here, I love the water." Several months later, when Donna was looking out the window and saw patches of snow, she was reported to have said, "It looks like sheep in the meadow." Each of these expressions carries with it the expectation that the other will recognize and validate her internal experiences and fantasies. She was also developing a repertoire for coping with a range of potentially upsetting events, which included dealings with her older siblings. She sometimes left the scene if it felt too overwhelming; she sometimes distracted them, or made a game out of a "teasing sequence," and at one point, she stepped into the middle of their fighting saying, "You are my brother and sister. Be happy."

Later on in this period, as strains in the family built up, resulting in the mother's going to work, Donna was left with babysitters more often and began to attend nursery school with her sister five mornings a week. These changes were stressful for Donna and elicited both creative solutions and the beginning of temper tantrums. At the arrival of yet another babysitter, Donna began to whimper, but then went and got a book and asked the sitter to read it to her. She also found a way to draw her mother into a fantasy play, during an ongoing, somewhat tense discussion between her parents about their taxes. As her tantrums increased, her mother and she began to develop a way to process these episodes afterwards. For example, when Donna had a tantrum over taking a nap, the next day Donna was able to explain, "I wanted to come downstairs. I cried hard." Here we see Donna's capacity to reflect on a prior state of upset, and her recognition that both she and her mother knew it had been upsetting and could now discuss it.

On our last visit, at 33 months of age, she and her sister got into an intense fight over a prized blanket. In the aftermath of this upsetting fight, Donna was still feeling vulnerable, when she and her mother were in the kitchen. Her mother asked if she wanted to use the potty. Donna began to have a temper tantrum. Her mother did not pursue the potty issue, and instead asked Donna what she wanted to drink for lunch. Donna, still caught up in her anger, misunderstood at first, thinking her mother was still talking about the potty. When she realized, that her mother had given up the potty issue, she then made a joke and said, "I want Cheerios to drink!" Her mother joined in the game, saying in a mock voice, "You can't have Cheerios to drink!" Donna then put on a mock temper tantrum, at which they both could laugh. Here we see Donna intentionally disrupting their mutual coordination, followed by her unspoken recognition of her mother's acceptance of her need to work through her anger, which then enabled her to creatively act out a fight, and resolve her earlier upset with her sister in a playful way. Both partners had communicated an awareness of Donna's upset state and what she needed and the recognition that they were each now invested in helping her to restore good feelings. This investment indicated that they both expected from past experience to be able to work things out together, which now enabled them to trust in their capacities to use humor and skill and to believe that their efforts would result in bringing about this highly creative and rewarding solution.

There was one example in the Boston–Denver longitudinal study in which the child was observed to intentionally defy the mother, but seemed to know just how far she could go before complying with the mother's demands. At times, when she went too far, and the mother became punitive, this pair always found a way to come back together. At one point during this phase, this child was having trouble falling asleep in a new bed, and the mother reacted punitively. But after several episodes of persistent distress on her child's part, the mother finally relented, saying, "I just had to." We coined the term "selective empathy" to describe this mother's response style. In this family, the experience of feeling recognized by the other and restoring continuity, seemed to be present in the ability of each partner to "read" the other. In other families, where a punitive pattern had already been established, the child involved had already learned to comply out of fear, or had become more defiant. In one family, the child learned to defy the mother and to fear and comply with the father. In these families the experience of the recognition of one's states, intentions, and fantasies was either consistently in the negative direction, or was inaccurate.

This concludes the presentation of longitudinal case materials used to illustrate the gradual unfolding of infant abilities to maintain cohesive affect states and to actualize agency in the context of the various transactions with the human and inanimate environments that they encountered. Sander's epigenetic series of issues were used to organize the data and to emphasise the increasing complexity and idiosyncrasies such processes entail. The primary importance of the vicissitudes of affects, namely the regulation of negative affects to achieve cohesive states, and the role of enjoyment and interest in creating "mini plots" of "being with," and in sustaining initiatives and agency, was demonstrated, as well as the importance of the ongoing role of the social environment in shaping these processes. Perhaps, at this point, it is redundant to state once again that from birth on, each newborn infant is fully equipped to attempt to make sense of his or her world in order to maintain psychic coherence and to exercise his or her agency, and that in these first few, very important, years, an enormous amount of psychological organization is occurring and being shaped both by the infant's innate capacities and their social environment.

Part II

Critical review of psychoanalytic theories of motivation, integration of current neuroscience, and Silvan Tomkins' comprehensive affect theory

Chapter 4

Motivation theory reformulated

This chapter is the first of three chapters that comprise Part II of this book, which focuses on the central issue of human motivation. It will briefly trace the evolution of Freud's dual instinct theory, and his conceptualizations of affect, with an emphasis on significant unresolved issues. It will then provide a critical review of a variety of psychoanalytic motivational formulations that seek to amend Freud's theory and their efforts to incorporate affects. It will also discuss recent findings from the neural sciences that assign a central motivational role to affects and a far more limited role to drives. This review will conclude with a summary of both the remaining important theoretical issues that any theory of motivation must be able to address, as well as the criteria that such a theory must meet.

What has impeded the development of an affect theory in psychoanalysis?

Freud, in articulating his dual instinct theory, followed in a long line of philosophers, theologians, and the common man, who throughout the centuries have struggled with the question of human motivation, and have regularly linked it to the biological drives, which at their most basic, encompass the need to survive and to reproduce. Perhaps most if not all psychoanalytic theorists today would agree that Freud's dual instinct theory, including his later shift to a pair comprising libido and the death instinct, needs major recasting, if not replacement altogether, with a comprehensive affect theory, in the light of our increasing knowledge and methodological advances in a variety of related fields. Simply put, instincts and drives as opposed to affects can no longer stand as a major source of motivation. It is widely recognized that the clinical work of psychoanalysis is in fact focused on the dynamics and vicissitudes of affects and the defensive organizations they engender, and yet the psychoanalytic theory of affects and their relation to drives is far from satisfactory.

How has such a state of affairs come about? In an excellent review of psychoanalytic thinking about affect, Green (1977) suggests two sources of difficulty. One lies in the nature of affect itself, which has not lent itself easily to conceptualization. Indeed, affective phenomena have challenged the intellectual, adaptive, and creative powers of human beings since the beginning of time, and have truly inspired a wide variety of formulations (see Hillman, 1961, for a comprehensive review of approaches to affect). Nevertheless, over the last several decades, in an atmosphere of lively controversy, substantial progress has been made in psychology and in neuroscience with regard to theoretical clarifications of affect, drives, and motivation (see Panksepp, 1999a, 1999b; Tomkins, 1962, 1963a; White, 1959), and with regard to empirical techniques for defining and measuring affects (see Ekman & Friesen, 1975, 1978; Ekman, Levenson, & Friesen, 1983; Izard, 1971 on facial expressions, and Levenson, Ekman, & Friesen, 1990 on demonstrating specific autonomic activity related to specific affects).

The second difficulty mentioned by Green (1977), "lies in our preconceptions and in the very manner in which the problems were posed from the beginning of Freudian theory" (p. 129). Modell (2005) argues that Freud understood the etiology of hysteria in two ways,

> as a disorder of energy transformation and as a disorder of meaning. Freud's initial epistemological bifurcation has had profound implications for the future of psychoanalysis as it created a tension between "scientific" theorizing and a "hermeneutic" interpretation of meaning that has never been fully resolved.
>
> (pp. 559–560)

Modell goes on to say that Freud focused more on the vicissitudes of energy transformation, describing repression in energic terms as a withdrawal of "cathexis," but using a term that implicitly also contains "the idea of meaning in the sense of selecting what is of significance" (p. 560).

Westen (1979), in reviewing these preconceptions, suggests another reason for the continued adherence to some form of instinct theory, namely that "theorists have recognized that to move from Freud's dual instinct theory to an affect theory of motivation would signal the demise of two of Freud's most central and 'cathected' models: his libido theory . . . and the structural model" (p. 524). He goes on to say that "[a]ttempted revisions of Freud's theories of affect and motivation have too long reflected a compromise between the desire for fidelity to the data of clinical observation and the fear of infidelity to Freud" (p. 524). Thus we need to explore Freud's changing conceptions of affects, and the compromises referred to by Westen (1979) in order to understand what within psychoanalysis has hindered both the development and the acceptance of a comprehensive theory of affects as the primary motivational source.

Freud's changing conceptualizations

Freud (1893/1966) originally conceptualized affect as a "quantity (of energy), which accompanies the events of psychic life" (Green, 1977, p. 130). He subsequently assigned to the ego the function of moderating excessive fluctuations in psychic life by regulating the quotas of affect through a variety of discharge mechanisms. Quotas of affect were conceptualized as perceptions of unconscious drive energies calibrated in degrees of pleasure and unpleasure, "reaching the mind, as a measure of the demand made upon the mind for work in consequence of its connection with the body" (Freud, 1915/2001, p. 122). The subjective quality of affect was subordinated to its objective expression, which placed the emphasis on quantity. This emphasis was consistent with a central tenet in Freud's theory building, namely, that the primary function of the psychic apparatus was to rid itself of excessive excitations, so as to return to quiescence, and a bodily homeostasis, in order not to disrupt smooth effective functioning. Hence, affect, as the perception of building internal tensions, was conceived of primarily as a disorganizing factor in psychic functioning, resulting in detrimental consequences for the capacity to think. Here is one of those basic preconceptions, of which Green spoke and to which I will return.

In a later, but still early version of Freud's theory (1905/2001),

> affects were seen as derived from the instinctual drive pressing toward realization of its biological aim, as determined by the zone of origin. In comparison, the object of the drive, linked with secondary process concepts, was by no means as significant.
>
> (Arlow, 1977, p. 158)

Holt (1976) pointed out that in Freud's early work (1900/2001, 1905/2001) he relied on wish, not the concept of *Trieb*, as his motivational term, which was defined in terms of "affect-charged, repressed memories" (Holt, 1976, p. 179) that were related to memory traces of earlier, real gratifications. But by 1916–1917, Freud described two components of affect, namely motor innervations or discharges and two feelings, namely, perceptions of motor actions and direct feelings of pleasure and unpleasure, giving the affect its "keynote." Freud went on to say:

> We seem to see deeper in the case of some affects and to recognize that the core which holds the combination we have described together is the repetition of some particular significant experience. This experience could *only* be a very early impression of a very general nature, placed in the *prehistory not of the individual but of the species*.
>
> (Holt, 1976, pp. 395–396, italics mine).

This idea that prior experience of the species is contained in the unconscious is another of those basic preconceptions.

Gill (1978) suggested that when Freud adopted the dual drives of libido and the death instinct as the source of all motivation, he closed the door on the role of *repressed real experiences*, independent of drives, as possessing equal motivational power. For some time, Freud continued to stress the separation of ideas or representations from feelings or affects. Both were understood as elements of instincts, but ideas were subject to repression whereas quotas of affect were subject to suppression, or were transformed into anxiety, although he acknowledged that he had no explanation of how this qualitative transformation of undischarged libido into anxiety took place.

In his final major revision of the theory of anxiety, Freud (1926/2001) introduced a cognitive element, namely, the idea of danger. In this model, anxiety now originated in the ego as an adaptive (phylogenetically inherited), organizing, motivating signal, functioning to alert the psyche to danger and to set in motion defensive maneuvers or escape behaviors. This allowed Freud to distinguish between realistic anxiety related to external dangers and neurotic anxiety related to instinctual dangers. At about the same time, Freud differentiated anxiety from other states of unpleasure, such as mourning and guilt.

This later model represents several important shifts in Freud's thinking about affects. By introducing the signal function of anxiety, affect is no longer viewed solely as a disturber of thought, a change that reduced the gulf between affect and thought. And by distinguishing between realistic and neurotic anxiety, he opened the door to viewing affect as adaptive and as a source of motivation independent of instinctual fluctuations. Finally, in this later model it was the negative quality of signal anxiety, not its overwhelming quantity, that motivated defensive action, which is what perhaps led Freud to consider the qualitative differences between anxiety and other unpleasant affect states, such as mourning and grief. Unfortunately, Freud never pursued the broader theoretical implications of these distinctions for re-working his ideas about the relationship between affects and instinct. His earlier views of the overwhelming quantity of affect were still present in his discussion of separation anxiety in infancy (Freud, 1926/2001), which he conceptualized as traumatic anxiety, namely as a source a psychic disorganization, experienced as traumatic helplessness, leading to anticipatory anxiety to avoid repetition of the trauma.

Compton (1983b) alludes to this dilemma when he notes the consequence of Freud's (1920/2001) revision of the relation of pleasure and energy:

> [T]he relation between the subjective experience of pleasure and the pleasure of the principle – metaphychological pleasure – is obscure; the two are somewhat dissociated . . . Pleasure and distress – or even unpleasure – are certainly affect terms. Sexual feelings and angry . . . feelings are also affects with particular qualities (which

> are part of the quality of affects). We have conventionally discussed these feelings in the context of the theory of drives, rather than in the context of other affects. *Affect theory in psychoanalysis has essentially meant anxiety theory.*
>
> (Compton, 1983b, p. 412, italics mine)

Freud was aware of the contradictions in his two formulations of anxiety – anxiety as traumatic, disorganizing, pathological, and anxiety as an adaptive, motivating signal, which might be seen as only one among several motivating signals. But he could neither resolve these contradictions and integrate them into a comprehensive theory of affect, nor dismiss the importance of the various phenomena he had observed. Indeed, as Green (1977) states, "Freud struggled with the problem of affect all his life" (p. 129). Green further pointed out that in "The Ego and the Id" (Freud, 1923/2001) Freud described affect as "an original subjective modality" (Green, 1977, p. 137), and as sensations arising

> in the deepest strata of the mental apparatus, belonging to the pleasure-unpleasure series ... more elementary than perceptions arriving externally ... (capable of having) different or even opposite qualities ... a qualitative "something" in the course of mental events ... either conscious or unconscious that may or may not be attached to "word-presentations."
>
> (Freud, 1923/2001, pp. 21–23)

As we will see later, Freud's insights about affect as "an original subjective modality," etc. as stated above are still pertinent today, and close to Tomkins' definition of an affect, but given the neuroscience of his day, he could not imagine their scope or their distinct qualities, beyond their connection to instinctual impulses. Thus as several authors (Green, 1977; Rangell, 1967; Rapaport, 1960) have pointed out, Freud used increasingly similar formulations to describe affects and instinctual impulses, thereby creating conceptual confusion in psychoanalytic writings for many years.

In "The Economic Problem of Masochism," Freud (1924/2001) articulates the difficulty in trying to sort out how experiences of pleasure and unpleasure, increases and decreases in tension and libido and the death instinct are related or separate from each other:

> Pleasure and unpleasure therefore, cannot be referred to as an increase or decrease of a quantity (which we describe as "tension due to stimulus"), although they obviously have a great deal to do with that factor. It appears that they depend, not on this quantitative factor, but on some characteristic, which we can only describe as a qualitative one. If we were able to say what this qualitative characteristic is, we should be much further advanced in psychology. Perhaps it is the rhythm, the temporal sequence of changes, rises and falls in the quantity of stimulus. We do not know.
>
> (p. 160)

A few pages later in the same paper, Freud argued that the principle governing all mental life was a special case of Fechner's "tendency toward stability," namely, the death instinct, which seeks to reduce all excitation to nothing or to as little as possible, or to destroy and disintegrate the organism into separate cells tending finally "into a state of inorganic stability" (p. 163). He then had to argue that in living organisms this tendency has been modified by the life instinct or libido, but he also acknowledged that,

> we are without any physiological understanding of the ways or means by which this taming of the death instinct by the libido may be effected. So far as the psychoanalytic field of ideas is concerned, we can only assume that a very extensive fusion and amalgamation, in varying proportions, of the two classes of instincts takes place, so that we never have to deal with pure life instincts or pure death instincts but only with mixtures of them in different amounts.
>
> (p. 164)

Freud made no further progress in resolving the conceptual contradictions and confusions mentioned above, or in understanding how such fusions and amalgamations of the two classes of instincts took place. Accounting for the full range of human experience in terms of these two powerful forces has been highly problematic, for while nothing can compete with their sheer grandeur and appeal, nevertheless, explanation at such an exalted level is, in the end, not adequately informative and is far removed from clinical data, as well as from the growing data from infancy studies, psychology, and neuroscience. That Freud chose to conceptualize the data of psychoanalysis in such "mythological" terms is, as Erikson (1964) said, "a matter of the history of concept formation," and a measure of the "immensity of the problem to be comprehended" (p. 212).

Is the continued retention of such concepts useful? It is my belief that the practice of evoking the death instinct, or libido as primary motivational factors in clinical phenomena, creates the illusion of an explanation often leading to intellectual closure, which then obviates the need to struggle with systematic and precise definitions that would clearly differentiate the functions of drives and affects, and that would allow an acceptance of affects as the primary motivational system.

One of the most admirable qualities of Freud's mind was his ability to acknowledge contradictions embedded in his theories as well as the limits of his understanding and to continue to ask probing questions. He could go no further in resolving these contradictions given the science of his day. But if Freud could live in this era of dynamic systems conceptualizations, powerful new technologies, and research methods that are generating a vast array of findings in the human sciences, I firmly believe that he would have been far more open to the scientific findings of today and not have been as loyal to his earlier theories as his followers have tended to be. It is important to remember, as Yorke (1999) reminds us: "Freud himself always thought his ideas open to modification and even replacement in the light of further discoveries" (p. 75).

Efforts to modify Freud's dual instinct theory

Freud ascribed central relevance to the biological aspect of the drives. Compton (1983a) raises serious questions about attempts to create purely psychological formulations of the construct of instinctual drive and suggests that

> it would seem to be the essence of Freud's drive concept that certain physiologic processes which commence ... outside of the central nervous system have a special relation to psychological phenomena, mediated ... through structures and pathways of the central nervous

> system ... it is this special relation that is intended to account for *driven-ness*.
>
> (p. 373, italics mine)

Compton (1983a) goes on to say that, "dissatisfaction with the concept of psychic energy was one of the main ideas in which Freud housed the mind–body ambiguity. It was Freud's device for 'getting the mind started'" (p. 374). Compton agrees with Brenner (1980), who states that, "there should be some term to designate the concept that drives have a capacity to impel the mind to activity" (p. 211). What is being addressed and sought after is a "conceptual device to account for the sense of more or less" (Compton, 1983a, p. 375). Again, Compton notes that "the motivational impulsion to activity, reflected in the subjective sense of tension and relief, is the very essence of the drive concept" (p. 384).

Brenner (1974) focused on the development of affects, relating this process to the development of the drives, and thus touched on the problem of the ontogenetic origin of the mind. He argued that

> affects are complex mental phenomena which can best be understood in developmental terms. Their antecedents are sensations of pleasure and unpleasure, the most important of which are the sensations associated with the lack of gratification of a drive derivative, so-called drive tension, and the gratification of a drive, i.e. with drive discharge.
>
> (p. 41)

The entire gamut of affects, in Brenner's view, emerge from this undifferentiated matrix of sensations of pleasure and unpleasure through a process by which memories and other ideas gradually become associated with the sensations of pleasure and unpleasure. The resulting complex of sensation and ideas is an affect. In this formulation it must therefore be assumed that affects are nonexistent in early infancy. In fact, Brenner (1974) states "the development of affects from infancy to adult life means the development of the ideas which are a part of the affects" (p. 41).

Arlow (1977) elaborated on Brenner's ideas:

> The range of affects is enormous and they vary from individual to individual, depending on the precise way in which *feelings of pleasure*

> *and unpleasure are combined with ideas* ... Precursors of affect are sensations of pleasure or unpleasure connected with *drive tension or drive discharge*. They constitute the undifferentiated matrix from which affects later in life develop when ideas become associated with these sensations. The critical memories, traumata and fantasies serve to determine the nature of the individual's affective life.
>
> (pp. 168–169, italics mine)

In these formulations we are offered an essentially cognitive theory of affects wedded to drive theory. The strong cognitive bias evident here is a departure from Freud, who, as noted earlier, recognized affect as an "original subjective modality" that may or may not be attached to word presentations. Many academic psychologists, who also insist on defining affect as a combination of a feeling and a thought, and who define early experience in terms of affect precursors, share this cognitive bias. It is also found in the neurosciences, which have found it easier to study cognitive processes in the brain than emotional ones. Both disciplines have ignored the increasing affective data from animal studies as well as the increasing evidence from infant studies reviewed in the previous section of this book that clearly demonstrate the presence of several distinct affects and learning at birth, and even in utero. Nevertheless, in other respects, these formulations carry on the legacy of Freud's thinking, retaining the notion that affects are derivatives of drives, connected to the central dynamic of drive tension and drive discharge, and stressing the role of traumata in psychic life.

This traditional psychoanalytic focus on anxiety and pathology is another major reason for the difficulty that psychoanalysts have had in attending to and giving theoretical scope to the full range of affective experience and to the power of *nonpathological affect dynamics*. Hartman (1958) and others have written about "conflict-free" spheres of ego functioning, utilizing neutralized energies and sublimated creative activities, and Parens (1979), in struggling to account for the non-aggressive, but motivated efforts and attention of young children to master their inner and outer environment, later argued for a primary autonomous ego activity fueled by a non-instinctual, neutral ego energy. These various theoretical expansions are examples of the felt need mentioned earlier to compromise between observational data and loyalty to Freud, and thus have stopped short of altering the basic premises of Freud's theory. Erikson (1964), one of the most eloquent psychoanalytic writers about human strengths and "virtues" has described psychoanalytic terms such as "conflict free" and "neutral energy" as "*miserly ways of characterizing our ties to actuality and to the world of deeds*" (p. 198, italics mine). To the extent that this reticence to alter Freud's metapsychological theory prevails, it has limited the scope of psychoanalytic theories of motivation, by seeming to either rule out the relevance of, or to not fully integrate the data derived from other conceptual frameworks, methodologies, and subject areas that have contributed substantially to our knowledge of the nature of the origins and functioning of the mind and nervous system.

Robert White (1959), an eminent psychologist not bound by such loyalty to Freud, in his seminal article entitled "Motivation Reconsidered: The Concept of Competence" critically reviewed a variety of drive models, including Freud's and psychoanalytic ego psychology's solution of neutralized ego energies and concluded:

> [I]t seems to me an awkward conceptualization, one which in the end is likely to lead ... to a "metapsychological snarl." The theory requires that instinctual energies can completely change their aims, which makes one wonder what purpose was served in the first place by defining them as having aims. It preserves an image of mobility of energies that seems much out of line with recent research on animal motivation, where energy is being conceived in a constantly closer relation to special structures. To my mind it thus compares unfavorably with its quite straightforward alternative, which is *that the alleged neutralized energies are there in the first place as part of the natural make-up of an adaptive organism.*
>
> (p. 310, italics mine)

White (1959) provides a deep integration of the data from animal research and studies of young children current at that time, and argues for a different kind of motivational concept, which involves "action systems, motility, and a sense of industry ... behavior which can scarcely be contained in the old bottle of instinct theory and which *is engaged in for its own sake*" (p. 312, italics mine).

He offers the concept of effectance and concludes:

> Effectance motivation need not be conceived as strong in the sense that sex, hunger, and fear are strong when violently aroused. It is moderate but persistent, and in this too, we can discern a feature that is favorable for adaptation. Strong motivation reinforces learning in a narrow sphere, whereas moderate motivation is more conducive to an exploratory and experimental attitude, which leads to competent interactions in general, without reference to an immediate pressing need. Man's huge cortical association areas might have been a suicidal piece of specialization if they had come without a steady, persistent inclination toward interacting with the environment.
>
> (p. 330)

Here is a powerful theoretical mind at work. His formulation prefigures some aspects of Tomkins' (1962) thinking about affects, particularly his description of the affect of interest/excitement as supporting all sustained intellectual work, which I will present in the next chapter, as well as Panksepp's findings, which I will present later in this chapter. White's formulation is also consistent with the two basic priorities that I proposed in Chapter 2, namely, enhancing a coherent understanding of one's world and one's capacities to affect that world.

Within psychoanalysis, another source of revisions has come from object relations theorists, who argued that the libido theory, with its focus on orifices, failed to capture the powerful motives for relatedness. Fairbairn (1952), for example, argued that libido was object seeking not pleasure seeking. But perhaps the most sustained and deepest challenge to Freud's dual instinct theory has come from the work of Heinz Kohut (1971, 1977, 1984) and his many self-psychology followers (to mention only a few: Ornstein, 1974, 1985, 1991, 1998; Ornstein & Ornstein, 1993; Stolorow & Lachmann, 1980, 2000).

Kohut proposed that the fundamental pathology consisted of the lack of self-cohesion, resulting from failures in parental empathic attunements to the developing child's psychological needs for mirroring. Such a deficit leaves the "enfeebled self" vulnerable to self-fragmentation that may be manifested by narcissistic rage or compulsive sexuality. From this perspective such outcomes have been mis-identified by other psychoanalytic approaches as evidence of aggressive and libidinal forces, rather than as affective reactions evoked by failures of growth enhancing empathic attunements. Lachmann (2001) has stated:

> Nowhere is the distinction between Freud's and Kohut's theories of development clearer than in their differing formulations of the Oedipus complex ... Kohut's postulation of a normal oedipal phase that can become conflicted due to parental pathology and misattunement stands in stark contrast to the Oedipus complex postulated by Freudian theory in which the way the person manages powerful erotic aggressive feelings toward the parents, that is, the characteristics of the Oedipus complex, is basic to subsequent personality organization. These differences point to irreconcilably different visions of human nature that lead to diverging clinical theories.
>
> (p. 5)

Psychoanalysis continues to be divided between conflicts involving the innate drives as the primary factor in pathology or failures of attunement leading to deficits in a cohesive self. Much of the debate seems to be focused around the two different views of aggression. Is it a primary drive or a secondary response to frustration and/or trauma? Self-psychologists argue the latter position, derived from the work of Heinz Kohut (1971, 1977, 1984). Lachmann (2001) provides the most clinically detailed rebuttals to those who claim that self-psychologists do not deal with aggression in their clinical work.

Kernberg (2011) is a good example of a gifted clinician and clear thinker, who accepts basic dual drive theory, stating: "at the bottom, all unconscious conflicts involve conflicts between love and aggression at some level of development ... with the warning that the only thing we know about these two drives is their expression in mental representations and affects" (p. 1010). But at the same time he acknowledges that Freud was unable to link psychological functions and structures with underlying neurobiological developments given the primitive nature of the neurosciences of his time, and that given today's developments of neurosciences, "it emerges that the primary motivational systems consist of affects of a positive and negative kind" (p. 1010). Yet, he goes on to say:

> clinically, the replacement of drive theory by affect theory does not do justice to the stable organization of unconscious conflicts ... on the other hand, a pure drive theory that does not consider the specific vicissitudes of affects ... does not do justice to the complexity of clinical experience. I propose ... that affects constitute the primary motivational system, and that they are integrated into supraordinate positive and negative drives, namely, libido and aggression ... and the drives, in turn, become activated in the form of their component affectively valenced representations manifest as unconscious fantasies.
>
> (p. 1011)

Here we see how the differences between Freud's metapsychological theory, which Kerberg acknowledges is premised on the unknowable nature of drives (encompassed in such terms as "the stable organizers of unconscious conflicts"), and his clinical theory, which for Kernberg is an affect theory, are glossed over and *remain unresolved*. Thus in severe cases of psychopathology that seem to be unresponsive to clinical interventions, Kernberg argues that the death drive is the dominant unconscious motivation propelling the patients toward self-destruction. He cannot seem to imagine that such phenomena might involve a combination of several powerful, persistent negative affect dynamics involving disgust, fear, rage, and contempt, which might be the result of earlier empathic failures or of unresolved, debilitating trauma. If the patient's psychopathology is not understood by the clinician as the result of powerful affect dynamics, then a misattunement is highly likely, and could result in a clinical impasse.

Those clinicians working from an intersubjective perspective have been most articulate about the source of clinical impasses. They argue that "[i]n the establishment of a therapeutic alliance, *two heads are surely better than one*" (Stolorow & Atwood, 1992, p. 101, italics mine). They go on to say, "From the continual interplay between the patient's and the therapist's psychological worlds two basic situations repeatedly arise: *intersubjective conjunction* and *intersubjective disjunction*" (p. 103, italics mine). In this framework, conjunctions occur when the meanings expressed by the patient are closely similar to those of the clinician. Disjunction occurs when the clinician processes the patient's material through formulations that greatly alter the meaning for the patient, which can lead to clinical impasses. Thus the clinician must always be aware of the impact of his own theories on the direction and course of the treatment, by continually investigating the patient's responses from the patient's subjective framework and asking himself: "*How is the patient right*?" "Only this can enable patient and analyst to distinguish between a 'pseudoaliance' based on compliance with the analyst's view point and a therapeutically mutative alliance based on an empathic inquiry into the patient's subjective world" (p. 101).

Lichtenberg (1989) provided an alternative motivational model that in many ways moved beyond Freud's dual instinct model by arguing for five motivational systems: physiological regulation, attachment, exploration/assertion, withdrawal or antagonism in response to aversive events, and sensual/sexual pleasure. He incorporated a great deal of empirical work from infancy and child studies, Tomkins' affect theory, the neurosciences, and clinical examples. Yet, several writers have pointed out compromises with drive theory in these formulations. Westen (1979) argues that Lichtenberg

> offers a somewhat mixed model, since his last two motives, like Kernberg's, essentially map an affect theory on to a modified drive theory of sex and aggression. The seeking of pleasure (his fifth motive) is, like Freud's ego motives, really inherent in the first three of his motives, as is the avoidance of unpleasure (his fourth motive). As in Freud's theory, the question again is whether the regulation of affect states (seeking pleasure and avoiding pain) is an underlying *mechanism* involved in all motivation – for sexual gratification, aggression, attachment to others, exploration, self-esteem, and the like – or whether it constitutes a separate and parallel motive system.
>
> (p. 523)

Ghent (2002), in an article distinguishing between needs and wishes derived from drives, and from the advantages of a dynamic systems theory approach, pointed out what he felt was confusing or inconsistent in Lichtenberg's usage of these terms, namely, that he describes his five motivational systems as representing the five basic needs, but then states:

"when these basic needs are met, the result is a self-object experience . . . a particular affective state characterized by a sense of cohesion, safety and invigoration" (Lichtenberg, 1989, p. 12, cited in Ghent, 2002, p. 795). Ghent goes on to say:

> Lichtenberg, in this context, is using "need" to mean something like *drive*, as used in classical psychoanalysis; whereas the need for self-coherence does not fit in the framework of classical metapsychology and is, therefore, assigned a different category in much the same way as Balant (1968) and Winnicott (1966) tried to resolve the problem.
>
> (p. 795)

In a more recent formulation Lichtenberg, Lachmann, and Fossage (2011) have shifted their thinking by incorporating a non-linear dynamic systems theory. Thus they are now in agreement with Ghent and others (including this author) that: "*Development is an intrinsically active process that creates its own categories, meanings, intentions, and goals*" (italics mine). But in their formulation this leads to the development of: "*its own emergent motivational systems*" (pp. 15–16, italics mine), which I don't agree with. They state further that, based on Edelmann's concepts of values and biases, "*we believe groupings of similar biases and affect exist in the neonate and form the basis of discrete but interrelated interacting motivational systems*" (pp. 15–16, italics mine). Thus, they have added two more motivational systems based on new evidence from infancy, namely affiliation and caregiving.

> Each system self-organizes and self-stabilizes as a loose assembly of categorized experiences having similar but not identical affects and purpose. A predominant similarity of affect, intention, and goal provides the basis for our proposal of each motivational system as a conceptual entity.
>
> (p. 30)

Dynamic systems theory has added some flexibility to the formulations of Lichtenberg, et al. (2011) but the contents of their first five motivational systems remain the same and thus the earlier criticisms that they fall easily into a pleasure–unpleasure framework of instinct theory still hold. They give priority to affects, but they do not differentiate the distinctive quality of each negative affect, namely that some are more bearable and less lethal than others, and thus might engender distinctive general coping strategies; instead, they are lumped all together in the aversive motivational system leading only to the two goals of withdrawal or antagonism, which can sound too much like the old anxiety model of Freud. Finally, their use of the term affect is imprecise; they propose a "predominant similarity of affect, intention and goal" (p. 30), thus the goal of effectance can be seen as an affect. I will argue later, when presenting Tomkins' affect theory, for the theoretical and clinical advantage in both defining the distinctive experiential quality of each affect, particularly the important difference between shame, distress, disgust, and anger and terror, which can, over time, be organized into different enduring, affectively driven motivational strategies that Tomkins calls "scripts." I will argue also for the added flexibility and the gain in our understanding of human psychological dynamics by separating the affect from any predetermined goal.

Westen (1979), following Brenner, has offered his own revision of Freud's motivational theory, based on the idea that early affective proclivities can through learning and later cognitive and developmental advances, lead to the formation of motives. He criticizes Lictenberg for deriving his motivational systems from infancy research and for assuming that all motives must have their origins in infancy. Westen (1979) also points out that: "natural selection operates at the level of specific mechanisms, not at the level of broad instinctive goals; the latter are constructs, which are selected by theorists, not by nature" (p. 527). Others have also pointed out the importance of this distinction (see Panksepp below). Westen also describes the problem of lumping multiple motives into a single category such as pleasure or unpleasure, namely, the lack of attention paid to the specific conditions for the activation of particular motivational processes. This last point is extremely important, for the associative links activating any motivational process can be *highly idiosyncratic*, which is precisely why the psychoanalytic method is so well suited to exploring the complex functioning of the human psyche.

Westen (1979) seems to give a nod to early affective proclivities and natural selection, but argues that new motives occur later in life based on advances in cognition and developmental changes, once again, tilting toward a cognitive theory of motivation. Thus in his formulation, the issue of psychic continuity is not addressed, nor is the complex relationship between innate affect dynamics and cognition clarified. Here is where I part ways with him, and join Freud in the need to *ground a motivational theory in our evolutionary history and our nervous system.* Such a requirement obligates us to formulate dynamic concepts that articulate how early experiences are organized and continually reorganized over time so as to influence later developments. This is exactly the challenge that my colleagues and I faced in trying to make sense of our longitudinal data. And here is where dynamic systems theory comes into play, *by articulating the dynamics of continuity and change, and how change preserves some continuity.* Thus studies of infant capacities are important, as demonstrated in previous chapters, along with current neurological understandings of how our nervous system works.

Lachmann has been involved in infancy research through his collaboration with Beatrice Beebe, described in the previous chapter (Beebe, Lachmann, & Jaffe, 1997), in which they ascribe a central role to affect in regulating the complex processes that occur within and between infant and mother in face-to-face transactions. They also differentiate their approach from that of Stern (1988), who assigns a greater role to the mother in regulating such transactions. I would add that Stern (1988) does not give affect a privileged position among other variables involved in the infant's lived experience, and states: "it is considered as one of the attributes of experience, among many (cognition, perception, motive, action) and cites research on infant memory, showing no difference between positive affect and 'neutral affect'" (p. 238). This latter term seems inexplicable, and can only make sense if a quieter affect is involved, such as when the affect of "interest" is present. He also never defines what constitutes a motive; it is simply listed as an attribute at the same level as other attributes. Thus we are left with an additive model, with no clear understanding of the differentiated contributions of the different "attributes" or of their dynamic combinational possibilities, or of the distinctive nature and role of motivation.

What does a theory of motivation need to provide?

Freud understood the need to ground motives in the neurological functioning of the body, but was limited by the science of his day.

He understood that the brain was hierarchically organized, and proposed that the lower level, the id, was unconscious, and the upper levels, the ego and superego, were conscious and regulated the lower level. But he gave up the project over a century ago, realizing there were too many questions he could not answer at the neurological level, and thus he could not realize this goal during his lifetime. Yet he never gave up on the belief that someday there would be answers at the neurological level. He also understood that there was a distinctive quality of affects, as well as a quantitative aspect that somehow produced the conscious experience of "drivenness," but he was unable to separate out the affective phenomena from his formulation of the instinctual drive processes, which in his day seemed to contain the deepest strata of our mental apparatus.

While nearly all the revisions of Freud's dual instinct theory agree that the vicissitudes of affects comprise the most clinically relevant phenomena for understanding our patients' motivations, yet none of these revisions clarify what any theory of motivation needs to provide, namely a clear understanding of how affects are activated and function and how they relate to drives and to cognition. Such a theory would also need to answer the following questions: *How is the distinctive quality of each affect produced? How is that quality related to quantity or to the psychological experience of feeling motivated? How does affect get organized over time? How does it create a continuity of experience over time*? And finally, *what would it mean to accept a comprehensive affect theory as a viable replacement of Freud's dual instinct theory, as the primary motivational factor in psychological organization?*

How does current neural science conceptualize these issues?

The neuroscientist who seems most interested in trying to establish a neurobiological theory of the mind and to relate his brain research to Freud's ideas is Jaak Panksepp (whose ideas are most elaborated in his book entitled *Affective Neuroscience: The Foundations of Human and Animal Emotions*, 1998). But a very interesting discussion with Panksepp and several psychoanalysts occurs in the first volume of the journal *Neuropsychoanalysis*, published in 1999 (Panksepp, 1999b). It includes a useful summary of Freud's formulations of affect provided by Mark Solms and Edward Nersessian, and then a longer presentation by Panksepp of the findings of neuroscience, including his ideas about what in Freud needs revision and what in Freud has no correlates in the brain. This is followed by commentary from several analysts, Andre Green, Allan Shore, Howard Shervin, and Clifford York, and the neuroscientists Joseph LeDoux and A. R. Damasio. The discussion closes with extended responses to each commentary by Panksepp. The discussion throughout is respectful, thoughtful, and deeply informative. I would highly recommend this reading for anyone interested in these issues. More recently, in 2012, Solms and Panksepp published a very important article in the journal *Brain Science* entitled "The 'Id' Knows More Than the 'Ego' Admits: Neuropsychoanalytic and Primal Consciousness Perspectives on the Interface Between Affective and Cognitive Neuroscience." What follows is a summary of the main points of these discussions and ideas.

First of all, among the participants in the evolving dialogue, there is general agreement on the need for this kind of collaboration, as well as an appreciation of how the very different methodologies of neuroscience and psychoanalysis can deeply inform and benefit each other. This book is also dedicated to the necessity of collaboration with current neuroscience in order to preserve the essence of Freud's insight. I heartily agree with this effort as stated in the Introduction of this book.

Panksepp (1999b) believes that even though Freud's conjectures about neurophysiology currently have little substance, Freud "may have perceived certain psychological dimensions with a clarity that was sufficient for us to now consider how they might be related to brain mechanisms" (p. 70). Psychoanalysis excels at exploring subjective emotional experience, while neuroscience studies the brain mechanisms that help create those states. The study of emotion in the brain is in its early stages, thus psychoanalysis, has a role in framing some of the important issues. Panksepp (1999b) recognizes that there is resistance on both sides, and that trying to relate mental views to neural views will be the most difficult theoretical task for both disciplines. Nor are the grounds for such a rapprochement self-evident: "The issue of what is the most fruitful level of synthesis for linking these levels of analysis, for truly understanding emotions, is rarely discussed in modern science" (p. 84).

He believes that we must learn to cultivate the following idea: "that there are important relationships to be clarified among the very different levels of analysis" (p. 81), and states that:

> some of the major bridges between the two would presumably arise from our conceptions of how emotional feelings actually emerge from brain matter, and it is hard to imagine that these kinds of mechanisms can be revealed without animal research. At present we need to establish measurable relationships between affective states and neural dynamics.
>
> (p. 82)

Thus, Panksepp's strategy would have us put "the study of behavioral changes, brain functioning, and psychological processes on an equal footing, and see if a theoretical triangulation among these lines of evidence can reveal credible predictive relationships across species" (p. 82). Later, in the same passage, he says:

> I think the single most important joint problem for both neuroscience and psychoanalysis is to provide a true and lasting understanding of affective processes and their fundamental role in behavior and the nature of consciousness. I personally do not think those goals can be achieved without animal brain research or a vigorous attempt to make first-person experiences open to analysis by third-person approaches.
>
> (p. 82)

Panksepp states that many of the difficulties in trying to relate the functions of the mind that Freud described to neural processes will hinge on how terms such as consciousness, drive, pleasure, and unpleasure are defined. He highlights Freud's monolithic use of the concept of drive to emphasize the problems that must be faced if one tries to retain, in their original form, all of Freud's insights. *Since there is no unified substrate in the brain to fit such a concept, Panksepp makes the radical suggestion of discarding the drive concept in practice if not in principle*. He states further that in neuroscience, "drives", namely homeostatic phenomena related to body energy, like hunger, thirst, temperature, and sexual issues have been clarified in the second half of the twentieth century with a high degree of precision, and are vital to our survival (see Tomkins, 1962, for a similar formulation). However, Panksepp (1999b) believes that a more general concept of "drive" is less durable and states:

> [I]n the crucible of neuroscience, it may fragment into many subsidiary processes, so that it only becomes a class-identifier like "motivation," retaining no more unified brain substance (at least at the neuroscientific level) than many other psychological terms. *In other words, all too many of the concepts of psychology are the cultural creations of our minds rather than the creations of nature.*
>
> (p. 81, italics mine)

In discussing Freud's concept of pleasure and drive, Panksepp (1999b) argues that one could find some correspondence in the emotional system he calls "seeking," which "is essential for organisms to become engaged with the world when they have any of a variety of motivational urges, whether eating, drinking, cruising for sex, retrieving lost babies, or seeking to play" (p. 74). He points out there are also many other emotive systems in the brain, and asks: "Should we incorporate all of them in a singular 'drive' concept or should we distinguish among them?" (p. 74). He does not believe that the differences in these emotive systems emerge "simply from ego or superego functions acting upon a single undifferentiated drive process" (p. 74). On the basis of his evidence, he argues that *these distinct systems are mediated by distinct genetic mechanisms, not through social learning.*

Panksepp (1999b) raises the question of why we need affects and suggests:

> Affects may be the ways that certain genes and their various interactions inform us of fundamental evolutionary values that are not only the harbingers of intended actions, but also the processes that allow social creatures like mammals, who depend on each other for survival, to communicate efficiently and urgently their needs, desires, and intentions to others . . . I do not think it can be overemphasized that the basic affects need not be learned: They emerge

> directly from the evolutionary epistemology of the brain . . . If this analysis is on the right track, the therapeutic enterprise needs to be imbued with much greater appreciation for affective processes.
>
> (p. 75)

This statement is very important and is in agreement with Tomkins' formulation of affects, described fifty years earlier, based on facial expressions, which also emerges directly from the evolutionary epistemology of the brain. I will present Tomkins' theory in the next chapter.

Panksepp (1999b) argues that the arousal of the various emotional systems in the brain is located in the evolutionarily earliest and lower components of the brain, which contain a great deal of learning and plasticity. The area on which he has focused much of his work is the midbrain periaqueductal gray or PAG region, whose components he states

> appear to be essential for coordinating and orchestrating the many outputs of emotional arousal including, I believe the generation of primal affective experience/consciousness. Hence, the vast neural pathways between higher areas such as the amygdala and lower areas such the PAG are better conceptualized as integrative systems rather than a mere output systems.
>
> (p. 74)

The existence of these different hierarchical levels of control suggests the following:

> [T]he distinction between conscious and unconscious processes may need to be more multidimensional than has been traditional. For instance, cognitive and affective forms of consciousness may each have several distinct levels of hierarchic organization. To accommodate these emerging views as well as new neuroscientific findings, Freudian theory certainly needs to be molded and updated . . . (to) allow some of Freud's original insights to be crafted into scientifically testable ideas that continue to evolve.
>
> (pp. 74–75)

In the later article by Solms and Panksepp (2012), in summarizing Freud's conceptions of the external and internal aspects of the body, and the functional properties of the id, or the lower parts of the brain as unconscious, and the ego or cortex as conscious, conclude that these formulations "reveal a stark contradiction between current affective neuroscience concepts of mind and those of Freud" (p. 159). Solms and Panksepp (2012) then present considerable evidence demonstrating that consciousness exists *without* the cortex, e.g. when the insula is totally obliterated and in hydraencephalic brains; in both circumstances both affect and consciousness are present. This represents unequivocal proof, they state, "that affective consciousness is both generated and felt subcortically" (p. 163). They argue that affect is not dependent on working memory, agreeing with LeDoux who argues: "It is an intrinsic function of the lower regions of the brain" (cited in Solms & Panksepp, 2012, p. 163). These findings do not apply only to affective consciousness: "The state of consciousness as a whole is generated in the upper brainstem. We have known this for many years" (p. 163). They cite the work of Penfield and Jasper (1954), whose work has stood the test of time and who discovered that removal of large areas of cortex, either under anaesthea, or even a total hemispherectomy had limited effects on consciousness, and did not interrupt the presence of a conscious self or being, even though it did deprive the patient of some kinds of information (Solms & Panksepp, 2012, p. 65). More recent studies indicate that the PAG seems to be the nodal point in the upper brain stem that generates consciousness, as well as: "the core quality of subjective being. *The primal conscious 'state' of mammals is intrinsically affective*" (Solms & Panksepp, 2012, pp. 163–164, italics mine), Panksepp (1999a) believes "it is this realization that will revolutionize consciousness studies in future years" (p. 21). This formulation is in agreement with the evidence I presented in neonates, who are capable of feeling, and thinking and using their agency to bring about desired events, long before language occurs.

Solms and Panksepp (2012) also provide a lengthy discussion on the role of the neocortex in refining, and re-representing perceptions, or "to put it metaphorically, the cortex transforms the fleeting, fugitive, wave-like states of consciousness into mental solids. It generates objects" (p. 165), although much of this processing is unconscious. One of the objects that the cortex represents as a thing is the external body, which emerges as

> a detailed representation of the subject of consciousness. It is not the subject itself. It is important to recognize that this conception of the self is an illusion, albeit an everyday one. The external body is not the owner or locus of consciousness. It is not really the subjective self; it is an objective representation of the self.
>
> (pp. 166–167)

This reasoning supports Sander's proposition, stated in earlier chapters of this book, namely that *the ego (subjective self) begins as a state ego, not as a body ego*. Solms and Panksepp (2012) go on to present evidence demonstrating that the locus of Freud's bodily ego can be experimentally manipulated. They suggest the use of different terms to indicate the primary subjective, affective self as the "core" anoetic affective self, and self of everyday cognition the "declarative" noetic self.

This leads them to conclude that "*the core self, synonymous with Freud's 'id,' is the front of all consciousness; the declarative self, synonymous with Freud's 'ego,' is unconscious in itself*" (p. 168, italics mine). However, because the ego stabilizes the core consciousness generated by the id, by transforming affects into object representations and more particularly verbal object re-representations, we ordinarily think of ourselves as being conscious in the latter sense. This obscures the fact that our conscious thinking (and exteroceptive perceiving, which thinking re-represents) is constantly accompanied by low level affects (p. 168).

> We may safely say, without fear of contradiction, that were it not for the constant presence of affective feeling, conscious perceiving and thinking would either not exist or would gradually decay. This is just as well, because a mind unmotivated (and unguided) by feelings would be a hapless zombie, incapable of managing the basic tasks of life.
>
> (p. 168)

Panksepp (1999b) laments that cognitive processes have been easier to explore in the brain than the "global state variables, such as emotions and other affective states of the brain" (p. 74). Later on he states:

> In fact, in order to really understand emotions and moods, we may need to cultivate conceptions that deal with *primitive global state variables, which are far more embodied and fundamentally analog*, than is easy to envision in traditional information-theoretic terms [here he is once again in agreement with Tomkins]. Emotions may have a logic of their own (some call it an irrationality) which is distinct from that normally seen in cognitive systems. Certainly bottom-up "affective neuroscience" is not intended simply as an antidote to cognitive views, but as an equal working partner with the more established top-down cognitive perspectives to mind.
>
> (p. 80, italics mine)

He goes on to say: "The ancient evolutionary processes that established priorities in the brain, prior to the emergence of more subtle and sophisticated cognitive abilities are just being conceptualized in neuroscience for the first time" (p. 81). Thus far Panksepp has found evidence for what he calls a "seeking" system, and has discriminated fear, rage, separation distress, and pain, involving different complex unities of reticulating circuits, neuropeptide chemistries, and the involvement of the visceral-limbic tissues, as well as a "play" system, and a care-giving system. He concludes by saying:

> In any event, powerful valeneced states, of positive and negative affect of various forms are built into our brain. First we need to know how many of them there are, then their precise neural causes, then their interactions and consequences for consciousness, thought, and other mental activities. This scientific journey has just begun.
>
> (p. 86)

These findings are not only consistent with the infancy data presented in Part I of this book, which argued for primary consciousness and early affective experience, but they clearly call for the acceptance of a comprehensive affect theory as a viable replacement of Freud's dual instinct theory, for which Panksepp can find no supporting evidence in neurology. His work is essential in finally putting to rest drive theory and providing important data confirming the central role of affects in motivation.

But by focusing on the PAG, he cannot answer the questions of how many primary affects there are, their neural causes, and their interactions and consequence for consciousness, and cognition. Or to put the questions another way, how affects capture consciousness, causing the human to care about what is happening and how they get organized over time into enduring motivational complexes. *Thus, it is not a complete affect theory.* His focus on the PAG, has also prevented him from recognizing or incorporating the extensive evidence demonstrating the existence of biologically based patterned facial expressions, and their related autonomic patterns, which contribute the essential quality of the distinct experience of each affect.

In the next chapter, I will present Silvan Tomkins' work, published fifty years earlier, which argues that these distinctive, facial, and autonomic programs contain a clear answer to the question of how many primary affects there are, and goes further in arguing that affects function not only as analogs, but as analog amplifiers of all the forms of stimuli impinging on the organism, and that this amplification is designed, through these distinctive autonomic global states, to capture consciousness. As analog amplifiers affects make good things better or bad things worse so as to make the organism care about what is happening. Tomkins' work also demonstrates how these affective experiences get linked over time into enduring affect scripts that shape the individual's motivational approach to life and are major factors in shaping the individual's distinctive personality.

Chapter 5

Silvan Tomkins' affect theory

This chapter will focus on Silvan Tomkins' comprehensive theory of affect. It will address why it has taken so long for his ideas to take hold, and provide a brief biography of his ideas. It will demonstrate not only how closely his theory corresponds to the recent findings in biology, infant research, and neuroscience, all of which point to affect as the essential organizing factor in human motivation and thought, but it will also demonstrate how his theory articulates the essential components of affect and its function as an urgent, general, abstract analog amplifier that causes us to care about what is happening. The function of each primary affect will be described in detail. This chapter will also present Tomkins' polarity theory, which relates affect socialization to the wider world through ideology.

As described in the previous chapter, clinicians are increasingly aware that affects comprise the major source of motivation, and although, some have made attempts to incorporate Tomkins' classification of the primary affects, never the less, letting go of drive theory continues to be a problem. It is as if (as I have argued before, see Demos, 2001) one could simply "cut and paste" these new ideas into the old theory, even though the two theories are derived from totally different basic assumptions, and are therefore neither compatible with drive theory nor internally consistent. Thus few clinicians have grasped the novelty and the full scope and dynamic implications of Tomkins' theory as providing *a different, internally consistent set of ideas* that articulates a clear distinction between the function of the drive mechanism and that of the affect mechanism, and offers an explanatory framework that can account for the dynamic interactions of the biological, psychological, and social influences that shape a human life. As Brewster Smith, a personality theorist, stated in his introduction to my edited volume of Tomkins' work "There are better and worse ways of being a person, and Tomkins' theory can be articulate about them" (Smith, 1995, p. 10).

In the previous chapter, we also presented in some detail the newest findings in neuroscience, namely the work of Jaak Panksepp, who stated clearly and unequivocally that there is no evidence in the brain to support Freud's conceptualization of the two primary instincts, namely the death instinct and libido, as viable motivational sources for all our human capabilities and psychological experience. He also argued that we begin life with the capacity for phenomenal consciousness, experienced as rewarding and punishing affect states prior to the development of a capacity to reflect on such states. This was demonstrated both by the neonatal findings discussed in Chapter 2, and in Chapter 3, which followed the development of two infant girls, from birth into their third year

According to Panksepp, affects, as global states, operate as an analog, which permeates all of our experiences and sustains all of our endeavors. He lists several basic affects, namely, a seeking system, fear, rage, separation distress, pain, play, and a care-giving system, and states that he does not know how many basic affects there are. As we shall we see, in Tomkins' theory, affects operate not just as analogs, but as analog amplifiers. He based his theory on our biologically inherited facial expressions, and lists the following as innate affects: fear/terror, anger/rage, and distress (which can be about many things, not just separation); Panksepp's "seeking system," is conceptualized by Tomkins as motivated by the affect of interest/excitement; pain is conceptualized as a drive that needs *amplification* by an affect; and play is seen as a combination of the affects of interest and enjoyment, affects that would also motivate a caregiving system. One of the benefits of Tomkins' classification is that he separates the affect from any specific purposes, such as play or caregiving, which might be motivated by different affects. Tomkins adds to this list the affects of surprise/startle, and the affect auxiliary responses of shame, dissmell, and disgust.

Perhaps, because of Panksepp's focus on the brain stem, he was not in a position to recognize that our patterned facial expressions are connected to distinctive global autonomic patterns, which create amplified analogs of stimuli impinging on the organism, and therefore are just as much a part of our evolutionary history, and thus are also lodged in our brains. These affect complexes can provide the answer to how many primary affects there are. In his major book entitled *Affect Neuroscience: The Foundations of Human and Animal Emotions* (1998), Panksepp has only a few sentences devoted to the facial expression of human emotions. Thus he does not seem to take seriously or to know about the extensive literature on the role of the face in our experience of emotion, e.g. Tomkins' work on the face, and the physiological patterns that combine with each facial expression, as well as Darwin's treatise entitled *The Expression of the Emotions in Man and Animals* (Darwin, 1872/1965), and all of the cross-cultural validation of universal emotional expressions in the work of Ekman and Freison (1975, 1978), as well as their work in linking these expressions to distinctive autonomic patterns (e.g. Ekman, 1972).

These facial phenomenon and their related autonomic patterns led Tomkins to be the *only other theorist* to recognize that affect operated as an analog. But Tomkins theorized that in order for affect to be the primary motivator it had to function as an *analog amplifier* of the different patterns of stimuli impinging on the organism, so as to *capture consciousness and to cause the organism to care about what is happening*. The concept of an analog amplifier captures both the qualitative and quantitative aspects of affects, aspects that troubled Freud for many years. Tomkins' ideas predated Panksepp's work by over fifty years. Combining Freud's earlier insights with the recent work of Panksepp on the upper brainstem, and with Tomkins' earlier work on the emotional, patterned responses led by the face, *we are now finally in the position to put together a more scientifically grounded understanding of the basis of human and animal emotions and how they function as our primary motivational system!*

Why has it taken so long for Tomkins' discoveries to be recognized?

How is it that the contributions of such a creative thinker and researcher are so little known and understood? Several reasons can be offered. Tomkins was working in the decades beginning in the 1940s well into the 1980s when in psychology the dominance of psychoanalysis, cognition, and behaviorism were well underway, and affect was sorely neglected as a viable field of exploration. Thus, when his first two volumes of *Affect, Imagery, and Consciousness* appeared in 1962, and 1963, his ideas went against the major psychological paradigms of the time. As Smith (1995) stated,

> Tomkins threw down the gauntlet to both psychoanalysis and neobehavorism in his attack on drive theory – also departing in this respect from his Harvard mentor and source of personological inspiration, Henry A. Murray. He thumbed his nose at all behaviorisms in his emphasis on imagery and consciousness, and by putting more weight on consciousness than on the unconscious, he further departed from his Freudian roots.
>
> (p. 2)

One form of the cognitive dominance he was up against was Schachter and Singer's (1962) theory, which stated that emotion depended on an increased state of a general arousal, which then required an interpretation of the situation one was in, in order to be experienced as a specific emotion. Here, in Tomkins' words, is the unlikelihood of such a formulation:

> Surely no one who has experienced joy at one time and rage at another time would suppose that these radically different feelings were really the same except for different "interpretations" placed on similar "arousals." Only a science which had come to radically discount conscious experience would have taken such an explanation seriously . . . Further, if emotion depended on an increased state of arousal, then nightmares and indeed any emotions in dreams would have been impossible to occur.
>
> (Demos, 1995, p. 35)

Tomkins points out that even at that time, there was experimental work demonstrating that arousal was not a unitary system and that the body was fractionated into many specific subsystems regarding arousal (e.g. the reticular system regulating wakefulness, as distinguished from emotional arousal. See Moruzzi & Magoun, 1949 and Sprague, Chambers, & Stellar, 1961).

A second reason for the delay in recognizing Tomkins' theory, may lie in the fact that Tomkins' first two volumes were published without a bibliography (which was to appear in volume 3, and that did not appear until the publication of volume 4, after his death in 1991), making it all too easy for academic psychology to dismiss his ideas. Also, given the cognitive bias at the time, the publication of Tomkins' study on the recognition of facial expressions, which reported an intercorrelation of .86 between faces posed representing affects based on his theory and the judgments of untrained judges, the first such study ever to find such a significant consensus, was rejected by a leading psychological journal. It finally appeared in the journal *Perceptual and Motor Skills* (Tomkins & McCarter, 1964), an unlikely place to be read by psychologists.

Perhaps another reason many are not familiar with Tomkins' work is that there was no easy way to access the full scope of his theory and all of its implications. Tomkins' thinking and presentation of his ideas is complex and embedded throughout his four-volume opus, *Affect, Imagery, Consciousness* (1962, 1963a, 1991, 1992), which contains his continual process of revising and refining his theory. Tomkins had a powerful theoretical mind and he read widely in many fields, and given his training in philosophy and logic he had the ability to both integrate and abstract the most important ideas from these many sources. As Irving Alexander stated in his introduction to Tomkins' work on affect and ideology, in my edited volume of Tomkins writings, "He possessed one of the most active minds I have ever encountered. I harbor an image of him with an overloaded brain flooding him with information, new ideas, and profound insights, all at the same time" (Demos, 1995, p. 105).

But perhaps the deeper reason for the inability to let go of drive theory in psychoanalytic thinking, besides the loyalty to Freud, discussed in the previous chapter, is that there did not seem to many Freudian analysts, to be any other explanation besides the death instinct that could account for the powerful negative forces involved in the organization of psychic events, particularly when all therapeutic efforts seemed to fail. Tomkins is perhaps the only theorist who has provided a comprehensive explanation of the different functions of drives and affects, by articulating the process of the amplification provided by affects, and the different ways in which drives are amplified by affects. This explanation finally resolves the problem of accounting for the imperiousness of the drives, a problem that Freud struggled with throughout his life. In Tomkins' theory the imperiousness of the drive signal has been confused with its amplifier, namely the affect that is recruited and designed to boost the gain of the drive signal. Tomkins' theory also identifies several other distinct negative affects, e.g. shame, distress, and disgust that are not as toxic or as urgent as anxiety. His theory, therefore, allows for an understanding of all the complex ways that the drive and the affect mechanisms interact. I will return to this issue of urgency later in this chapter.

Tomkins' commitment to a theory of motivation and affect

Tomkins described his intellectual journey as "a love affair with an idea: "What do human beings really want?" (Demos, 1995, p. 27). He was born in Philadelphia on June 4, 1911, the son of Russian Jewish immigrants, and grew up in Camden, NJ, where his father was a dentist. He received a BA in three years from the University of Pennsylvania with a major in playwriting, and wrote plays that reflected his early interest in human motivation. He connected this interest in later years to his development of script theory, which describes how affect-laden scenes are linked together over time, finally systemizing his interest in human drama and in human feelings. In the following year, still at the University of Pennsylvania, he switched to psychology, receiving an MA in psychometrics. He said he left psychology and entered the doctoral program in philosophy, "because psychology seemed to lack a persuasive theory of motivation" (p. 28). He received his PhD in three years, specializing in logic and value theory. His dissertation dealt with what he called the psychology of knowledge, which for him represented

> a field that would concern itself with the personal as well as social influences of the ebb and flow of affect invested in ideas and ideology, in methods and styles of investigation, and in what are considered acceptable criteria of evidence.
>
> (pp. 27–28)

Tomkins was concerned with ideology throughout much of his career and made a major contribution in this area, which I will return to later in this chapter.

Tomkins received his PhD in 1934, landing him in the midst of the great depression and jobless. He worked for a racing syndicate, handicapping horses for a year or so, before arriving at Harvard to do postgraduate work with Quine, and Sheffer in logic and with Ralph Barton Perry, Whitehead, and Prall in the theory of value. But after two years, he returned to psychology, partly because of the difficulty of empirically validating basic questions in philosophy, and partly because of a renewed excitement in understanding human beings in the work that Robert White and Henry Murray were pursuing in their study of lives in the Social Relations Department at Harvard. But he soon realized that although these new mentors had adopted a humanistic ideology, which resonated in some ways with his own, they were discussing philosophical issues as if they were empirical psychological realities. Given his training in both philosophy and logic, as well as in psychometrics, this seemed to him to be a confusion of disciplines that could not lead to a clarification of important issues.

By the early 1940s he was becoming vaguely aware of the centrality of affects, and in the early 1950s had included faces drawn as happy, sad, and angry, in the design of the Tomkins–Horn Picture Arrangement Test in the tradition of Rorschach, and Murray's use of the TAT, but at that time, he could not find any rationale for doing so. In retrospect, he felt his own intuitions were masked by what he called a pseudo-resonance, which accepted a restricted range of options that was the closest to his own ideo-affective posture.

> Since theories develop slowly, it is common for the theorist as a young apprentice to accept relatively gross mismatches between what he has learned and what he intuits only vaguely at the outset. I was persuaded by Freud that the primary drives were powerful motivators and by Murray that his several psychogenic "needs" were equally important. I also intuited that whether a person was happy or sad, angry or afraid, or ashamed was also important, but I could not at that time find either an empirical or a theoretical base for this intuition.
>
> (p. 30)

Drawing on his background in logic and value theory, and as a former psychophysicist, Tomkins came to believe that personality theory had to be grounded in a *biopsychosocial* view of the person. In the 1930s he had had an earlier fantasy of creating a human automation, which he called the humanomation. During this earlier period he had come across Wiener's early papers on cybernetics, which had exposed him to the concept of multiple assemblies of varying degrees of independence, dependence, interdependence, and control and transformation of one by another. He states that one day in the late 1940s he suddenly understood the role of the affect mechanism as a *separate amplifying co-assembly* that could amplify the mechanisms of perceptual, motor, memorial, cognitions, as well as drives, e.g. oxygen, hunger, sex. "Freud's id suddenly appeared to be a paper tiger since sexuality, as he best knew, was the most finicky of drives, easily rendered impotent by shame or anxiety or boredom or rage" (p. 32). He describes this moment as a major breakthrough in his understanding of affect and motivation.

The second major discovery about affect came in 1955, when his son was born, and like other theorists before him, such as Piaget, he observed his son daily, soon after his birth. Here in his own words, he describes the impact these experiences had on him.

> I was struck with the massiveness of the crying response. It included not only very loud vocalization and facial muscular responses, but also large changes in blood flow to the face and engagement of all the striate musculature of the body. It was a massive total bodily response, which, however, seemed to center on the face. Freud had suggested that the birth cry was the prototype of anxiety, but my son didn't seem anxious. What, then was this facial response? I labeled it distress. Next, I was to observe intense excitement on his face when he labored after the first few months of his life to shape his mouth to try to imitate the speech he heard. He would struggle minutes on end, and then give up, apparently exhausted and discouraged. I noted the intensity of the smiling response to his mother and to me, and again I became aware that nothing in psychoanalytic theory (or in any other personality theory at that time), paid any attention to the specificity of enjoyment as contrasted with excitement.
>
> (pp. 32–33)

Tomkins went on to identify several other primary affects, namely startle/surprise, fear/terror, and anger/rage, as well as an affect auxiliary response, namely, shame, an auxiliary to the affect interest, and two drive auxiliary responses, which over evolutionary time, have attained the status of a more general motivating signal, namely disgust, and dissmell (I will describe the role of each specific affect later in this section). Tomkins' theory not only addressed the number of primary affects, but, given his earlier understanding and acceptance of Werner's concept of multiple assembles, he also saw the necessity for the following:

> A general theory of affect activation must account for both the innate and the learned activation of affect ... Further, the affects must be capable of being activated ... by *any* other mechanism (be it perceptual or motoric) as well as the cognitive one.
>
> (p. 45)

From this he also inferred that:

> Each affect had, therefore, to be activated by some general characteristic of neural stimulation, common to both internal and external stimuli, and not too stimulus-specific like a releaser ... they had to be correlated with biologically useful information ... some had not to habituate while others had to be capable of habituation, otherwise a painful stimulus might too soon cease to be distressing and an exciting stimulus never let go – like a deer caught in a headlight.
>
> (p. 45)

Here we see the systematic working of his logical, theoretical mind. What follows is the result of his explorations.

After examining many instances observed by others and himself of infant affects for commonalities in feeling states that could be correlated with known external stimuli, he believed it was possible to account for these major phenomena with a few basic assumptions about the characteristics of neural events activating innate affect as well as events involving cognitive, motor, or perceptual mediation:

> I would account for the differences in affect activation by three variants of a single principle – the density of neural firing. By density I mean the frequency of neural firing per unit of time. My theory posits three discrete classes of activators of affect, each of which further amplifies the sources which activate them. These are stimulation increase, stimulation level, and stimulation decrease.
>
> Thus any stimulus with a relatively sudden onset and a steep increase in the rate of neural firing will innately activate a startle response . . . if the rate of neural firing increases less rapidly, fear is activated, and if still less rapidly, then interest is innately activated. In contrast, any sustained increase in the level of neural firing, as with a continuing loud noise, would innately activate the cry of distress. If it were sustained and still louder, it would innately activate the anger response. Finally any sudden decrease in stimulation that reduced the rate of neural firing, as in the sudden reduction of excessive noise, would innately activate the rewarding smile of enjoyment.
>
> With respect to the density of stimulation and neural firing, then, the human being is equipped for affective arousal for every major general contingency. The general advantage of affective arousal to such a broad spectrum of levels and changes of levels of neural firing is to make the individual care about quite different states of affairs in quite different ways. It is posited that there are both positive and negative affects activated by stimulation increase, but that only negative affects are activated by a continuing unrelieved level of nonoptimal stimulation and that only positive affect is activated by stimulation decrease.
>
> (p. 46)

It is important to notice that this theory can account for all kinds of voluntary responses, such as a sudden contraction of bodily muscles as in an avoidance response that is intense enough to innately trigger fear, even though the motor response itself is not innate, but occurs because of an inference of danger. Here he offers an ordinary example of the complex relationship between the affect mechanism and other basic mechanisms by describing how drive, cognition, and muscle movements can combine to evoke anger:

> Again, an individual who comes into a restaurant hungry might become distressed as the density of neural firing of the hunger signal increases to a level sufficient to trigger distress. But now the individual is subjected to the conjoint, elevated level of neural firing from two sources, the stomach in hunger and the facial and vocal muscles contracted in distress. It would require only a small additional contraction of the fist (occasioned perhaps by an inference of inequity on seeing a waitress attend someone who came in to the restaurant later than she or he did) to reach a level of neural firing adequate to activate anger. Such an arousal of anger is based on part drive, part affect, part inference, part contracted fist, conjointly adding up to the density level of neural firing required to innately trigger anger. To the extent to which such rates and levels of neural firings themselves become habitual and overlearned and located in ideas or muscle movements they radically increase the frequency of specific affect activation.
>
> (p. 48)

He goes on to articulate that in a multi-mechanism organism like the human being, each mechanism must be minimally matched to all other mechanisms as well as being mismatched in varying degrees, so that all mechanisms can, at the same time meet varying environmental demands. "Play" refers to this looseness of fit between mechanisms, and the system as a whole and its environment. But for survival, evolution also requires enough of a match to meet a satisficing criterion, so that the system as a whole can reproduce itself:

> Contrary to Freud, it is extremely unlikely that any motivational mechanism could have been so blind and mismatched to reason and reality as the "id." Contrary to cognitive theory, no motivational mechanism could have been so altogether docile and reasonable as we are being asked to believe. *Affect is a loosely matched mechanism designed to play a number of parts in continuing changing assemblies of mechanisms*. It is in some respects like a letter of an alphabet in a language, changing in significance as it is assembled with varying other letters to form different words, sentences, paragraphs. Further, the system as a whole has no single "output" …

> Affect is the bottom line for thought as well as perception and behavior ... Affect is an end in itself, with or without instrumental behavior.
>
> (p. 5, italics mine)

It may be difficult or confusing for the reader to fully embrace the implications of Tomkins' approach to affect and motivation. He therefore goes on to name several assumptions about affect and motivation that have to be "surrendered." What follows is a brief version of these assumptions: (1) that affect has to be cognitively activated; (2) that affect and motivation have to be "about" something; (3) that affect has to lead to some kind of "response," usually behavioral; (4) that motives are "pushy" or "pully;" (5) (given number 4) that motives are severely limited in the degree of their transformability; (6) that the degree of abstraction is limited in motives – "Thus hunger as a motive is about food, pushing and pulling the individual to eat and only eat, or to do whatever is instrumental to the consummatory response" (p. 52); and (7) that an identifying internal organization exists that is motivational. How then are we to understand motivation? Tomkins offers the following conceptualization:

> In contrast to these assumptions I will argue that what we ordinarily think of as motivation is not a readily identifiable internal organization resident in any single mechanism but is rather a crude, loose, approximate conceptual net we throw over the human being as she or he lives in her or his social habitat. It is as elusive a phenomenon as defining the locus of political power in a democracy. Is political power in the executive, the legislature, or the judiciary? Is it in the mass media, the people, big business, big labor, the universities, the states, or the cities? The answer is that political power is everywhere and nowhere and never the same in one place for very long.
>
> The affect mechanism has evolved to perform multiple vital functions in continuing assemblies with other vital mechanisms. Because of the principle of "play" it is imperfectly adapted to serve these multiple functions, but by virtue of the satisficing principle of good enough matching affect, it "works" biologically, psychologically, and socially. *It works by virtue of three major conjoint characteristics – urgency,*

> *abstractness, and generality.* In its urgency it is insistent. It is insistent in a very abstract way – that matters are increasing rapidly, or decreasing rapidly, or have increased too much. In its generality it is capable of very great combinational flexibility with other mechanisms that it can conjointly imprint and be imprinted by, thereby rendering its abstractness more particular and concrete (so that it can become an automobile that is coming too fast and too frightening rather than more abstract awareness of something too fast.
>
> (p. 52, italics mine)

Affects amplify the urgency of anything with which they are co-assembled, by being an analog amplifier. He uses the example of the pain mechanism, activated by a cut on the hand, which functions as an analogue to the injury, namely, it hurts! This concentrates powerfully the mind. He goes on to say:

> Affect receptors are no less compelling than pain receptors or sexual pleasure receptors. Our hair stands on end and we sweat in terror. Our face reddens as our blood pressure rises in anger. Our blood vessels dilate and our face becomes pleasantly warm as we smile in enjoyment. These are compelling analogs of what arouses terror, rage, and enjoyment. A second form of amplification occurs by virtue of the similarity of their profile, in time, to their activating trigger. Just as a pistol is a stimulus that is very sudden in onset, brief in duration, and equally sudden in decay, so its amplifying analogue, the startle response mimics the pistol shot by being equally sudden in onset, brief in duration, and equally sudden in decay. *Affect thereby either makes good things better or bad things worse by conjointly simulating its activator in its profile of neural firing, and by adding a special analogic quality that is intensely rewarding or punishing.*
>
> (p. 53, italics mine)

He states further that this amplification happens in an abstract way, so that any responses that occur (whether cognitive or motoric) will contain the analogic quality in the activator. Take anger as an example, which is activated by a continuing non-optimal level of neural firing, so too then, any angry response will have this same high level of neural firing. Or in excitement, which is activated by an increasing rate of neural firing, so too is an exciting response accelerating in speech, gesture, or activity. And as enjoyment is activated by any decrease in neural firing, so too are enjoyable responses relaxing as in savoring responses. *The main function of the urgency of affect by these analogic amplifications is to make the human being care by feeling.*

But because these urgent, analogic amplifications are complex responses, they can also have *syndrome and involuntary characteristics*, organized neurlogically via the bloodstream, with innervations occurring in all parts or in rapid succession, and therefore can offer resistance to control, as in a startle response or an organism. Also affects may be triggered outside of the individual's control, or be controlled only with difficulty, or continue for periods of time that again may not be easily controlled. They may then in all of these respects and at some times, feel alien to the individual. Perhaps because of these probable characteristics of affects, it has made it hard, all these years, to distinguish them from drives.

If we now look at the third major characteristic of the affect mechanism, namely its generality, by which Tomkins means its transformability or degrees of freedom, all of which allows for a great flexibility of co-assembly with other mechanisms, so "that the abstract features of affect are made more particular and concrete and the more urgent features are made more modulated" (p. 54). He gives the example of the game of twenty questions in which the first question contains the most information and the last question contains the least.

> The affect mechanism similarly invests its urgency first of all at just such an abstract level. Other information, either simultaneous or sequential, acts a like a zoom lens to specify more concretely the vital area that has first been magnified by affect.
>
> (p. 55)

It is because the innate activators of affect are urgent and abstract (e.g. too much, increasing fast, or decreasing) and do not function as specific releasers, but as signals that cause the human being to care about what is happening, that it then becomes possible for all the resources of the more detailed, differentiated mechanisms to come into play and that can then be used by the human being to solve whatever problems or situations have arisen. It is this transformability of the affect mechanism that allows these more complex organizations and coordinations to happen.

Tomkins argues that by contrast, drives contain considerably less transformability. The drive mechanism has built in "vital information of where and when to do what" (p. 55). This increases greatly "the probability of finding the correct consummatory response" (p. 55). He gives the following examples: hunger and thirst are space and time specific; they are felt in the mouth and or stomach, and tell one when to start and when to stop drinking or eating. Whereas one need not feel a particular affect for days or weeks, or could feel affect momentarily, or for a lifetime, as anxiety. Pain is space specific, but is time general, and sex has more space variability but is also time general; one may or may not have pain or sex for long periods of time. As was stated earlier, sex normally requires excitement, *but excitement does not require the sex drive; one can be excited by anything*. This is a good example of how the multi-mechanism model of human functioning provides much more freedom for affective phenomena to amplify human experience without depending on a connection to a drive. Affects also have a greater generality of both intensity and density than is true for drives.

> One day I might not be at all angry until quite suddenly something makes me explode in a rage ... Affect density (the product of intensity x duration) can vary from low and casual to monopolistic and high in density – intensity and enduring ... It is by virtue of its structurally based generality of space and time that affect can readily co-assemble with and therefore impart its urgency and lend its power to memory, to perception, to thought, and to action no less than to drives. Not only may affects be widely and variously invested they may also be invested in other affects, combine with other affects, intensify or modulate them, and suppress or reduce them. Neither hunger nor thirst can be used to reduce the need for air, as a child may be shamed into crying or may be shamed into stopping his or her crying.
>
> (p. 56)

It is this generality of co-assembly that constitutes the power of the affect system. He goes on to say the following:

> It is well suited for membership in a feedback mechanism, since from moment to moment its role in the causal nexus can shift from independence to dependence to interdependence. It is free of the unidirectionality of billiard ball causal sequences (as would happen in a reflex chain or to some extent in a drive chain). Affect can determine cognition at one time, be determined by cognition at another time, and be interdependent under other circumstances. This permits one person to become truly more "cognitive" and another to be much more "affective" via the differential affective magnification of other mechanisms including affect magnifying itself.
>
> (p. 56)

Tomkins further extends the generality of affects' combinatorial co-assembly to the differential magnification of cultural, social, historical events, so that excitement cultures in which change is magnified can be distinguished from enjoyment cultures in which sameness is powerfully magnified. He also states that because affects are extremely contagious, all cultures need to exercise control over the free vocal expression of affects, although the degree and nature of control may differ from society to society. In this context, he cites the work of Lomax (1968), who correlated the tightness of the voice box as revealed in song, with the degree of hierarchical social control in the society, and the looseness of the voice box with permissive societies. Nevertheless, given the need for all societies to suppress affect in some manner, Tomkins believes there is a universal confusion with, what he calls the experience of "backed-up" affect and the experience of biological and psychological innate affect. "What the price of such suppression is we do not know because we have confused 'stress' with backed-up affect, and both with authentic, full-throated affect" (Demos, 1995, p. 57). But whatever the physical effects of backed-up affect may be, Tomkins argues that any suppression of affect results in a bleaching of the experience of affect and thus to some impoverishment of the quality of life.

Finally, he addresses another consequence of the affect mechanism's generality of co-assembly, namely that it imprints both the activators of and responses to affect equally in an abstract and urgent way, so that

> the range of connectedness of experience is radically increased. Thus via temporal overlap there may be produced S-S equivalences, S-R equivalences, and R-R equivalences mediated by affects and affect analogs. A pleasant person becomes a relaxing, warm, enjoyable, helpful person. An angry person becomes an angering hurtable person. As affect density increases it provides an increasingly viscous psychic glue that embeds very different phenomena in the same affective medium. Thus are produced many of Freud's "primary process" phenomena, as well as many of the "fusion" phenomena of both abnormal and normal identity of self and other that are more compelling than either "identification" or "object choice." As at the moment of intense affect and orgasm, in experienced fusion there is no "self" or "other.
>
> (p. 57)

This connection between the activator and response is not learned; it occurs simply because of the brief overlap in time. Tomkins' use of the word response here does not imply a restriction to motor responses; it may include retrieved memories or thoughts which carry the same abstract, urgent analogue as a physical response, e.g. relaxed, or accelerating, or intense, etc.

This concludes the discussion of the three conjoint characteristics of the affect mechanism as an analog amplifier, namely urgency, abstractness and generality, and how it has evolved, in its degree of being matched or mismatched to other mechanisms, to play a number of different parts in these continually changing assemblies. Thus the experience of affect can take on many different qualities, as described by Tomkins,

> making it seem sometimes blind and inert, other times intuitive and flexible; sometimes primarily biological, other times largely psychological, social, cultural or historical, sometimes aesthetic, other times

instrumental; sometimes private and solipsistic, other times communicative and expressive; sometimes explosive, other times overcontrolled and backed-up.

(p. 58)

A description of the primary affects

Affects are organized sets of responses widely distributed throughout the body involving changes in the blood flow in the face, changes in breathing and vocalizations, in the heart, in the endocrines, and in the skeletal muscles, which generate feedback that is experienced as either positive or negative. There are specific programs for each distinct affect stored in subcortical centers that are part of our genetic inheritance. Thus the infant does not have to learn how to cry in distress when hungry, or how to startle to a loud noise. Tomkins sees the viscera as secondary to the face in importance as a part of the affect mechanism for several reasons. First of all the face responds faster and with more precision than the slower viscera, therefore it leads the viscera, just as the fingers lead the slower muscles of the forearm or shoulder. Second, the face not only communicates to the self, but also communicates to others, which is of great significance, because it represents a motivational signal that can be read at a distance.

In his last public lecture, entitled "Inverse Archaeology: Facial Affect and the Interfaces of Scripts Within and Between Persons," presented at the annual meeting of the International Society for Research on Emotions, on July 15, 1990, Tomkins elaborated further on the importance of the face. By inverse archaeology he meant

> that the surface of the skin is where it is at, not deep within us, that the *skin is the major motivational organ*, and that a smile is where it appears to be. It is not in a group of happy cortical neurons, nor in the folds in the stomach. But like the pain of torture, the pleasure of sexual seduction, or the irresistible sleepiness at the site of the eyelids, that region is the site of exquisitely sensitive receptors on the surface of the skin, whether we're talking about drives or pain or affects or whatever.

(Demos, 1995, p. 284, italics mine)

He cites other evidence indicating that the skin in diving birds, namely the beak leads in widespread autonomic changes, in order to conserve oxygen. "When the beak of a diving bird is stimulated by the water as it dives for fish, this change produces profound general changes such as vasoconstriction within the body as a whole" (p. 91). He states further that similar changes are found in humans when submerging the face in water (see Elsner, Franklin, Van Citters, & Kenny, 1966). He goes on to say: "Inverse archaeology not only locates motivation on those surfaces where it appears to be, but it also says that facial affect is at once individual and private and social and shared nonverbal communication" (Demos, 1995, p. 285). He argues further that such affect communication is continually being shaped and reshaped as both partners continually respond to the other. Thus he insists on the following: "Facial affect is also at once biologic and innate and leaned and transformed. This is no debate whether it is one or another. It is always both and it has to be" (p. 285). He goes on to give the following examples of how we learn to use voluntary affect as a symbol,

> as in a slow or too fast smile, which communicates "I am not amused," or a slow raising of the eyebrows, which says "I don't believe you." "What you say is too surprising." These responses work on the assumption that there a consensual knowledge about what an innate joyful, or surprise affect response is.
>
> (p. 285)

The function of each specific affect

The three affects of surprise/startle, fear/terror, and interest/excitement are all activated by an increasing rate of the density of neural firing. By density is meant the frequency of neural firing per unit of time. The affects are listed in their weak and strong form. Because these three affects differ only in the rate of neural firing that activates them, an unstable equilibrium exists between them. Any one of these affects can activate the other.

Surprise/startle

The startle results in a sudden jerk of the body, which amplifies both the suddenness of the onset and the decline of the stimulus. The function of the startle is like that of a circuit breaker, in that it interrupts all other ongoing processes: "it orients the individual to turn his attention from one thing to another" (Demos, 1995, p. 69). Surprise, which is slightly less sudden, involves a quick raising of the eyebrows and perhaps a jaw drop as well. Any other affect can then follow. Thus a sudden tap on the shoulder may evoke surprise. If the person tapping one's shoulder is familiar, one might then feel interest; or if it is a policeman, one might feel fear. Also the following common sequence has been observed, both in animals and humans, when suddenly spotting any strange object or situation. The suddenness may initially trigger surprise or startle, upon a closer look this strange object may trigger fear or terror, but with further examination, this same object may now arouse interest. Also interest can activate a startle or a surprise as in a "double take" when one's initial perception or thought suddenly takes on a shocking or surprising meaning.

Fear/terror

Fear and/or terror are activated by any rapidly increasing threat to the person, as in a powerful approaching storm, or a rapidly approaching automobile or animal, or by a wide variety of rapid changes in internal events, e.g. a sharp pain, or a quick avoidant motion, involving muscle contractions. Drugs can also activate fear by producing rapid and unfamiliar changes in the internal environment. Fear/terror involves an increase in heart rate; the skin can become white and cold with sweat, and one's hair can stand on end; one's muscles may tense, or freeze up, which can temporally paralyze one's ability to think straight or to defend oneself. The eyes widen, and the lips tremble. Sustained fear/terror is toxic, as in trauma.

Sedatives can be used to decrease fear by relieving the chronic muscle tension and increased heart rate due to chronic anxiety. Social fears and inhibitions are often relieved by alcohol, through its relaxation of the skeletal muscles and the blood vessels lying close to skin, so that the face becomes warm and relaxed. Fear/terror can also be activated by any rapid increase in one's thought processing, either about an external event or the recovery of a disturbing memory, either when awake or asleep, as in a nightmare. One awakes from a nightmare not only from the terrifying imagery, but also because of the activation of the patterned fear program that involves the viscera, e.g. such as a pounding heart, cold skin, a tensing of the skeletal muscles, etc.

Interest/excitement

Interest/excitement is also activated by any increasing source of the density of neural firing, but the rate of increase is slower than in either fear or startle. Yet the experience of excitement can be intense enough to amplify the sensations during sexual intercourse or athletics, but it is also capable of more graded and flexible amplification as when it is matched with cognitive activities. A state of interest involves a quieting of the body, except in more active moments of excitement, and a focus of attention, which facilitates an exploration of whatever has evoked this state. Tomkins describes the flexibility of interest as a necessary condition for the early formation of the perceptual world in the following passage:

> In learning to perceive any object, the infant must attack the problem over time ... The object must be perceived in some detail, but it must also be perceived in its unity. Attention must steer a middle course between extreme distractibility from one aspect of the object to some other aspect of an adjacent object, and extreme stickiness and compelled attention to the same object ... In order to make such graded sampling possible, there must be the continuing support of interest or excitement to the changing sampling of the object.
>
> (Demos, 1995, pp. 71–72)

He goes on to say: "Excitement lends more than spice to life. Without zest, long-term effort and commitment cannot be sustained, either physiologically or psychologically" (pp. 71–72).

All learning is dependent upon the sustaining motivational amplification of the affect of interest/excitement. In Chapter 3 of this volume, we could see how, in Cathy's early life, with so little support from her family for her interests, by the end of our observations she was unable to generate much initiative, curiosity or creativity, in comparison to the ongoing family support of Donna's interests, resulting in her expanding initiatives, curiosity and creativity.

Distress/anguish

Distress/anguish is one of two affects that is activated by a sustained, non-optimal level of neural density. In distress, the inner corners of the eyebrows go up, the corners of the mouth go down, the head lowers, the body goes into a slump and sobbing vocalizations may occur. In Tomkins' theory *distress is a fundamental human affect because human suffering is so ubiquitous*. What follows is his reasoning based on our evolutionary history:

> It seems very likely that the differentiation of distress from fear was required in part because the coexistence of superior cognitive powers of anticipation, with an affect as toxic as fear, could have destroyed man if this were the only affect expressing suffering. What was called for was a less toxic, but still negative, affect which would motivate human beings to solve disagreeable problems without too great a physiological cost or too great a probability of running away from the many problems that confront the human being and which would permit anticipation of trouble at an optimal psychic and biological cost. Such we think is the cry of distress.
>
> (Demos, 1995, p. 73)

Since distress/anguish is activated by any continuing source of non-optimal neural stimulation, there are a wide variety of sources, both internal or external, which can trigger the cry of distress, such as enduring pain, hunger, fatigue, ongoing noise or lights that are too bright, or a valued loss of various kinds, such as the death of a loved one that increases one's longing and misery.

Distress crying is perhaps the first vocalization infants make, because of the over stimulation of the birth process, and hunger and fatigue crying are perhaps the most ubiquitous expressions of negative affect in infancy. The primary function of crying is first to inform the self through the face and the cry, that all is not well, and second, through the cry, which is an auditory signal, to inform others. Thus any caregiver can hear at a distance that the baby or a person needs help in some way. But in and of itself the cry does not indicate the cause of the suffering. Generally, from past experience, a caregiver can sort out what the baby or the other needs. In Chapter 2 of this volume, when discussing infant capacities for maintaining coherent states, I emphasized the infant's limited repertoire of responses for modulating increasing levels of distress, and thus how important it is for the caregiver to intervene so as to protect the infant's psyche from increasing densities of distress, which can escalate into anger, and if continued can result in a disorganizing, overwhelming experience for the infant.

In Chapter 2, we also discussed the various factors that influence a caregiver's ability to respond to her infant's distress in a helpful way. Since all affect is contagious, and infant affect is full voiced and bodied, these factors included the caregiver's tolerance of hearing the distress cry, given her own socialization of this affect, and the various meanings the cry evokes in the caregiver. In Chapter 3, I also discussed the importance of the socialization of distress early in life in determining the fate of this affect later on in a person's life, as it effects the development of the capacity to self-soothe when falling asleep, as well as the capacity to regulate daytime distress enabling one to signal the need for help. The learned capacity to tolerate distress allows one to engage in short-term or long-term problem-solving when necessary and to seek help, without undue shame. Without this capacity to bear one's distress, one might learn to hide one's suffering or to build powerful defenses against any awareness of distress, because one has learned it is uncontainable, or is unimportant to others, or is a sign of weakness, or unmanly to cry, and thus develop no tolerance for one's own or others suffering.

Throughout life, then, the experience of distress can either continue to be a bearable and important source of information to the self and/or to others, motivating one to solve problems, and/or to share one's distress, thereby obtaining help or solace; or one's distress may become a deeply denied or inhibited, foreshortened, or unrecognizable, alien experience, evoking shame, anger, anxiety, disgust, or contempt, which may then impair one's capacity to empathize with other's suffering or with one's own suffering, and thereby interfere with one's ability to persist with a difficult task, prevent one from seeking help, or lead to angry attacks on others, or on oneself, as internal stress builds. Without the capacity to bear distress, one may turn to substances to alleviate suffering, a solution that could eventually lead to addiction.

Anger/rage

Anger/rage is the only other affect that is activated by a continuing source of non-optimal neural stimulation, but at a higher level of stimulation, than distress. Thus many sources of distress, if continued, without relief for any period of time, will summate and reach a level sufficient to activate anger. The function of anger is to increase the urgency about whatever is creating the feeling of "too much, and is not stopping!" It communicates this urgency both to the self and to others, by means of its correlated responses of a squared mouth, lowered eyebrows, a tensing of the eyes into a focused, hard glare, a tensing of the skeletal muscles, as in the fist or an arching of the back, as in infancy, as well as autonomic responses involving a rise in blood pressure, producing a red face. Any accompanying vocalization will tend to be loud and forceful, as the vocal cords tighten and any action will tend to be forceful.

Given the general contagion of all affects, combined with the intensity of angry responses that increase the potential for destructive actions, every society has strict rules and laws about the need to control the expression of anger. Tomkins (1991) states the following: "The socialization of anger is characteristically vigilant, insistent, strident, and pious, because of its real and believed toxicity. Given its potential for harm, no society can be indifferent to its socialization" (p. 218). Later in this same volume Tomkins describes how throughout history and in different societies there have always existed different values around the use of aggression to rid the world of disbelievers, or to promote a social revolution, or the lack of a universal consensus on "an optimal degree of *difference* between the values of the individual, the society and the total social community." He then concludes the following:

> Having confronted the deep, unresolvable value conflicts inherent in the socialization of anger, we will nonetheless argue that there yet remain some nontrivial directives for considering some aspects of anger socialization that are better and more rewarding than their opposed, more punishing modes of anger socialization. Such would include any learned incapacity to detect anger in the self or other, as well, as any learned incapacity to detect the presence of non-anger. It is equally critical that one neither deny nor exaggerate the presence of anger in the self or in the other.
>
> Again it is critical that one be capable of *feeling, expressing*, and/or *acting* on ego-syntonic anger so as to be capable of *not* feeling, *not* expressing, and *not* acting on anger to the extent that the individual's values and circumstances dictate such control.
>
> Further it is critical that anger and its expression and its action be capable of being *differentiated*, graded, and modulated. This is a learned skill . . . The modulation of anger extends the possibilities both in the direction of more finely nuanced anger appropriate to varying degrees of seriousness of the problematic and in the direction of a more sustained and deeper violence against violations of central values.
>
> Such modulation is also critical in the ability to move from positive affect to anger and from anger back to positive affect through a graded series rather than in volatile explosive affect.
>
> (p. 228, italics mine)

Earlier he described this capacity in the following way:

> Most important, his self is not split into a bad, angry self and a good loving self, nor are others divided sharply into nice, loving people and bad, hating people. He is capable of seeing himself and others whole. After intense anger he knows the way back to the pre-anger self and the pre-anger relationship. To show anger and to aggress upon someone can be followed by physical survival for both parties, by mutual love between both parties, by mutual respect between both parties, by excitement and enjoyment once again. In short, anger can be an incident and accepted for what it is, a temporary flash of lightning which may sear and burn but which may also

> illuminate and clear the air, which has been oppressive. This individual might also sustain anger if the cause is just and the sources are deep and stubborn and require a lifetime of revolutionary activity to uproot.
>
> (Tomkins, 1991, p. 224)

Tomkins (1991) argues that: "the differential consequences of the rewarding and punitive socialization of anger are considerable . . . The whole spectrum of psychopathology is intimately linked with the punitive socialization of anger." He goes on to say the following:

> There is no affect whose punitive socialization can more jeopardize human development. Depending on the particular negative sanctions employed, the experience or the possibility of the feeling of anger can come to evoke utter humiliation or guilt, or anguish or overwhelming terror. There are single and multiple anger binds depending on whether the anger of the child was contained primarily by one or another negative affect or withdrawal of positive affect. Thus, there are anger-shame binds, anger-fear binds, anger-distress binds in which the child is finally reduced to the tears of impotent rage. There are also the multiple binds such as the anger-shame-fear-distress bind [which involves an escalation of child and adult anger, ending with] a final challenge to parental authority, which was punished with [a] slap on the face, which produced further shame at being beaten, fear at the possibility of a more severe beating and tears of anguish at the impotence against overwhelming force.
>
> (p. 225)

Given the potential danger of unregulated anger, its socialization often begins early. In hierarchical homes or societies, any expression of anger by children in the home or at school, is likely to be experienced by the adults as insubordination and not be tolerated and may be severely punished, in an effort to teach obedience to authority, which may lead to any or all of the negative binds described above. In more egalitarian homes or societies, a child's anger is likely to be tolerated and understood as an expression of a protest about something that feels overwhelming to the child, and therefore is heard as a plea for help. The child is thereby taught tolerance for anger and offered help to cope with the sources of his or her anger, which tends to enhance the ability to modulate the expression of anger, and to develop the expectation that one's frustrations can be managed and solutions can be found. In such families, if parental anger occurs, the parent offers restitution to the child.

The psychic cost of suppressed anger over a life span has been linked to several health problems, such as high blood pressure, or ulcers. Given both the negative potential for unregulated anger, or the over control of anger, it may be difficult to see the usefulness of such an affect. Yet anger often contains important information about serious problems. Thus the ability to tolerate it and develop the capacity to feel moral outrage at violations that hurt others, and express it in constructive protests, as in the non-violent civil rights protests in this country, can lead to fairness or to necessary reforms. In its modulated form, throughout one's own life, anger can be the catalyst providing the motivation for a needed change, for example in finally dealing with an ongoing serious problem, by taking action to improve the situation, as in naming and working through difficult problems with others, or if all else fails, in seeking a divorce, or by leaving an abusive employment or discriminatory situation.

Enjoyment/joy

Enjoyment/joy is the only affect that is activated by a reduction of the density of neural firing. The face relaxes into a smile, and becomes warm with increasing blood flow; the skeletal muscles relax, as in a savoring response. Given the different sources of the decrease in neural firing, there can be a variety of different kinds of smiles. A smile of relief occurs with a decrease in negative stimulation from a wide range of sources, as in a decrease of fear, or distress, or shame. A smile of triumph may occur with a decrease in anger, as in remembering a crushing retort to an annoying other, or as in a decrease in frustration in being unable to solve a difficult problem, and suddenly finding a solution. A smile of pleasure may follow a decrease in stimulation after an orgasm. A smile of joy follows a decrease in excitement in seeing a favorite person who has been away.

The decrease from any source of stimulation has to be steep enough for joy to occur. If the other is too familiar, joy is not activated. Too gradual a decrease in the density of neural firing can lead to indifference. Joy requires some novelty for the smile to occur, as in first hearing the punch line of a joke, but not on a repetition of the same joke. Indeed, Tomkins (1991) argues that: "Anything that can capture the excitement or interest of a human being can also produce the smile of joy" (p. 83).

A smile of joy can also be activated by memory in several ways, as in remembering the smiling face of another and how it felt to receive that empathic response, or in seeing another's smiling face and remembering how one's own smiling face felt. Smiling between two people creates a joy that is similar to but different from the joy created by sexual intercourse, which involves drive satisfaction. Both involve mutuality, but a shared smile does not require physical contact or drive satisfaction (e.g. libido), but rather involves visual receptors that can operate at a distance. This frees the individual from requiring body contact and stimulation as necessary for positive reward.

The paradigm at the affect level is the early joyful smiling between the mother and the infant and child. Here in Tomkins' words is the significance of this early joyful exchange:

> Because the infant will smile at the face of the mother and thereby reward itself, and because the mother will in turn smile at the smile of the infant and thereby reward herself, concurrent smiling is mutually rewarding from the outset. Later, when the child's development is sufficiently advanced, both parties to this mutual enjoyment are further rewarded by the awareness that this enjoyment is shared enjoyment. This is mediated through the eyes. Through interocular interaction both parties become aware of each other's enjoyment and of the very fact of communion and mutuality. Indeed, one of the prime ways in later life that the adult will recapture this type of communion is when he smiles at another person, who smiles back at him and at the same time the eyes of each are arrested in a stare at the eyes of the other. Under these conditions one person can "fall in love with" another person. The power of this dyadic posture is a derivative of an earlier unashamed fascination-and-joy smile. The power of the earlier experience is essentially innate: the match

> between the stimulus characteristics of the human face and the conditions necessary for innately arousing the reciprocal affects of interest and joy biologically equips the infant, no less than the mother, to be joyous in this way.
>
> (pp. 79–80)

Such intimate, joyful, eye-to-eye engagements with infants and young children may not be possible for adults for whom closeness feels threatening, e.g. if it evokes a feeling of being too exposed in some way, or feeling too shy/shameful, or too inadequate.

These early infant experiences quoted above from Tomkins' writings in the 1960s, describing the mutually created and highly rewarding transactions between infants and mothers, both anticipated and fit beautifully with the descriptions, nearly thirty years later, of the rewarding experience of "being with" described in the recent findings of infant-mother researchers (Beebe, Lachmann, & Jaffe, 1979) reported in Chapter 3 of this volume. Tomkins' ideas were way ahead of his time.

When we compare joy to the experience of pain, danger, fear, anger, distress, disgust, or the intense interest involved in difficult challenges, the joy response can seem to feel like a luxury. This can happen because the contents of consciousness are limited, and since the essence of joy is a savoring and relaxing response, it may, given the press of life events, lose out in the competition with all these other, more urgent affects, in capturing the attention of the individual.

Shame, disgust, and dissmell

Shame, disgust, and dissmell are defined as auxiliary affects, but they function as innate affects in that they have the motivating and amplifying properties of affects, with somewhat different characteristics and mechanisms.

Shame

Tomkins' formulation of shame is seen as an auxiliary to interest/excitement. He states that the innate activator of shame is the incomplete reduction of interest or excitement, which functions as a specific inhibitor of one or both of these affects, thus its activation leads to a barrier to the continuation of interest or excitement. This barrier to interest/excitement can occur in the following ways:

> [O]ne is suddenly looked at by one who is strange, or because one wishes to look at, or commune with, another person, but suddenly cannot because the other is displeased by one's presence, or one smiled expecting the other to be familiar, but suddenly the other appears unfamiliar, or one started to smile, but found that one's smiling was mocked in some way.
>
> (Demos, 1995, p. 84)

The shame response includes lowering the head, lowering the eyelids, lowering the tonus of all facial muscles, and in children a protrusion of the lower lip, and a unilateral tilting of the head in one direction. If one is fearful of showing a shame response, or feels angry at being shamed, one is likely to push the chin up as defense against lowering the head in shame, or as a defiant anti-shame response.

Tomkins states that shyness, shame, and guilt are identical as affects, even though the experience of them feels different. The difference consists of its coassembly with different causes and consequences.

> Shyness is about strangeness of the other; guilt is about moral transgression; shame is about inferiority; but the core affect, namely the felt barrier to the continuation of interest/excitement, in all three is identical, though the coassembled perceptions, cognitions, and intentions may be vastly different.
>
> (p. 85)

Thus whatever these differences in coassembly are, shame and guilt can *only* be activated after interest and excitement have been activated, and that activation then results in the *incomplete reduction of interest and excitement by inhibiting or creating a barrier to their continuation.* This barrier to further communion is the essence of shame and guilt.

> In shame the individual wishes to resume his or her commerce with the exciting state of affairs, to reconnect with the other, to recapture the relationship that existed before the situation turned problematic.

> *In this respect shame is radically different from the drive auxiliary responses of disgust and dissmell.*
>
> (p. 400, italics mine)

Both of these latter two responses reject the object, without a wish to reconnect. *Thus shame in its essence is an affiliative response*, indicating the existence of a valued positive connection with another. Without the existence of such a valued positive relationship, a person may become "shameless" in thoughts, actions, and deeds.

Although shame can be evoked at any age, it becomes particularly salient to the young child somewhere in the middle of the second year of life, when they first become self-reflective, and thus becomes aware of their own smallness in comparison to an older sibling or adults, or in comparing their abilities with an older child or adult. In such situations feelings of inferiority are easily evoked (see Chapter 3 for an example, Kagan, 1981). If a child is continually made to feel incompetent or small, throughout the child's development, this affect can become dominant in a personality, and lead to pervasive social inhibitions and shyness.

Disgust and dissmell

Disgust and dissmell are innate defensive responses related to the hunger, thirst, and oxygen drives. If something smells bad, the upper lip and nose are raised, and the head is pulled back from the offending odor. Or when one ingests food or liquid that turns out to be toxic in some way, it will evoke disgust, which may result in nausea or vomiting. In the first example the warning sign is in the nose, and in the second it is in the mouth or stomach. If these responses were only limited to these functions, then they would not be defined as affects. However, Tomkins describes their stature as unique because they "also function as signals and motives to others as well as to the self of feelings of rejection and revulsion. They readily accompany a wide spectrum of entities that need not be tasted, smelled, or ingested" (Demos, 1995, p. 84). Disgust and dissmell towards others or the self are more likely to be learned and feel acceptable in hierarchically ordered families or societies.

It is important to focus on how destructive these affects can become. When, either through the socialization process or learning, dissmell and disgust are combined with anger, the result is the compound experience of contempt, which is manifested by a unilateral sneer. This combination can be lethal when it is directed towards the other, who can now be perceived as less than human, an abominable, foul smelling, and disgusting other whose existence is no longer tolerable. Our human history is filled with religious crusades, genocides, lynchings, burnings at the stake, and other inhuman acts toward those who are no longer seen as part of the human family and must be expelled or exterminated, lest the social polity become contaminated.

Dissmell, if greatly magnified, can become problematic on its own. As one ages and becomes increasingly isolated by the death of friends, family, and the loss of meaningful work, dissmell can become corrosive when joined with physical ailments and the distress connected to rapid cultural changes that can increase one's alienation and feelings of uselessness. Tomkins describes this possibility as follows: "Magnified dissmell is an alienation deeper than rage, which is still hot and engaged in the preservation of hope. Such terminal dissmell is perhaps the deepest sickness of the human spirit" (pp. 203–204).

The evolution of the affect system

Evolution, according to Darwin, concerns the way a population of genes maintains itself through reproductive success and adaptation. Tomkins argues the following:

> From this position, in addition to a strong sex drive, such characteristics as sensitivity to novel stimuli, sensitivity to social stimuli, aggressiveness, timidity and other affects *become no less important* foci for natural selection than the development of a homeostatic autonomic system and an adapted drive system.
>
> (Demos, 1995, p. 64, italics mine)

He also points out, that even without an understanding of specific genes, animal breeders have been able to breed rats who are tamer and more able to run mazes, and dogs who are more aggressive, or less dominant, and sheep who are more or less social, depending on how spread out their feeding sites are. Thus he argues that natural selection could have produced specific affective and behavioral characteristics in man.

> It is our belief that such was indeed the case and that natural selection has operated in man to heighten three distinct classes of affect – affect for preservation of life, affect for people, and affect for novelty . . . he fears threats to his life, is excited by new information and smiles with joy at the smile of one of his own species.
>
> (p. 66)

He goes on to say:

> If this is so, it is clear that his integration of these needs cannot be perfect, nor can he be more than imperfectly adapted to his changing environment. There could be no guarantee that selection for social responsiveness might not conflict with selection for self-preservative responsiveness and with selection for curiosity and responsiveness to novelty and thus complicate the problem for the integration of these characteristics. Nor could multi-dimensional criteria of any kind guarantee adaptation to a changing environment. No animal, of course, is completely adapted, but some animals have been able to attain a closer fit within a narrow niche by combining specialization of characteristics and restriction of movement to an equally specialized environment. In the case of man, natural selection was operating on a broad spectrum of characteristics for adaptation to a broad spectrum of environments.
>
> (p. 67)

Tomkins' polarity theory

Thus far we have focused on affect as the primary motivational system and its interactions with other inherited biological mechanisms. We have described each of the six basic affects and the three auxiliary affects that Tomkins has identified. And in Chapter 3 we followed the longitudinal affective experiences in two infant girls in their families of origin and the gradual motivational effects of these familial transactions on their capacities for self-regulation of distress and fear (inner cohesion), and on their abilities to develop their interests and their capacities for engagement with others and with objects (agency), all within the family context. But as the child grows, so too will their participation in the world of others and of ideas expand. Tomkins argues that in order to have a complete science of human beings, we also need to focus on *the affective investment of humans in their cultural products, such as their social, artistic, economic, religious institutions*, which is part of what he means by his focus on the "psychology of knowledge." He is particularly interested in knowledge that is on the edge of verified evidence and is therefore primarily based on faith, thus one part of this exploration involves the structure of ideology. By ideology, he means the following:

> Any organized set of ideas about which human beings are at once most articulate and most passionate, and for which there is no evidence and about which they are least certain. The foundations of mathematics, the philosophy of science, metaphysics, theology, epistemology, the theory of value, aesthetics, jurisprudence, government, theory of education and finally theories about child rearing, more recently called socialization – these have all evoked the most coherent and passionate controversy ... At the growing edge of the frontier of all sciences there necessarily is a maximum of uncertainty, and what is lacking in evidence is filled by passion and faith, and hatred and scorn for the disbelievers. Science will never be free of ideology, though yesterday's ideology is today's fact or fiction.
>
> (Demos, 1995, p. 111)

> *The issues are simple enough. Is man the measure, an end in himself, an active, creative, thinking, desiring, loving force in nature? Or must man realize himself, attain his full stature only through struggle toward, participation in, conformity to a norm, a measure, an ideal essence basically prior to and independent of man?*
>
> (p. 117, italics mine)

Through the socialization of affects, individuals adopt what Tomkins has called *ideo-affective postures*, by which he means *a loosely or organized set of feelings about feelings and ideas about feelings*, which in turn cause the individual to resonate to the right, left, or middle-of-the road positions in the ideological polarity. *The differences in socialization involve differences in tolerance or intolerance of the basic affects, which in turn effects how negatively or positively the person learns to feel about oneself and others.* Here is Tomkins speaking about the choices open to parents in their interactions with their child:

> At one pole is that return of the parent to his own golden age through identification with the child in play and shared delight. The child's zest for life, and obvious joy in simple human interaction and in elementary curiosity and attempted control of his body and his world in general can vitalize the adult personality. Such a parent bestows on the child the feeling that he is an end in himself and that shared human interaction is a deeply satisfying experience. Further, such a parent will not puncture the child's conception of his ability to control his parent. Eventually such a child must come to the awareness that the world presents endless opportunities of varied positive affects: joy, excitement, love of people, of places, of activities, and of things. He becomes addicted to creating satisfaction for himself and for others.
>
> There is another possibility open to any parent: the conjoint opportunity and obligation to mold the child to some norm. The norm may be a moral norm, a norm of "manners," a norm of competence, or a norm of independence. In any case, the parent sets himself in opposition to the child and bestows upon the child the sense that positive satisfaction is necessarily an epiphenomenon, consequent to effort, to struggle, to renunciation of his own immediate wishes. His own feelings and wishes are devalued in favor of some kind of behavior which is demanded of him. When the child wishes to do one thing and the parent wishes him to do another, the normative parent must set himself in opposition to the child's wishes. The parent must convey to the child that want he wants to do is of no consequence when it is in opposition to the norm. What is expected of him, in opposition to his own wishes, may be presented with all possible attractiveness and

> positive sanctions, but the fundamental necessity of renunciation and devaluation of his own wishes, thereby of his self, cannot in a normative socialization be sidestepped.
>
> (pp. 168–169)

Tomkins also describes several types of middle-of-the road socialization stances. One parent can take a left-wing stance and the other a right-wing stance. The child then has to find a way to deal with this clash of ideologies, and is likely to be focused on reconciling opposites in the world, or within his or her own divided self. Another possibility is that within each parent there is a mixture of left and right, which might result in being loving and playful at one moment or about some things, and stern and insisting on norm compliance at another moment or about other things. In the third variant the parents don't switch from one pole to the other, but instead stiffen the left-wing stance with right-wing overtones, or temper the right-wing rules with left-wing softening. An example of the first might be, "You and your friend can play, but don't make too much noise," and of the second, "You need to clean up your room before you can go and meet your friend, but if you hurry, I'll give you a ride there." A fourth option is that parents may not have developed a clear ideological stance.

There have been several validations of the ideology polarity. Nesbitt (1959) in his study of friendship, love, and values, studied ninety, paid college freshman and found significant differences between person identifiers, and norm identifiers. The person identifiers showed no responses on measures of conformity, superego, or social restlessness, and a higher score on sociophilia, and a more situational variation of scores on a measure of optimism and pessimism; whereas the norm identifiers were higher on conformity and superego measures, and low on sociophilia responses and relatively low on optimism and pessimism measures.

Since Nesbitt's study, Tomkins and several other collaborators intensively studied nearly 500 subjects of both sexes, ranging in age from high school, up through university students, as well as "normal" adults aged 45–60, and also psychotic depressives, and schizophrenics, using an extended battery of procedures. Much of this work was not published, but is reported in the *Selected Writings of Silvan S. Tomkins* (Demos,

1995). During the course of this work, they constructed a 59-item Polarity Scale covering a variety of subjects – science, government, responses to other human beings, human sympathy, children and play, feelings about feelings, pluralism versus hierarchy, and life. Item #38 of this scale presented the choice: "Human beings are basically good" versus "Human beings are basically evil." They found that if a person believed humans are basically good, they agreed with 80 percent of all other items keyed as humanistic; and if they believed that human beings are basically evil they agreed with 80 percent of all other items keyed as normative.

Here are some examples of the choices, several have been shortened from the original items, but contain the gist of the polarity. The humanistic response is presented first.

- *In terms of science*: "The important thing in science is to strike out into the unknown – right or wrong" versus "The important thing in science is to be right and make as few errors as possible." Or "Science enables man to realize himself, by gaining understanding and control of the world around him" versus "Science enables man to separate the true from the false, the right from the wrong, and reality from fantasy." Or "Great achievement requires first of all great imagination" versus "Great achievement requires first of all severe self discipline." Or "Numbers were invented" versus "Numbers were discovered."
- *In terms of government*: "Government's main purpose is to promote the welfare of the people" versus "Government's main purpose is to maintain law and order." Or "It is not always best for society and the person, for a law breaker to be punished" versus "All law breakers should be punished for the good of society." Or "Anger should be directed against the oppressors of mankind" versus "Anger should be directed at those revolutionaries who undermine law and order."
- *In terms of sympathy*: "To every lover, his beloved is the most beautiful person in the world" versus "Love is blind. Otherwise no one would ever fall in love." Or "To assume that most people are well-meaning, brings out the best in people" versus "To

assume that most people are well-meaning is asking for trouble." Or "It is distressing to see an adult cry" versus "It is disgusting to see an adult cry." Or "Those who err, should be forgiven" versus "Those who err should be corrected." Or "Familiarity like absence makes the heart grow fonder" versus "Familiarity breeds contempt."

- *Sympathy towards children and play*: "Play, no matter how old one gets, is enjoyable and exciting" versus "Play is childish, adults should attend to more important things." Or "Parents should first of all be gentle with children" versus "Parents should first of all be firm with children." Or "A child must be loved so that he can grow up to be a fine adult" versus "A child must be taught how to act so that he can grow up to be a fine adult."
- *Attitudes towards feelings*: "To act on impulse occasionally makes life more interesting." versus "To act on impulse is to act childishly." Or "Man must always leave himself open to his own feelings – alien as they may sometimes feel," versus "If sanity is to be preserved, man must guard himself against the intrusion of feelings which are alien to his nature." And finally, "Life sometimes leaves a bad taste" versus "Life sometimes smells bad".

(Demos, 1995, pp. 149–155)

Tomkins and his colleagues also collected data from these same 500 subjects on the Tomkins–Horn Picture Arrangement Test, in which the subject is asked to order three pictures, involving different kinds of activities, in which a person is either alone or together with others, so that in the third picture the person is either alone or together (Demos, 1995, p. 156). The results confirmed their expectations. The humanistic ideology is significantly correlated with general sociophilia, and the normative ideology is significantly correlated with sociophobia that involved an avoidance of physical contact between people, with an expectation of aggression from others.

In another study, involving the eighty-seven high school students of both sexes, who were given the Polarity Scale and the Tomkins–Horn

Picture Arrangement Test, they presented photos of the same face expressing six different affects – happy, sad, angry, ashamed, contempt, and fear. In each trial the subject was presented with one affect on the right eye and another affect on the left eye in a stereoscope. In addition, after each stereoscopic presentation, each affect was randomly presented simultaneously to both eyes and the subject was asked which affect they had previously seen. Each affect was put into conflict with every other affect, resulting in thirty-two pairings of affects. They assumed that the same attitudes evoked in the two other tests, would be activated to resolve the perceptual conflict in the stereoscope, and that it would result either in a fusion of the two affects, or a preference for one affect over the other. They expected that the humanistic orientation would produce a dominance of the smiling face over all other affects, and that the normative orientation would produce a dominance of the contempt face. Both predictions were validated.

In another study by Vasquez (1975) previously selected subjects on the basis of their scores on the Polarity Scale were videotaped in conversation with an experimenter and when alone. The focus in this study was on the use of the face, whether conscious or unconscious, whether voluntary or involuntary. The humanist subjects smiled more frequently than the normative subjects while talking to the experimenter, although there was no difference in their spontaneous affect expressions when alone. Also the humanist subjects responded more frequently than normative subjects with shame when there was any perceived barrier to intimacy, while the normative subjects not only smiled less frequently, but also displayed disgust on their face more frequently when the other was tested and found wanting. In summarizing the results of all of these studies, Tomkins concluded the following:

> Thus, whether we put the question to the brain faced unconsciously with conflicting perceptual information or to the fully conscious subject asked to decide in what order to place three different scenes to make sense of them, or whether unbeknownst to the subject we take moving pictures of his complex and ever-changing facial displays, the individual continues to respond as though he lives in one world, consistent in behavior, cognition, perception and affect. It is,

> however, one world that is systematically different if he views it from the left or from the right.
>
> (Demos, 1995, p. 159)

These results, taken together, represent *highly significant findings* that demonstrate the enduring effects of the socialization of affects in childhood. I will describe Tomkins' script theory in the next chapter, which details how these affects become organized into enduring personalities.

We certainly see this polarity operating in the current highly divisive political divisions and discussions so prevalent now in this country. Tomkins suggests that polarities of any kind did not exist until some kind of scarcity or danger to the group occurred and resulted in social specialization and stratification. He bases this idea on the work of Sanday (1981) who surveyed 150 societies, beginning with hunters and gatherers and throughout the globe. Thus different societies vary in their degree of stratification and the costs involved and in their mixture of male and female roles, therefore the normative and humanistic polarity is universal and different for each society. After describing the changes in the content of this polarity over time in China, Tomkins goes on to say the following about the United States:

> In radical contrast, the focus in the United States is on individualism, egalitarianism, freedom, the pursuit of money in a capitalistic competitive economy coupled with the transcendental Christian good works for those who fall behind, and the Christian sense of sin for both winners and losers, and the endless hot pursuit of the infinite and the transcendental in science, politics, love and religion. The left-right polarity now centers on the relative importance of big business versus big government, the relative importance of the environment versus the need for economic growth, the relative importance of nuclear energy versus "natural" energy sources, the relative importance of military power versus peace, the relative importance of caring for the sick, the aged, the poor, versus self-help or turning the responsibility over to business, presumably more "efficient" than government.
>
> But a left-wing American is more like a right-wing American than either is to any member of Confucian China. A protestant is

> more like a Catholic than either are similar to a Hindu. A Marxist is more like a capitalist than either are to a hunter-gatherer. Polarities occur within extended families of ideologies ... The polarity appears to function as a universal *moderator* of widely differing ideologies. It is the variations *within* ideologies that are best described by the polarity.
>
> (Demos, 1995, pp. 166–167, italics mine)

James Gilligan, in his recent book entitled *Why Some Political Parties Are More Dangerous Than Others* (2011), compiled data on measures of violence and economic inequality in the United States dating from the early 1900s to the early 2000s. He found that on every measure of violence: rates of domestic violence, murders, suicides, capital punishments, lynchings, and incarcerations, were higher in red states under Republican leadership than in blue states under Democratic leadership. These measures of violence as well as economic inequality were also higher under Republican presidencies, than under Democratic presidencies, with the exception of Eisenhower, who did not undo the policies comprising Roosevelt's new deal.

Gilligan frames his findings in terms of shame and guilt cultures. But given Tomkins' formulation of shame as an affiliative affect, it cannot carry the load of anger, contempt, and hatred that is reflected in the rhetoric of Republican statements such as "bleeding-heart liberals," "welfare cheats," or "shit-hole countries" embedded in a normative, hierarchical ideology, and in which punishment is preferred to empathy, and military action is preferred to diplomacy and building coalitions. Compassion, an end to racism, and diplomacy are part of the Democratic Party platform based on the humanistic values that hold that all human beings are worthy of respect. A normative stance also leads to an inner alienation and an intolerance of the negative affects of shame, distress, and anxiety. Given the current stresses of unemployment, racial inequalities, and poverty, all of these affects are increasing and as a result, we are seeing alarming increases in addiction rates, suicides, and violence in the United States.

Chapter 6

Silvan Tomkins' script theory

A theory of personality

This chapter will begin with Tomkins' question of how we build a science based on the data from the face. This involves the distinction between affect as an amplifier, which is of brief duration, and affect as magnification, which involves the formation of a script, which is a condensed set of rules that binds time. The difference between recurrent habitual scenes that are not psychologically magnified and affect-powered scripts will be described. A detailed description of the formation of a script will be presented, which will be followed by a description of each of the affect scripts. The chapter ends with a description of affect control scripts that can lead to addiction.

Tomkins has used the term inverse archaeology to describe the centrality of the skin on the face as the major motivational organ. He goes onto say: "Further, in contrast to archaeology, inverse archaeology is not restricted to the past but rather embeds the present in an extended past and an anticipated future ... That is what our faces show" (Demos, 1995, p. 286). He then asks how do we build a science on the data from the face? What kind of data should be most promising? He suggests the following: "What will be needed is a nonexistent unified theory of affect, as a part of an integrated biopsychosocial science, because affects are at once biological, psychological, social, cultural and historical" (p. 286). He describes science "as the fine art of making a mountain out of a molehill" (p. 286), and elaborates further in the following statement:

> Science is not magical, but it does involve two conjoint things going on at the same time: tremendous compression of information which

> is capable of extraordinary expansion. We call that expansion explanation or prediction or control ... *We cannot have science which does not correspond to reality. We cannot have science which does not achieve a coherent corpus of propositions. And we cannot do any of this without invention.*
>
> (p. 288, italics mine)

He then goes on to describe what this would mean for affect:

> Now, such a theory, if we could develop it in this field, would enable us to infer from small bits of facial information, important other characteristics for any individual, of any historical period, of any gender, intelligence, age, class and society. This would not mean that the particular diagnostic response was a universal, not at all. But rather that the model compressed enough information in the ordering rules to be expandable to a great variety of differences in particular human beings. Much as any equation has an infinitely large number of instances that can be solved for by that equation, science is explicative of variety and change. It neither denies heterogeneity, individuality, or conditionality, nor is it reductive, but it is *informationally advantageous by requiring fewer propositions than it explains, predicts, or controls*. I am not urging that affective responses across time, in different historical periods, in different cultures, for people of different ages, gender, and intelligence all show the same thing. That is absurd. We know that is not so. But that says nothing whatever about the kind of theoretically informed science we need to develop to be able to contain this variety and to account for it with as few primitive assumptions as may be possible. Needless to say, we are remote from any such theory. But I will offer my script theory as a first approximation, stressing both "first" and "approximation."
>
> (p. 289, italics mine)

In script theory he makes an important distinction between affect, which is elicited as an amplifier of changing rates or levels of abstract neural patterns, and affect magnification in the following way:

> [I]n affect magnification, cognitive, motor, perceptual and memorial processes are centrally involved, because magnification requires the

> formation of a script, which is time binding. Affect is momentary; in general it is of short duration. That is inherent in the mechanism. Were we dependent upon that all of our life, we would be very impoverished human beings. But we are not impoverished. We are not impoverished because we can bring all of our resources to bear on the scenes we experience, co-assemble them, consider their relationships, and design strategies to deal with them in the future. This I have called a set of rules – compressed rules – and labeled them scripts.
>
> (p. 289)

He goes on to say:

> A script is a minitheory and as such has all the properties that we are looking for. But it has more. *It is maintained by and controls dense affect.* No theory does that normally. But the scripts and theories which we develop are affect powered. That is one of the major reasons for the urgency of achieving this degree of economy and power in our constructions. They are entirely centered on what will make us happier or make us less sad: That is the vital ingredient of these theories.
>
> (p. 290, italics mine)

Tomkins points out that a form of psychological magnification begins very early in life when the infant replaces the innate sucking reflex with voluntary sucking (see Bruner & Bruner, 1968), which Tomkins has called *autosimulation*, namely the imitation of one's own reflexes. Another example of early psychological magnification is the neonate's ability to imitate facial expressions experienced passively (see Field, Woodson, Greenberg, & Cohen, 1982). These phenomena were cited in Chapter 2, when discussing agency in early infancy, and in that context I quoted Tomkins' suggestion that the infant acting as if it were imagining "I'd rather do it myself" is not inherited, and Tomkins' (1978) statement that: "It represents an extraordinary creative invention conjointly powered by primitive perceptual and cognitive capacities amplified by excitement in the possibility of improving a good scene by doing something oneself" (p. 215). Tomkins adds a third example of the infant actively imitating its own reflexes, namely the orienting reflex and ocular motor reflexes involved in innate tracking of a stimulus, and the infant's voluntarily moving the head and neck, thereby making a good scene better.

But in the early months of life, the infant can only link scenes that happen very close together in time. Thus the power of magnification in early life is constrained by the infant's limited memory capacities. For example, David Levy (1960) has show that when infants initially receive inoculations in the first six months of life, and cry in pain, when they return a few months later, they do not cry at the sight of the doctor or the needle, and show no signs of being afraid or distressed or of having remembered the earlier experience. In this second visit, they do cry again at the pain of inoculation, but nothing new has been added; it appears to be no worse than the first time.

But several months later the infant now remembers the pain of the last inoculation, and will cry at the sight of the doctor and the needle, as well as during the inoculation. Here is Tomkins' description of the psychological process involved:

> This is psychological magnification, the phenomenon of connecting one affect-laden scene with another affect-laden scene. Through memory, thought, and imagination, scenes experienced before can be co-assembled with scenes presently experienced, together with scenes which are anticipated in the future. The present moment is embedded in the intersect between the past and the future in a central assembly via *a constructive process we have called co-assembly.*
>
> (Demos, 1995, p. 318, italics mine)

Tomkins argues that not all amplified scenes are magnified, even though the affect may be amplified. He gives the example of what he call *transient* scenes, as in hearing an automobile horn, which may startle, but have no further consequences, or hearing a very funny joke that may be intensely rewarding in the moment, but again remains a transitory a scene, and may not be remembered later. As Tomkins states, thus: "All experience is not necessarily connected with all other experience" (p. 319). Our lives are made up of large numbers of such transient scenes.

Tomkins defines another contrast to the scenes that lead to psychological magnification and script formation, which he calls *recurrent habitual scenes*. These involve habitual skills, which contain learned programs representing a good deal of compressed information, so that it can be expanded effectively, but with only minimal consciousness and affect. He gives the example of shaving every morning; another example might be knitting, or becoming so familiar with a piece of music or with a spouse's presence, that one's experience of the music or of the other becomes impoverished. Any skill, which works well, will reward us the least. He states further that:

> Skills may become temporarily magnified whenever they prove inadequate or permanently magnified as a result of brain damage from a stroke, when the individual must now exert himself or herself heroically to relearn and execute what had once been an effortless skill.
>
> (p. 319)

He describes another kind of habitual scene that he calls the "as if" scene, such as walking across street as if we were afraid.

> Everyone learns to cross streets with minimal ideation, perceptual scanning, and affect. We learn to act as if we were afraid but we do not, in fact, experience any fear once we have learned how to cope successfully with such contingencies.
>
> (p. 320)

The same might be said about driving, once we have learned how to manage a car, follow road signs, how to go in reverse to park, how to drive at higher speeds on the highway, etc. Even though we know driving can be dangerous, most of the time we drive "as if" we were afraid, using ordinary caution and with minimal fear. If our lives were restricted to transient scenes combined with habitual scenes, they would be greatly impoverished, by insufficient psychological magnification. But we are not impoverished because we experience some events with more intense affects that require greater attention, which results in psychological magnification and the formation of scripts.

An example of script formation

Tomkins uses the example of Laura, a young girl studied by Robertson, in England (an unpublished document). Laura was hospitalized for a week, and as was customary in England at the time, she was separated from her parents as she went through a variety of medical procedures and was also being photographed by a moving picture camera near her crib. Like many young children, she cried a good deal, and missed her parents. So clearly the quality of her life went from good to bad during this week. Will there be permanent effects of such an upsetting experience? Tomkins says the following:

> First, the answer to such a question will depend critically on the degree of magnification which *follows* this week. How many times will she rehearse these bad scenes? Will such rehearsals co-assemble them in such an order and with such spacing that they are experienced as magnifying or attenuating the negative affects connected with these scenes? Further, apart from her own imagination, what will be the quantity of good and bad scenes she experiences at home when she returns? Will her parents further frighten or reassure her, or in attempting to reassure her give her an implicit message that she has been through hell? Further, will this be the beginning of further medical problems, or will it be an isolated week in her life?
>
> (pp. 324–325, italics mine)

Tomkins explains further the factors involved in script formation, first:

> What is important from the point of view of script theory is that the effect of any set of scenes is *indeterminate* until the future happens and either magnifies or attenuates such experience. The second point is that the consequence of any experience is not singular but plural. There is no *single* effect but rather there are *many* effects which change in time.
>
> (p. 325)

This latter phenomenon he calls the principle of *plurideterminancy.*

When Laura returned home she seemed to be upset. If we assessed the effect at this point, we would say it was "deleterious." But after a few days, she was her normal self again. Now we might say, it was no so bad after all. Some time later, Robinson visited her home in order to interview her parents, and Laura became upset again. Tomkins argues that the magnification of the bad scene has now been increased. He then explains a further principle of script formation:

> This illustrates a very important *third* principle of psychological magnification and script formation: Scenes are magnified not by repetition, but by repetition with a *difference*. It is, as in art, the unity in variety which engages the mind and heart of the person who is experiencing a rapid growth of punishment or reward.
>
> (p. 325)

He argues that mere repetition results in either adaptation or attenuation of the connected scenes. If we return to Laura the difference is that Robinson has now invaded her home, a place of love and security, and her parents seemed unable to prevent his coming and maybe even agreed to it. Up until this point the only danger was that her parents might take her to another strange place and leave her there. Now, things seem to have become more problematic. Yet, once again, in a few days, things seem to go back to normal. So, as before, we might now conclude there are no serious long-term effects of the hospitalization

Things go well for quite a while. Then her parents take Laura to an art museum, where they want to see an exhibition of paintings. They leave her in a white crib, which in England at the time, the museum provides. How will Laura experience this event? Once before, they took her to the hospital and left her in a white crib. However, on this occasion she does not cry. So perhaps the effects of the hospitalization were short term. As Tomkins says, "She had been left by her parents in a white crib, but the deadly parallel escapes her" (p. 326). But a few minutes later a man comes by with a camera and takes a picture of her, and now she does cry. And so, once again the family of connected scenes has been critically enlarged. Tomkins argues the following:

> This man is not Robinson. He has a camera, not a moving picture camera. It is an art museum, not a hospital – but it smells like danger to Laura, and her own crying becomes self-validating. The scene, whether dangerous or not, has been made punishing by her own crying. Any scene which is sufficiently similar to evoke the same kind of affect is thereby *made more similar*, and increases the degree of connectedness to the whole family of scenes.
>
> (p. 326, italics mine)

This represents a fourth factor in script formation. Things have now become sufficiently magnified to create a script. Tomkins asks, "What will this script be like?" (p. 326).

He notes that none of these scenes have involved much action on the part of Laura; this indicates that she has not yet developed any action strategies that would provide ways for her to avoid or escape such scenes. Therefore this represents a more simplified case of script formation. A more complex case of script formation would involve all of our capacities, namely perception, cognition, memory, affect, and action. Initially, once an upsetting event has occurred, the individual attempts to focus on the most salient feature as sharply differentiated from the background. This differentiation can involve affects, sights, sounds, thoughts, imagery, words, or actions taken or with action potentials, which results in "an organization of a simple scene into a salient figure differentiated from a more diffuse background" (p. 327). Subsequent scenes may shift from the initial figural to another aspect of the same scene, e.g. the person involved, the place, the time, the actions, how it began, how it ended, etc. The person can then connect one scene to another, producing a family of scenes, *which now need to be organized so as to maximize the most important information with the fewest possible assumptions*. Tomkins describes this need in the following way:

> This is in part because of an enforced limitation on their ability to process information, and in part because some power to command, understand, predict and control their scenes is *urgently* demanded if they are to optimize the ratio of rewarding positive and punishing negative affect in their lives. In their attempt to order the information and produce a script from a set of scenes, they will first of all partition the variance in to what they regard as the major variance and the residual variance.
>
> (p. 328, italics mine)

In this search for the main effect, the individual is like the scientist who employs factor analytic procedures, whereby a general factor is first extracted, followed by more specific features, which account for less and less of the variance.

Tomkins asks,

> What is the general script factor, or the main effect script question likely to be? It is characteristically determined by three conjoint criteria: (1) What is experienced with the most dense, i.e. the most intense and enduring affect? (2) What are experienced as the sharpest gradients of change of such affect? (3) What are the most frequently repeated sequences of such affect changes? Whenever these three criteria are conjointly met in any series of scenes, they will constitute the first major partitioning of the variance within and between scenes ... The big picture must first be grasped before it can be fleshed in. An important, repeated change is the general script factor. This includes internal repetition, in past rehearsal and future anticipation.
>
> (p. 329)

So let us look at how these factors occurred in Laura's case. The most repeated, sharp, dense affect that changed for Laura was going from positive to negative affect and then a slower change from negative affect back to positive affect. This constitutes the main variance, and was repeated three times – going to hospital – back to home and normal; home invaded – return to normal; museum – back to home and normal. The residual variance involves place, cast, and action. Initially, the positive-affect scene occurs at home, with parents, talking and playing versus the negative-affect scene that occurs in the hospital, with a doctor and medical procedures. This set of features changed when the doctor comes to Laura's home, which then no longer feels quite as safe, the doctor is the same, but the action is talking, yet the distress is the same. In the third scene the place is not the same and seems initially good; *thus Laura has not yet begun to anticipate danger, and to scan the scene looking for it.* But it then becomes a bad place, the person is different, and his action is different, but once again it feels like danger and the distress is the same. The main effect remains, each scene goes from positive to negative affect, with a slower change back to positive, although the lesser variants are different. In such a way, the family of distressing scenes has now been expanded without violating this main variance. Tomkins argues the following: "As these variants grow in number yet continue to produce the more general changes in dense affect, psychological magnification increases" (p. 331). Eventually a script is developed to manage such scenes.

We could see that initially Laura did not react to being left in a crib at the museum; thus a script of anticipating of danger when left in a strange place had not yet become established. Perhaps the bias toward positive expectations was still very strong for her. It took the appearance of a different man with a different camera, before the connection between her past negative experiences and the present occurred. We do not know if this last event was enough to establish an enduring script for Laura, in which she would be on the look out for danger; but in this third event, the family of negative scenes has been enlarged, and psychological magnification has increased. Tomkins goes on to say: "In the early stages of magnification, it is the set of scenes which determines the script; but as magnification increases, it is the script which increasingly determines the scenes" (p. 333). Thus most scripts become more self-validating than self-fulfilling.

The major affective scripts

Tomkins had been thinking about various kinds of scripts for many years and had described distinctive kinds of organizations and rules for these scripts, but it was only in the last years of his life that he realized that these organizations fit very nicely with each of the primary affects that he had come to understand earlier. Here in his own words is his description of the coming together of his theory:

> All of these types of scripts, and there are many different types under each of these classifications, were designed, as I said with no thought to affect. Then one day a light bulb went on in my head. I realized that each of these types or scripts, while very complex in affect structure and composition, nonetheless had a primary affect which matched extraordinarily well my understanding of the nature of each of the primary affects. That was a bonanza for me, because it was almost like an independent validation of both the script theory and the affect theory that they should hang together so nicely . . . It was very exciting.
>
> (Demos, 1995, p. 392)

Before describing each of these scripts, Tomkins offers the following general principles it would be helpful to keep in mind:

> Any gratuity must be built upon to reward in the long run; any threat must be elaborated by further action to become traumatic. Thus a mugging may be shrugged off as a transient or built upon as a way of life if one elects to hire a bodyguard . . . When, however, the density of the ratio of positive to negative affect reaches a critical level, then it can become a relatively stable equilibrium, both self-validating and self-fulfilling. At that point the possibility of radical change, though always present, becomes a diminishing probability requiring ever more densely magnified countervailing forces of positive or negative affect.
>
> (p. 341)

What follows is a description of each of these primary scripts.

Affluent scripts

Affluent scripts deal with the positive affects of enjoyment/joy, and interest/excitement. In order for this script to become a stable equilibrium in a personality, the ratio of positive affect to negative affect must be high. This equilibrium cannot be achieved either by disconnected peak experiences of joy or excitement or by seeking joy or excitement, nor by the avoidance of suffering. Tomkins describes this script in the following way:

> From the viewpoint of strategy, the individual must neither attempt to minimize negative affect nor to maximize positive affect nor satisfice, but rather attempt to optimize positive affect to achieve the optimal stable equilibrium. The distance between the ideal and the actual must not be so great as to demoralize, nor so small as to trivialize.
>
> (Demos, 1995, p. 345)

Balance is the essential feature of a stable equilibrium of positive affect. The person must attempt to balance the use of all of one's functions, e.g. thinking, feeling, remembering, acting, perceiving, in the service of exploring a variety of sources of positive affect, e.g. family, friends, career, travel, nature, the arts, etc. Any focus in a single direction can jeopardize the balance, e.g. an excessive focus on work over family, an excessive focus on the past over the present or the future, any intense activity unrelieved by relaxation, etc. Tomkins insists on the following:

> The maintenance of affluence demands the capacity to understand and absorb negative affect when it is encountered. One cannot afford excessive specialization even of rewarding affluence without some capacity for the compensation of and absorption of the confrontation with the inevitable suffering by the self and by others.
>
> (p. 346)

In Chapter 3 we saw the beginnings of an affluent script in the case of Donna who experienced many sources of positive affect. She and her mother had many extended face-to-face playful exchanges in early infancy, and over the months these were repeated with her siblings and her father. As she developed her motor and verbal capacities these positive exchanges continued as her growing interests and activities were shared, supported, and encouraged. We also saw that her distresses were empathically responded to, as she adapted to babysitters and when she began to verbalize her distress and talk about her crying so as to work these through these experiences. In our last visit she and her mother found a way to use humor to help her through an upsetting argument with her sister, as she dealt with her anger and hurt, which ended in a shared positive moment. Thus her positive world was expanding, as well as her instrumental capacities to deal both with her positive affects and with her distress and anger. By the time our observations ended she was well on her way to establishing a stable equilibrium of positive affect.

Throughout life, when such a stable equilibrium of positive affect has been established, many sources of positive affect can converge, increasing the magnification of an affluent script, as in living with a cherished mate, in a cherished place, with cherished work, and with cherished friends and family. Tomkins offers the following example of such a convergence: "In the Middle Ages, the convergence of the building of great Christian cathedrals often represented the aggregation of the deepest motives and best energies of all members of a community in a celebratory, sacred, aesthetic, and educational enterprise" (p. 349).

Damage-reparation scripts

Damage-reparation scripts deal with the affect of shame. Tomkins understands shame as an affect auxiliary, which is triggered by any barrier to either excitement or enjoyment, resulting in an incomplete reduction of these positive affects. Thus he sees shame as an affluent affect, because it can only occur in the context of a positive bond with the other, and always contains the wish to re-establish that good feeling. This script then depends on the varieties of the innate and learned sources of the incomplete reduction of positive affect. Tomkins suggests that: "In effect this implicates all the positive values, but not to the extent of *complete* and *enduring* interference" (Demos, 1995, p. 400, italics mine).

Some of the early sources of shameful scenes that are likely to become linked and contribute to a damage-reparation script tend to occur more frequently in normative family settings. Toilet training is one such an occasion for repeated scenes of shaming if a mother taunts the child by calling him or her a "baby," when the child loses control of their bowels, or focuses on how bad the child smells. A child can then feel a loss of love, a loss of respect from the mother, too much turning away by the mother, a feeling that he or she has done something wrong, as immoral or as in incompetent, so that the competence of the mother and or the child is called into question. Tomkins describes this in the following way: "Such a scene's magnification implicates all varieties of violations of values: moral – 'soiling is wrong'; aesthetic – 'soiling is ugly'; truth – 'you promised to control yourself'; instrumental – you have no skill"; and they are all "shameful" (p. 403).

Some families may emphasize the child's incompetence through shaming in a variety of situations if the child's instrumental skills or performance disappoint the parent in some way, or they may shame the child for talking too loud, or acting too silly, or not eating their food, etc. In this script, the shaming cannot be so extreme that the parent cannot find ways to offer the child a way back into a positive relationship, such as expressing affectionate or proud feelings toward the child, so that the child can still maintain hope and experience that good feelings can be restored. Tomkins describes shame in the following way: "This experience of shame is inevitable for any human being insofar as desire outruns fulfillment sufficiently to attenuate interest without destroying it. 'I want, but . . .'" (p. 406).

Once this script has been established, the child and adult may approach each new situation, such as school or social groups in a shy and hesitant manner, wanting to join and be included, but unsure of what the "rules" are. In general, although the ratio of positive to negative affect is still biased toward the positive, some worries remain about just how one will be seen or heard, e.g. as inadequate or acceptable if one's behavior is not quite "right." Such a person may be cautious to stick their neck out in any way, or feel reluctant to express one's opinions or knowledge, fearing rejection if one's view is different, or worry that the other will experience them as incompetent. Yet beneath all of this worry, there remains a yearning to be accepted and a hope that good feelings can be established, or reestablished, as well as a readiness to respond to positive responses from the other.

The other area in which one can learn to feel shame is about sex. One may have learned to feel that bodily functions are dirty or bad in some way, or that one's body is inferior, or unattractive in some way, or that it is foolish or too risky to express vulnerable feelings towards another or that one's sexual preference is bad, immoral, or wrong. Unfortunately in some social situations, one can be victimized for one's sexual choices, which can lead to intimidation and either to defending oneself, or to a greater magnification of shame and inhibition, in which one part of the self may turn against the other part of the self. If shame has become too magnified, and one's head is in a permanent posture of depression, it can take on an extreme form of malignancy. In order to maintain this damage-reparative script in a stable equilibrium, one cannot become too discouraged and hopeless. The balance between positive and negative affect has to remain weighted toward the positive, so that the reparation part of the damage-reparative script remains a viable and real possibility, as in the resumption of positive feelings.

Limitation-remediation scripts

Limitation-remediation scripts are powered by the affect of distress, which is the primary affect of human suffering. It deals with the problems of life that are less than ideal, but that must be confronted and can be confronted. The remediation part of this script requires the development of instrumental skills combined with a tolerance for suffering. Tomkins suggest that for most people this script constitutes the realm of work and commitment, which bind a person to enormous investments of affect, energy, and activity over long periods of time. He describes this script in the following way:

> Although all limitation scripts are based on an assessment of the overall ratio of positive to negative affect, commitment scripts are distinctive in their bias toward positive affect. They originate in a favorable ratio of positive over negative affect and aim at increasing that advantage.
>
> (Demos, 1995, p. 358)

He states further that:

> People differ radically in their limit-remediation scripts, varying all the way from what I call commitment scripts to the resignation of slavery. If you are born a slave, you also have to script your life, and you resign yourself to be as good a slave as you know how to be. That is not much, but that is a limitation which you must face. Millions of people over thousands of years have faced lives less than perfect, to which they had to adapt in some way or other. This kind of script gets at that large class of human concerns.
>
> (p. 391)

In our own time there are a number of situations, besides work, which arise that must be faced and adapted to, while still maintaining a positive stance toward life, such as the limitations of various health issues; or the decreasing powers and capacities of all kinds involved in aging; or all the difficult issues and heartbreak involved in caring for a child with cancer, or with major handicaps; or the major challenges due to floods and the loss of one's home, or the loss of a job that provided a necessary income. These kinds of situations challenge a person to marshal and utilize all of their accrued strengths and positive powers, in order to bear, adapt to, and accept these limitations.

What kinds of early experiences contribute to the formation of such a script? In order for someone to develop the capacity to tolerate distress and develop instrumental skills and strategies to remediate it, they must have experienced throughout their childhoods sufficient understanding and support for their own expressions of distress, and help in finding solutions for whatever problems led to their distress. In Chapter 3, we saw how just these supports occurred repeatedly in Donna's life, and how, even as early as 3 months of age, she had developed a protest cry, which contained in it both the capacity to regulate her distress in order to "ask" for attention and her expectation that her needs would be met. By contrast, we saw in Cathy's life, that no matter what the cause of her distress, she was always nursed, thus she was not given the opportunity or support to develop her own capacities to cope with distress. This lack left her unable to fall asleep alone by the age of 3, without being nursed; her distress cry when her mother left the room, had no modulation in it or any expectation of relief; and she had not learned any instrumental means to cope with difficulties, such as how to ask for help, and thus she cried for hours when left with a babysitter. If things do not change later on in Cathy's life, she is likely to seek some form of sedation for the distresses and suffering in her life, since she will not have learned any other ways to cope with these feelings. I will describe affect management scripts later in this chapter.

Another kind of inability to cope with distress can occur in families in which the child's distress is seen as weakness or as disgusting, and not tolerated, as might occur in a normative family setting described in the previous chapter. In such a setting the child must develop powerful defenses against any awareness of such feelings, which can lead to an inability to feel compassion for another's suffering, and to a tough stance of blaming the other for their misfortunes, or if defenses fail, it can lead to affect management scripts.

Decontamination scripts

Decontamination scripts are powered by the affect of disgust, and deal with scenes of impurity. Here we are moving in the direction of a less favorable balance between positive and negative affects. These are scenes that were once enchanting or wonderful, but have become contaminated or spoiled in some way. The experience is not one of damage that can be repaired, or of distress that can be comforted, or of a limitation or problem that can be remedied; it is rather an experience of impurity or contamination that must be expunged, purified, or decontaminated. According to Tomkins, such scripts make use of a maximizing–minimizing strategy, which Tomkins describes as: "a combination of greed and cowardice." He goes on to say: "Greed requires a maximum of reward. Cowardice requires a minimum of punishment. Clearly a double maximum cannot be achieved" (Demos, 1995, p. 381). Thus, this strategy fails in both respects. "It neither attains the prize nor escapes defeat. It is a game that must be played even though the player knows the dice are loaded against him" (p. 381). The internal world of such a person has become polarized into the two idealized opposites of a heaven or a hell. In this script the balance between the ideal and the actual has become weighted heavily toward the ideal of goodness, namely perfection, while the actual or the real has become exaggerated into an impossible negative that feels too overwhelmingly unbearable, to ever be remedied or accepted.

How does such a script come into being? Tomkins suggests the following: "There can be no greed without a seductive other. There can be no cowardice without an intimidating, contaminating, or confusing other . . . and without massive collusive reciprocal magnification" (p. 380). Both ends of this polarity must be greatly exaggerated and idealized. In an earlier publication I suggested how this might happen in childhood (see Demos, 1998). The seduction has to come first, given that the affect of disgust is evoked when one has taken in something that was believed to be good, and even wonderful, but now has turned rotten. Thus there is always the sequence of enchantment followed by disenchantment. Such a person must have grown up with parents who themselves have been struggling with this same deeply, polarized split within themselves. But as parents they now attempt to hoard all the goodness and may present themselves as wonderful, loving, perfect parents.

The essential dynamics seem to involve (1) a seductive, even charismatic quality in the parent, who conveys his or her deep investment in the child with fervor, and/or with ideological conviction, and/or with intimidating and intrusive power. This is communicated in such a way that (2) the child's imagination is seized with the wish to please, to join, to be close to this idealized other, or the child feels compelled out of weakness to join, and may harbor secret revenge fantasies or of counteractive power.

This must be combined with (3) the parent's intolerance of any sign in the child of "failure or inadequacy or badness": not complying with the parent's needs, not validating the parent's goodness, or not measuring up to some higher standard, or simply acting so as to irritate the parent. So that when the child fails, as every child is apt to do, the parent both exaggerates the seriousness of the failure and conveys the unacceptability and their intolerance of such qualities, behaviors, and/or feelings. Thus these are very good scenes that have turned very, bad, which are extremely painful and confusing to the child. They are painful and confusing not only because disgust is a powerfully negative feeling and may involve the child's awareness of his or her own complicity in what transpires, but also because these children are often left alone to try to cope with their parent's devastating judgment and rejection of them, leaving them feeling helpless, inadequate, and devalued.

Furthermore (4) as all small children, these children cannot step back and accurately assess the appropriateness either of their own behavior or of their parent's reactions. And the more alone, helpless, confused, and devalued these children feel, the less they can imagine themselves as the source of anything positive or good, while at the same time, their parents seem, in contrast, all the more powerful, and desirable, and as representing the promise of everything good and wonderful. Indeed (5) as these scenes are repeated and elaborated in the child's mind, over time such children come to believe that these exaggerated failures, which have been projected onto them by their parents, now confirm their own experiences of weakness, inadequacy, helplessness, and unacceptable vengefulness, which include wishes to hurt, or blame others, and therefore, such feelings must now represent a valid assessment of their true nature.

Here we have the massive collusive magnification of the all powerful, wonderful parents and the all weak, inadequate child. Because of this congruence between the child's own feelings of inadequacy and vengeful wishes and the parent's judgment, the child comes to believe that he or she is truly the source of all the troubles and problems; such a reality feels both undeniable and impossible to face, and so the decontamination fantasy takes hold and this script is created. Such a person is then driven to continually seek an imagined paradise that never really existed in the past, in order to flee from a hell in which the self is imagined to be more disgusting and valueless than could ever have been true in the past. I will discuss the clinical implications of such a script in the next section of this book.

Anti-toxic scripts

Anti-toxic scripts are powered by the affects of terror, rage, and dissmell. In this script the goal is not to accept limitations and deal with their consequences, or to try to purify contaminated scenes, but rather to protect the psyche from any situations, relationships, or thoughts that could overwhelm it with terror, rage, or dissmell. These affects are toxic and intolerable; thus hypervigilance is maximized because the cost of experiencing them is too high. This script deals with scenes in which terror, rage, and/or dissmell are evoked and from which there is no escape. Such scenes can involve experiences by abusive others, as in beatings or sexual molestation; or they can involve destructive powers unleashed by nature, as in floods or storms; or by horror unleashed by man, as in wars, terrorists attacks as the September 11 attack and bombings. These are traumatic events that can happen at any time in life. Thus the response to trauma may depend on many factors, such as the age at which the trauma occurred, the pre-traumatic ratio of positive to negative affect in the person's life, and on how quickly the person can find help with processing traumatic events.

I would suggest that trauma, no matter when it occurs, by definition undermines both of the basic human priorities that I described in Chapter 2, namely the preference for psychic coherence, e.g. making sense of one's world, and the preference for being an active agent in effecting the course of one's life. Traumatic events *violate* one's sense of the way the world should work, e.g. "such things *should not happen*!" And they *render the person helpless*. They thereby evoke terror, rage, or dissmell. Such states overwhelm the mind's capacity to remain coherent, and render it incapable of producing effective actions. If the person is young and has achieved a stable balance between positive and negative affects, and receives early and effective help, an anti-toxic script may not necessarily develop. But without these assets, and perhaps even with them, depending on how severe or repetitive the traumatic experience was, when in life it occurred, and how long the traumatic situation lasted an anti-toxic script is likely to develop.

Ghislaine Boulanger (2007) in her book *Wounded by Reality* makes a very important distinction between the experience of trauma in childhood, when the psyche is still developing, and adult-onset trauma, when the core self is fully formed. She presents compelling evidence in support of her persuasive argument that adult-onset trauma, which involves the horror of a violent, near-death experience, *has catastrophic effects on the core self, independent of one's early experience.* It creates a collapse of this self that results in derealization, depresonalization, the loss of agency that feels like a paralysis, the fear of physical fragmentation, a flattening of affects, the loss of meaning, a disruption of the feeling of continuity in one's life, and a deep fear of annihilation. The core self has been "wounded by reality" and exists disconnected, and dissociated from its previous functional capacities. The realness of the horror is so overwhelming that such a person lives in the reality of the trauma, alienated from oneself, from others, and from the world. Such a person may experience repeating nightmares with terrifying images, or they may tell their story in an affectively flat manner repeatedly, without any relief, or they may go for years leading quiet, affectively numbed lives. Some never make it that far. The suicide rate has been high for many of the returning veterans of our recent wars.

Trauma that occurs in childhood, before the core self has become fully formed, leads to a very different kind of defensive organization. Sexual abuses, beatings, verbal abuses, neglect, are the kinds of traumas most clinicians are familiar with. These terrifying experiences *lead to a vertical split in the psyche, which protects the child's psyche from a total collapse.* Such experiences can remain outside of consciousness for many years, while the child continues to grow physically, mentally, and affectively. But some portion of their psychic powers continues to operate to prevent such overwhelming states of terror or uncontainable rage from recurring. Depending on the degree of terror, and its frequency, these efforts may then result in the formation of an anti-toxic script. Such a script is designed to create massive defensive psychic barriers, which almost always include a highly tuned hypervigilance that can become so automatic that such people cease to be aware of all the ways they have developed to avoid triggers and to protect themselves. They cannot be caught unaware or be surprised by internal or external events; thus control becomes primary and may include a rigid control of the contents of consciousness, thoughts, and feelings. For some, this may involve interrupting their sleep every two hours, in order to avoid the REM cycle of sleep, which might produce a nightmare. Some may develop brooding fantasies of persecution or fantasies of revenge and counter action, which may help them feel less helpless and terrified.

Such people may develop passable social skills, but if their traumatic scenes involved abusive others, or if the trauma is too close to the surface, they can not allow themselves to get too close to anyone. The unpredictability of spontaneous human exchange can feel too dangerous: they cannot trust themselves or others to keep things safe. They must also avoid certain TV shows and books lest their trauma be triggered. Such people may become aware of a deep sense of isolation, and loneliness, aware that they are living with an awful, unacceptable secret, which might shock others or lead to rejection or harassment by others. Thus they feel outside of ordinary life, with no way to fully participate.

If their anti-toxic script works and successfully protects them from intrusions of toxic affects, and they have not had to use alcohol or drugs to numb themselves, or other health threatening behaviors, such as cutting or eating disorders to help control their demons, and if they have not got into trouble with disruptive or odd behaviors, then they may be able to live emotionally constricted, but safe lives, without therapeutic help. But they remain walking time bombs.

Usually what brings people with an anti-toxic script into treatment is a breakdown in the effectiveness of the anti-toxic script. The events of their lives may have overwhelmed them, for example the death of an important person, or the ultimatum of a spouse who cannot accept excessive drinking or rages. For some, an event that had led to an unanticipated breakthrough of toxic affect has occurred, which has got them into trouble with cutting. For others they may have miscalculated the capacity of their body to function with long-term use of drugs or alcohol or anorexia, which has led to a physical breakdown, or because of injuries due to an unsuccessful suicide attempt. Any one of these reasons might land them in a hospital. Some times a first hospitalization will lead to therapy, but often as not, they are treated only for their physical symptoms and released. I will discuss the clinical implications of working with these patients in the next section of this book.

I would add one more category of the consequences of terror to this list, namely the terror of disorganization experienced by very young infants. Earlier in this volume I spoke about the capacity of young infants for coherent states of the affects of enjoyment and interest, and mild distress, and their limitations in managing states of increasing distress, which if not attended to can build up into anger, rage, and eventually lead to a disorganized state. I gave the example of the infants in institutions, studied by Provence and Lipton (1962), who were fed by the clock every four hours, even though they were hungry long before that and thus probably cried with no relief, leading eventually to a cessation of crying entirely. I speculated that this was a massive defense against the toxic build up distress, rage, and the disorganized, terrifying state of terror. Some case histories suggest the possibility that this early experience of an overwhelmed psyche can create a vulnerability for psychotic experiential processing. The infant has *no defense* against this kind of early disorganization.

Thus far I have described the scripts that are powered by the primary affects as formulated by Tomkins, which were derived from his study of facial expressions. Tomkins is unique in articulating the importance of the positive affect of interest/excitement in sustaining our engagement with the world, thus such engagement does not depend on sexual arousal; but equally important is his enumeration and articulation of the qualitative distinctions between the negative affects of shame, distress, disgust, terror, rage, and dissmell, greatly enriching our understanding of human experience. Thus not all negative affects need to become intolerable. And the dynamics of the stronger negative affects, namely disgust, terror, rage, and dissmell can be understood without reference to the death drive. When negative affect does become intolerable, some form of an affect management script then occurs.

Affect management scripts

This section is based on Tomkins' empirical research program undertaken in the 1960s, with the cooperation of the Clearinghouse for Smoking Information of the United States Public Health Service, then under the direction of Horn (Horn & Waingrow, 1966). It involved a stratified sample of 15,000 people in the United States, who were tested to determine the fit between Tomkins' model of affect dependency and the factor structure of that sample. Then in cooperation with Donald Frederickson, these models were further tested in a large-scale therapeutic program with the public health department of New York. In no case were his models disconfirmed.

In Tomkins' model, affect management scripts are focused *only* on the reduction of negative affect, regardless of the specific negative affect. In a sedative script:

> the first order of business was to attenuate or to reduce entirely the negative affect ... It is an escape script rather than an avoidance script, and what it aims to escape is not the problematic source of negative affect in the scene, nor does it seek the instrumental solution to the problematic source.
>
> (Demos, 1995, p. 364)

The conditions necessary for the formation of a sedative script are the following: (1) they occur only within a limited, middle range of the ratio of density of positive to negative affect, there is no need for sedation in affluent scripts, or damage-reparative scripts, or in limitation-remediation scripts in which the ratio of positive to negative affect is high and in which the main focus is on dealing with problematic scenes; (2) negative affect is the most salient problematic feature; (3) the sedative act is given priority over instrumental actions; (4) the sedative act must be used in an increasing variety of different negative scenes and experienced as effective; (5) the sedative act must become that of "a unique one-much type, in which one and only one act will sedate any of an infinite number of negative affects" (p. 366).

Once these conditions have been met, the individual now believes in the following: (1) the possibility of reducing negative affects versus suffering; (2) the desirability of comforting oneself versus being constrained by ideological norms; (3) now favoring the self as the agent of sedation versus passively hoping for help from others; and finally (4) that sedation must give way to other preemptive scripts, such as avoiding an automobile accident, or when hearing about the death of a loved one. This script is only used to sedate negative affects, thus its frequency and duration will depend on when negative affects occur. Thus, for example, it was found that when on vacation, and one is relaxed and enjoying oneself, this script is not activated, e.g. the person didn't smoke much at all.

I suggested earlier that perhaps Cathy (one of the children followed longitudinally in Chapter 3) may be headed for a sedative script because she had established a one-many, unique relationship with her mother, who held or nursed when she was in negative states, and thus she was not enabled to develop instrumental strategies or actions to cope with negative affects. It is difficult to know the quality of her positive affects, because she and her mother did not have extended face-to-face exchanges in infancy and because her parents took on instructional modes of interacting around her interests. Thus many of her positive experiences were either very short or she was a passive observer of the enjoyments of others, and without parental involvement, her play continued to be repetitive. Thus her positive experiences appeared somewhat constricted and of low intensity. Of course, she had not yet entered school, and perhaps there, with the help of teachers, she may be able to expand her capabilities and her interests further.

Preaddictive scripts cannot occur without the existence of a prior sedative script. "It represents a crucial step in the transformation of sedative to addictive dependency" (p. 368). This script happens when "sedation has been magnified by a substantial incremental urgency and required as a *necessary* condition to remain in the scene and/or to act in it" (p. 368). Tomkins gives the example of a person now believing they cannot answer the phone or meet others or be alone without this sedative. This represents a moving forward in time and anticipating the need for a sedative in a particular scene that will be intolerable unless *avoided* by a sedative. In a sedative script, one could wait until one actually felt a negative state and then sedate it. "It is no longer simply a response to any negative affect, but to a specific scene that promises unique punishment unless uniquely sedated in advance" (p. 369). The sedative has now become: "an *instrumental escape and avoidance* sedation script" (p. 369, italics mine). "What is *added* is an increment of urgency about a restricted set of scenes within the larger family of less urgent scenes" (p. 369, italics mine).

It is only one short step further to addiction, which will occur when one cannot find the sedative quickly enough before one must enter a negative scene, as in needing to answer the phone. Such events will increase the urgency sufficiently to create the need to sedate this worry and so to have the sedative at hand at all times. "Should her quest for a cigarette fail, deprivation affect grows in intensity, acceleration, and density, experienced as deepening of a crisis growing more and more intolerable. There are no viable alternates. There is very limited capacity for delay" (p. 371). Now the bias toward negative has been greatly increased. *Addicts are not happy people.* "One cannot become addicted until one has learned that to be without the sedative is much worse than any other negative affect that the sedative might reduce" (p. 372).

Once this last step in learning has occurred, the sedative has now become an end in itself. When this happens, the person becomes highly skilled at perceiving when they have a cigarette in their mouth and when they don't. It is not unusual for an addict to light up another cigarette when there is already one lit in the ashtray.

> The addictive script is both self-validating and self-fulfilling. It demonstrates again and again the necessity to be ever alert to the possibility of being without some X, the punishment that is inevitable should that X not be recoverable, the increased rate of punishment the longer one is without that X, its irreplaceability, nondistractability, or nonsubstitutability, and finally how wonderful it is to have it again no matter how brief such enjoyment continues to be.
>
> (p. 371)

In all affect management scripts, whatever the negative affect is, the crucial variable is the decision to reduce the affect through sedation, by the use of some substance, such as food or alcohol or cigarettes, rather than addressing the source of the negative affect by engaging in adaptive problem-solving. Such a choice in Tomkins' affect theory is based on the relative balance of positive affects versus negative affects, as well as on one's past experiences that have fostered the capacity to tolerate negative states and supported one's efforts to solve problems. This relates to my earlier discussion of learned affective sequences. Positive–negative–positive sequences foster an expectation that problems can be solved, and that help is available, all of which develop one's tolerance for negative affects and coping skills and abilities. A steady diet of positive–negative–negative sequences leaves one feeling helpless and defeated and can lead to a growing need for some relief from such a negative feeling; thus begins the search for sedatives.

In my descriptions of these scripts, I began with the positive-affect scripts and moved to scripts that dealt with increasingly negative affects. One of the clinical implications of this ordering is that whatever negative script is dominant at the beginning of treatment, the patient will move to the nearest script in either direction during the course of treatment. For example, if a person is living with an anti-toxic script, that person may either move towards suicide, or to a decontamination script first, and only then to a limitation-remediation script, and go through a grieving process. Or, if a person begins with a decontamination script, he or she can go in either direction, e.g. to an antitoxic script or to a limitation-remediation script, which involves grieving and working toward a more realistic acceptance of one's own limitations. In the last example, the direction the person eventually moves toward will depend to some degree on the earlier balance in his or her life between the positive and negative affects.

This ends the description of Tomkins' script theory and the variety of scripts he has formulated, which I believe is an enormous advance in our understanding of how our momentary affective experiences become organized, through the process of magnification into time-binding scripts, and slowly shape our enduring personalities. In the next two chapters, I will describe the treatment of a patient who had developed a decontamination script and a description of an anti-toxic script based on one of the longitudinal cases from the Boston–Denver study.

Part III

Two case presentations

Clinical case and longitudinal case from birth into adulthood illustrating an affect-driven script as defined by Tomkins

Chapter 7

Revisiting the repetition compulsion

In this chapter, I will describe the clinical implications of Tomkins' decontamination script, which is powered by the affect of disgust, and that Tomkins has described as "a combination of greed and cowardice" (Demos, 1995, p. 381). I will argue that his description of this script offers a way to understand what is occurring dynamically in what has been called the repetition compulsion. The repetition compulsion is one of the most difficult and tumultuous psychological problems to treat and can often result in a negative therapeutic outcome, or a stalemate. I will begin by reviewing the psychoanalytic literature about what Freud and others since Freud have meant by repetition and the compulsion to repeat and other formulations of this condition, before presenting a clinical example of the treatment of a young woman suffering from a decontamination script. This case is offered then, as an example of a decontamination script, powered by the affect of disgust as manifested in the dynamics of the repetition compulsion.

Perhaps the most useful and comprehensive review of this concept was written by Lazar and Erlich (1996). They present the different conceptualizations of this phenomenon in the various schools of thought in psychoanalysis. They have focused on the repetition compulsion as a "starting point for a theoretical discourse – on the very question of the possibility and appropriate modalities of conceptualization in the psychic domain" (p. 47). They go on to say: "The repetition compulsion thus refers to an experienced pattern, not to the events themselves . . . but an interpretation of psychic events. A psychic event is an occurrence that can be signified or testified to in consciousness" (p. 47). The authors argue that in Freud's formulation there is an inherent tension in combining somatic-economic concepts on the one hand, and mental/psychological concepts on the other: "This is the seam (the potential space) in which the repetition compulsion moves" (pp. 47 and 48), namely, the language of drive theory. They suggest that the following question remains to be answered, namely, why is it that a concept that refers to relatively common phenomena and at the same time to central and vital theoretical considerations finds itself in such a marginal position. They conclude the following:

> The issue is really whether our presence is an independent entity, unconditioned by our activity as a speaking subject, or whether it is contingent on an endless, interminable activity or emotional, cognitive and instinctual rereading – condensed in Freud's *nachtraglichkeit* – an obsessive activity of the human mind, *almost demonic by its nature.*
>
> (p. 50, italics mine)

Freud gave us the interpretative method that aims at psychic change, which as they conclude: "is not merely a restoration of a lost but wished-for phase, or the restitution of some mental state, but the recreation, through spiral-like psychic transformations of, meaningful events" (p. 51). In this last formulation Lazar and Erlich seem to focus on the repetitions that are necessary in therapy to bring about healing changes, but they do not address the phenomenon of the compulsive need to repeat as a symptom of illness, not based on drive theory. Their description of the curative process fits nicely with the dynamic processes articulated by dynamic systems theorists that describe the ongoing process of adapting to new situations by incorporating new strategies that retain something of older ones.

Wilson and Malatesta (1989) also provided a review of ongoing issues. They distinguish between a broad definition of repetition that occurs in the transference, and in all of our relationships, as well as in learning, such as in practicing, from the more limited or specific definition of the phenomena motivating a compulsion to repeat. Tomkins too makes a distinction between what he calls duplication, described as a biological process inherent in all living organisms as opposed to repetition that occurs in psychological perceptual experience. He argues that simple repetition leads to boredom and to sensory habituation, and that what captures the psyche and evokes interest is repetition with a difference. Thus, it would seem that whatever else is involved in the repetition compulsion, it must have this characteristic of the experience of repetition with a difference. This kind of repetition is what sustains interest and excitement, and can also be a definition of what can happen in therapy.

Wilson and Malatesta go on to focus on what is being repeated in a repetition compulsion, and review Freud's reasoning in "Beyond the Pleasure Principle" (1920/2001). In that writing, Feud struggled to reconcile his discovery that dreams contain wishes, whereas nightmares, which are also dreams, produce negative affects, thus it would seem that the person wishes for an experience of painful affects. Flashbacks of traumatic experiences also seem to contain wishes for a repetition of painful affects. Could these wishes be in the service of mastery? Freud understood such wishes as masochistic wishes and evoked the death instinct as an explanation. Wilson and Malatesta (1989) argued that this solution was so unsatisfactory that it led to an avoidance of this topic for several years. They then go on to propose their own solution, namely that the contents of the repetition compulsion consist of primal, preconscious, non-symbolic affective interactive patterns, occurring in early life, which remain outside of our awareness, beyond subjectivity. These early contents are believed to be in contrast to symbolic fantasies and wishes that occur with the advent of language and consciousness and thus are more amenable to therapeutic intervention and recognizable transference phenomena.

Given what we now know about early infancy reviewed in the first three chapters of this volume, I find their solution as unsatisfactory as Freud's. It contains several difficulties. First, since we all possess these early, presymbolic patterns, we must all, therefore, be struggling with some form of the *repetition compulsion*. Yet this is clearly not what clinicians are referring to. Second, there is no indication in their formulation that these early patterns are negative or disturbing, so the compulsion aspect, once again, is not accounted for. Third, they are assuming that presymbolic experience in infancy is "preconscious and primal," yet there is no evidence supporting that claim. All the recent data we have on infants indicates that infants are indeed conscious and processing their experiences in that state. Also, infants are continuously organizing and reorganizing their affective experiences. Thus when they become capable of language and self-reflection, such conscious experiences will continue to be reorganized. Clearly, not all experiences will be put into language, but that is also true of experiences throughout our lives; it is not unique to early pre-verbal experiences. Fourth, even if Wilson and Malatesta had limited their claim (which they did not), to the kind of aberrant early experiences described by Bion (1967) as beta elements, or by Mitrani (1995) as unmentalized experiences that are thought to remain unsymbolized, this would still be an unsatisfactory solution. Recall that Freud's criterion for the repetition compulsion involved experiences that had *achieved symbolic representation* in the form of images in dreams and flashbacks. The compulsion to repeat these experiences, which in their formulation are assumed to be primal and beyond subjectivity, then seems to occur mainly because we cannot get at them. Thus, the whole paradox of feeling compelled to repeat *painful symbolized experiences* is not explained.

Otto Kernberg, in an article entitled "The Concept of the Death Drive: A Clinical Perspective" (2009), includes the repetition compulsion in this category, and states the following: "Originally described as a 'resistance of the id,' clinical experience has demonstrated that the repetition compulsion may have multiple functions that have different prognostic implications" (p. 1012). He then offers several possibilities. At times, he argues it can simply be a repetitive working through of a conflict, which responds to patience and a gradual elaboration over time. Or it can involve an unconscious repetition of a traumatic relationship with the hidden hope that "this time" the other "will gratify the needs and wishes of the patient, thus being transformed, at last, into the much needed good object" (p. 1013). In post-traumatic stress disorder (PTSD) cases he suggests the compulsion to repeat is an effort to come to terms with an earlier overwhelming situation, and again in a context of a safe and protective environment, a "gradual resolution may obtain" (p. 1030). All of these examples represent repetition in the service of mastery (p. 1013).

But, he then goes on the argue that in other PTSD cases, where the trauma is an etiological factor behind "severe characterological distortions," then in an effort to overcome the trauma, the person unconsciously identifies with the perpetrator, and projects onto others the role of the victim. The world is then exclusively inhabited by perpetrators and victims, and the patient needs to repeat this triumphant reversal endlessly. A malignant variation of this last example is the repeated need by the patient to destroy a helpful relationship in order to unconsciously triumph over the helper who is envied for "not having suffered what the patient, in his mind, has suffered" (p. 1013). He cites Andre Green (1986) who described the unconscious identification with a "dead mother," namely a chronically depressed and frustrating mother, but a mother who cannot be abandoned and is clung to, so that the patient repeatedly denies the existence of all live relationships. Kernberg (2009) offers another example of a repetition compulsion that occurs in cases of severe narcissistic pathology in which the patient engages in what he calls "an active destruction of the passage of time" by a denial of aging and death, and combines this with "the triumphant destruction of the work of the envied therapist" in order to protect himself from the anxiety of his avoidance of his life tasks, as well as the work of the therapy. He calls this a manifestation of what Kleinians describe as a destructive narcissistic organization. He concludes with the following summary: "*Repetition compulsion, in short, provides clinical support to the theory of a relentless self-destructive motivation, one of the sources of the concept of the death drive*" (p. 1013).

The examples he has given run the gamut from working through conflicts to destructive malignant organizations. They all involve painful affects, but the specific affects involved are all subsumed under trauma, rage, envy, and anxiety. We are limited by the brevity of his descriptions. He speaks of PTSD and of destructive narcissistic disorders. PTSD involves the affects of fear/terror, and rage, and successful therapy does involve reworking the trauma in a safe protected place, often involving group work with other trauma survivors. In such settings, flashbacks are uninvited breakthroughs of intolerable terror and helplessness. He makes room for this possibility, except when severe characterological distortions are involved and then he calls this a repetition of a self-destructive motive at work, echoing Freud's solution to this problem. An alternative interpretation of PTSD phenomena such as flashbacks and needing to go through the traumas in order to heal from them, would argue that the effects of terrifying experiences are an indication of an overwhelmed, helpless psyche. In Tomkins' formulation this leads to an anti-toxic script, in which the person is *struggling to avoid the repetition* of states of terror, as distinguished from other scripts powered by other negative affects.

The narcissistic disorders discussed by Kernberg comprise a range of severity, and involve a variety of different negative states. For, example, in the identification with the dead mother, the person may have an undeveloped or enfeebled self, and thus feel totally unprepared to deal with live relationships, or they could be filled with rage at the "dead mother" and thus fear their destructive wishes toward others, so that in both possibilities the other must be avoided. Thus his concluding definition of the repetition compulsion as "a relentless, self-destructive motivation" and one of the sources of the concept of the death wish does not get us much further than Freud's formulation in understanding the dynamics of the repetition compulsion. Given the recent advances in neuroscience described in Chapter 4 of this volume, evoking *the death instinct can no longer be a viable explanation*.

I have argued throughout that Tomkins' articulation of the qualitative distinctions between specific negative affects offers us an enormous advance over previous formulations. I will argue that a person caught in a repetition compulsion is not seeking pain or negative affects, nor is he or she identified only with the destructive aspects of the perpetrator, and compelled to simply reverse the roles of perpetrator and victim, nor are they motivated by a wish for relentless self-destruction. Rather I believe such people are unable to grieve the loss of a relationship with an idealized good other, which was never so good, and that now, through repeated attempts to rejoin this goodness, they repeatedly fail, and then feel an equally exaggerated sense of themselves as "losers," "inadequate," or "unworthy" of care. But in my clinical experience, this refusal to grieve is only half the story. Therefore, the repetition of painful affects is not the goal. It is instead an *unanticipated consequence of a failed strategy*. Patients are not seeking painful affects; they are neither trying to hold onto the destructiveness of the caregiver nor to master painful affects. They are seeking something else entirely, and they seek it repeatedly. But their strategy is deeply flawed, and thus they fail repeatedly, thereby experiencing painful affect. What is this flawed strategy? We need to return to Tomkins' decontamination script for a possible answer, based on the dynamics of the affect of disgust as the primary motivation.

Tomkins described this script as a "*combination of greed and cowardice*," because *it adopts a maximizing-minimizing strategy* and, as Tomkins reminds us: "*Clearly a double maximum cannot be achieved*" (Demos, 1995, p. 381). Such a strategy can neither attain the prize nor can it escape defeat. This script seeks nothing less than purification, by joining in an exaggerated goodness so as to minimize the risk of feeling the *self-disgust* of utterly failing to live up to impossible demands, a failure that contains within it an exaggerated sense of a self that is wholly inadequate, and thus is believed to be sickening to behold and thereby unworthy of being loved. The *greed* involves the grandiose fantasy of a *perfect reunion with an idealized good other* (not a perpetrator) in the belief that one could actually escape the pain of such suffering, and the loading of each new situation with such unrealistic expectations. The *cowardice* comes with imagining that it would be *impossible to ever face one's failings, inadequacies, and limitations, which have been exaggerated into grandiose proportions, beyond the hope of ever being loved.* Herein lies the refusal to grieve for the ordinary limitations, failings, or losses in life. But both ends of this polarity of the good and of the failure must be *present and exaggerated* in order for repetition to become compulsive.

What kind of early experiences lead to such a script? In Chapter 6, I described how this script comes into being. I will quote again here Tomkins' formulation: "*There can be no greed without a seductive other. There can be no cowardice without an intimidating, contaminating, or confusing other ... and without massive collusive reciprocal magnification*" (p. 380). In brief, the exaggerated goodness of the parent, seduces the child into wanting to join the goodness, or the powerful, intimidating parent compels the child out of weakness to join. These experiences are combined with the parent's intolerance of any behavior in the child that does not validate this parental goodness, and thus the parent exaggerates the inadequacies and failures of the child, who is never allowed to disobey or express anger, and who is then left alone to try to make sense of these confusing experiences. *These are very good scenes that have turned very bad and they are repeated many times.* The vast middle ground of possibilities is not allowed and thus remains outside of this increasingly polarized world.

A small child cannot accurately assess either the validity of the parent's actions or negative judgments of his or her own behaviors or of the so-called "good" qualities of the parent. The child repeatedly needs to feel how wonderful the parents are, yet no matter how hard the child tries to please, he or she somehow keeps upsetting the parent and then ends up feeling weak, disgusting, inadequate, and unlovable. Over time, such children come to believe that their parents' judgment of their failures (which have been exaggerated and projected onto them by their parents), must be true, because it now confirms their own frequent experiences of feeling weak, dependent, helpless, confused, ungrateful, including forbidden angry wishes toward them. It must feel to these children that their parents can see into their secret, weakest, and worst selves. Herein lays the massive collusive magnification of the all-wonderful, wise, loving parent, and the all inadequate, failing child.

As the child comes to believe that he or she is the source of all negative events, *such a reality feels both undeniable and impossible to bear* and so the decontamination fantasy of once again joining with the all-good parent takes hold *at the heavy cost to the child of denying his or her own reality and dependency needs*. Such a person is driven to continually seek an imagined paradise, which never really existed in the past, in order to flee from a hell in which the self is imagined to be more disgusting, inadequate, ungrateful, and weak than could ever have been true in the past. Tomkins described this tragic dilemma in the following way: "It is a game that must be played even though the player knows the dice are loaded against him" (p. 381).

People who have had to construct this decontamination script are continually caught in *repeating cycles of enchantment and disenchantment*. They become enchanted or seduced by authority figures or powerful others who they can idealize and strive to please, or to join and feel special to. But sooner or later, this enchantment is inevitably *spoiled* by perceiving an undeniable flaw in the other, or a decrease in the attentions of the other, or a fear of rejection by the other if they are true to their own perceptions, their own feelings, or their own needs. These disenchantments can occur in the context of an unavoidable problem at work or in any relationship that matters in which there is a decrease in the attentiveness of or in the good feelings of the other, or some criticism by the other of their actions, evoking a fear of failing to live up to the expectations of a valued other. Any one of these events can activate real or imagined limitations of their very core. When such a spoiling, deflating realization occurs, it can produce a massive, rapid plunge into the depths of self-doubt, despair, disgust at their "weakness," cowardice, inadequacy, or of unacceptable feelings, such as, their dependency needs, or their anger. It is the unbearableness of the strength of the self-revulsion, brought on by the *conviction* that their needs, actions, or feelings are wrong or inadequate, or that they are to blame for whatever went wrong, failings that are greatly exaggerated in their minds and that compels the person to seek an escape into the fantasy of an idealized purification, which leads them to the next round of seduction and failure.

The deep dilemma is that to be real is to risk not being loved. There is little learning from one enchantment–disenchantment cycle to the next. Each time feels entirely new, different from the past, and ever hopeful that this time will be different, and a perfect union can be achieved. Here is the failure to tolerate, accept, and to grieve ordinary limitations and failures, which mean unacceptable weakness and evoke self-disgust.

A case presentation

This case is an exploration of how the stresses of being uprooted involved in the process of emigration, namely, separation, loss, and abuse, were transmitted across the generations in the form of a polarized world that was inhabited by the all-good parents and the ungrateful, bad children. Thus it is a demonstration of the dynamics of a decontamination script in one multi-generational family and of how in the latest generation, the eldest daughter was seduced into this polarized world and developed a decontamination script. It describes one young woman's painful struggle to come to terms with her parents' commitment to a family myth that obliterated her reality, to slowly disentangle herself from the wish to join that family myth and hang onto her special role, and to slowly begin to bear her suffering by learning to trust her own experience, and accept the normality of her own needs and limitations, by recognizing how she was in danger of repeating her parents' defensive patterns. Her story unfolded gradually.

The patient, who I will call Ms. L., was an attractive, articulate, engaging 20-year-old college junior, who had taken medical leave from a nearby woman's college because of her daily drinking, her inability to concentrate and function in the college setting, and her suicidal wish to jump in front of a train. She had consciously identified with the tragic fate of Anna Karenina, unaware that she may also have identified with her mother, who as a teenager had been hit by a truck. She was admitted to a residential treatment center in the late spring, after her therapist felt

Ms. L. was no longer safe enough to continue as an outpatient. At the time of her admission she described her troubles as follows: "Things have fallen apart and I don't understand why." But she knew she needed to be in a hospital and to get away from home in order to try to sort things out. Her defensive style was one of repression in the context of a false-self organization. It was difficult for her to explore her problems without her quickly feeling she was a total failure who would become non-functional, as she perceived her mother to be. At this point she was moving towards an anti-toxic script and wanting to die.

We began our work together by trying to develop an understanding of what had gone wrong and why she was so focused on jumping in front of a train and dying. It quickly became clear that she had always pushed herself hard to achieve, with little realistic sense of her physical and intellectual limits. She had easily done well in high school, but the work in a high-powered college was much harder. Things slowly began to fall apart in her sophomore year, but as the threat of failure increased in her junior year, her response was to take on more courses until the whole thing collapsed. Her internal world was rigidly polarized. The only alternative to being the "best," which she had strived to be at school but could now no longer maintain, was to feel she was lazy, worthless, and bad. She then embraced this negative identity by daily drinking, sexually acting out, and becoming increasing suicidal. This deep sense of badness was the most enduring and certain thing she knew or feared about herself. Thus, when this grandiose sense of her powers began to fall apart in mid-college, she was left with only this awful failure, a feeling of deep inadequacy and badness, and became more and more focused on suicide. She stated on several occasions that she really did not know who she was or what she wanted. She was disconnected from her own deeper dependency needs and the reality of her family life. Her only options seemed either to identify with her rageful, terrifying, yet idealized and successful father, or with her depressed, dysfunctional mother; yet neither option seemed workable to her. In this patient's mind, the two ends of the polarity are located in separate people, an idealized successful father and a depressed dysfunctional mother, and she no longer had a viable way to exist in such a world.

In the first weeks of her treatment we gathered a family history, which provided the basis for an initial formulation. Both of Ms. L.'s parents were children of immigrants to this country, three of the grandparents came from Europe. On the father's side, his grandmother and his mother and her two brothers were the only survivors out of seven children; the two brothers never married, and his mother married an alcoholic, who abandoned her when Ms. L.'s father was 3 years old. Nevertheless, his mother worked hard to graduate from college and pursue a career. This choice, however, meant leaving her young son in the care of her own mother and her two brothers, who beat their young nephew throughout his childhood.

Ms. L.'s father never felt close to his uncles or his grandmother, but he did feel close to and proud of his mother, yet according to Ms. L. he treated her badly, e.g. yelling and arguing with her a lot. After age 3, he only saw his father once, when he was 14, and he felt enraged, disgusted, and frustrated that his father was so drunk that he could not tell him how angry he was with him. Four years later his father died of a heart attack. Ms. L.'s own father went on to graduate from college, earn an MA in finance, and then became a successful businessman. Thus, on the father's side, the stresses of being uprooted and of loss were dealt with either through idealizing hard work and achievement, with little concern for nurturance of the next generation, and through denial of one's losses and helplessness, as in the two uncles, by physically abusing a younger, helpless other, Ms. L.' father. Thus generativity toward children took the form of being the breadwinner, which was highly valued, with little concern for their dependency needs.

Ms. L.'s mother had gone to a fashion institute, but did not want to work for others, fearing they would take credit for her designs. So she worked in a department store until she became a mother and a housewife. She met her husband through an ethnic youth group in her early twenties, and they married in their mid-twenties. When she was pregnant with Ms. L. (her first child), her own mother died, and she named Ms. L. after her mother, perhaps, thereby, not fully grieving her loss. This young family then moved into the mother's parents' two-family house to be close to Ms. L's maternal grandfather. Two more children were born to Ms. L.'s parents, eighteen months apart – first another daughter and then a son. After several years, the grandfather died and Ms. L.'s mother and the mother's older brother had a falling out over the settlement of their father's estate; they had not spoken since. Ms. L.'s mother, as a teenager, had been struck by a truck and broke her hip. The settlement from that accident enabled the family to buy the house they lived in at the time of Ms. L.'s hospitalization. Thus on the maternal side, Ms. L.'s mother seemed unable to make an emotional separation from her parents, or to establish herself independently in the outside world. Also intense disagreements remained unresolved, causing a permanent rupture.

According to Ms. L., once a son was born, her mother seemed to ignore her daughters, leaving Ms. L., at age 3, to care for her sister, aged 1½; otherwise the family seemed to function relatively well in the early years. The mother made school lunches, took the kids to and from school, and birthdays were celebrated with parties in the back yard. But one day, when Ms. L. was 8 or 9 years old, her mother did not arrive to pick them up from school; the father finally came. When they returned home, the house was dark and the mother was in bed. So began the mother's inexplicable, sudden, and dramatic decline in functioning. From that day on, according to Ms. L., her mother rarely left the house, no longer saw friends, and ceased to function adequately as a parent or as a housekeeper. "Why should I cook and clean for you!" *No one in the family has ever discussed the mother's problem*. The mother denied she was depressed or that there was anything wrong with her, and the father denied that anything had changed. There seemed to be no place for reality in this family. The timing of this event roughly coincided with the youngest child's (her only son) entry into school, which perhaps was experienced by this mother as a deep emotional abandonment, leaving her unable to function alone, all day, at home.

At this point in the treatment several powerful indicators of the potential for the intergenerational transfer of defenses against loss, separation, and dependency had emerged. First, the parents seemed unable to process intensely painful emotions, particularly helplessness, dependency, loss, and separations, a deficit perhaps passed onto them from their own parents, and leading to any or all of the following: over achievement, anger, and/or dysfunction. Second, they were joined in their denial that a very obvious, negative, sudden change had occurred in the mother. And third, there was an unacknowledged inversion of parental roles, as Ms. L., from age 8 or 9 on, had to take over the care of both of her younger siblings. Here we have the ingredients for the formation of a decontamination script – the refusal to grieve losses, denial of parental dysfunction or weakness, overvaluing of achievement, and shifting parental responsibility onto the eldest child, Ms. L., an unspoken seduction into a role as a co-parent, thereby exaggerating her role and importance, without any acknowledgment of this abdication of parental responsibility.

As the therapeutic work deepened and Ms. L. was eventually able to speak openly about the abuse and neglect in the family, these three dynamics became very prominent. I will focus my discussion on how they affected Ms. L.'s psychological development, her attempted solutions, and her painful struggle to free herself from her parents' attempts to lean on her psyche, in order to protect them from their own unresolved losses, hurts, and fears, and her struggle to give up her own wish to hang onto her *special role* in the family that represented a powerful unspoken seduction.

In the early part of our work Ms. L. focused on her deep ambivalence around dependency. This was manifested both toward her mother – alternating between hate and contempt for her neediness, and love and wanting to help her; and toward her own dependency needs – alternating between her fear that needing anybody represented being a loser, or the danger of being exploited, and on the other hand, these needs evoked painful longings to be taken care of and mothered. She was beginning to recognize her long-standing pattern of suppressing her needs and feelings, in order to please and take care of the other, and how this pattern dominated her relationships with friends and with men. *She hated herself for her lack of courage in being able to stand up for herself in relation to others*. Remember in Tomkins' formulation the decontamination script is a combination of greed and cowardice; a maximizing–minimizing strategy. Here is the cowardice the other side of the greed in wanting to be special. In this context, her school achievement looked like a desperate attempt to fend off these feelings of being a loser and a failure, like her mother, as well as a way to try to please her father. It also entailed her first attempt to separate from her family.

At the start of Ms. L's second month of treatment, we had our first series of family meetings. Given what I knew so far about the family, and my sense that the children had been abandoned by their parents, I wanted to strengthen the alliance between the siblings. Thus I arranged to meet with the three siblings first, before meeting with the whole family. I also knew that both of Ms. L.'s younger siblings had had academic trouble in school, and trouble with controlling their anger. In our meeting, Ms. L.'s younger sister and brother verified her story of their mother's collapse and their father's rages, but they were freer to express their anger and rebellion toward both parents than was Ms. L.; they simply wanted to get away from home as soon as possible, and could not understand her wish to die. Unlike her siblings, Ms. L., as the eldest, had been *seduced into the polarized world of her parents, by becoming the valued, adultified child, as well as the ungrateful, bad child*, and thus was now more trapped in a decontamination script that kept her more enmeshed with her parents than were her siblings.

Her social worker and I had two meetings with the parents and children. In these meetings, Ms. L.'s sister was most able to confront the parents. Near the end of the first session, the mother said she felt that Ms. L. did not respect her, seeing her as a loser, and stated that her marriage "sucked." Ms. L. could not acknowledge that these were her feelings and tried to take care of her mother in this meeting. In the second session, we tried to address the two versions of reality in the family: namely, the children's experience of their mother's collapse and dysfunction, and of parental fighting, as well as the effects these events had had on them, versus the parents' version, which denied the mother's collapse and focused on how troublesome and spoiled these children were and how they took advantage of their mother.

We also tried to articulate parental responsibility for managing marital problems and for childcare. The parents, after a brief acknowledgment of our formulation, again blamed the children, insisting it was their job to take care of the parents. The parents spoke with pathological certainty, presenting themselves as self-righteous and long-suffering, *hoarding all the goodness and projecting all the blame onto their "ungrateful and uncaring children.*" In this stance the parents manifested the same deep ambivalence about dependency needs that Ms. L. had articulated earlier, namely that to need others is to be spoiled or troublesome, qualities they located only in their children, yet, at the same time, they longed to be cared for and expected their children to take care of them and thus felt exploited. The children did their best to defend themselves against these charges; Ms. L. tried to placate her parents; by contrast, her two siblings argued and used angry retorts. These discussions were volatile.

Ms. L. reported later that she and her siblings found these meetings painful but helpful, in that they had *never* before discussed with each other or in the family the troubles they had been experiencing. Ms. L. said that during lunch, when the parents had tried to berate our formulation of the two realities in this family, the children had stuck together and reiterated their version of family dynamics. Also, at one point, when the parents fought and walked off in different directions, none of the children went after either parent to take care of them. *Ms. L. stated that this was a first for all of them*! Thus our initial attempts to re-establish generational boundaries seemed to have met with some success, at least with the children. The effect of this beginning of support for the children's experience in this family had opened up an *intense struggle* within Ms. L.

Although during the meetings, Ms. L. had continued to try to please her parents, later she expressed her *shock and disillusionment* at her father's defensiveness and closed mindedness, even calling his behavior "sleazy." Applying this label and expressing disgust for him was a powerful moment of disenchantment and the beginning of the slow process of validating her experience. She had also been surprised by her mother's ability to say as much as she did and by her own inability to speak up. As a result of her strengthened alliance with her siblings and her father's behavior in these meetings, she experienced a *massive and sudden de-idealization* of her father, *which confused her.* She no longer knew whom to look up to or to seek advice from. But *she did not feel entitled to her anger* at her father, and reported that she could not sustain it outside of our sessions. At the same time she noted that she could no longer switch into a happy mood either, and thus would go numb when she left my office.

This inability to hold onto her own reality versus her parents' reality represented one of the major effects on her psyche of her parents' *pathological certainty* by hoarding all the goodness, berating their children's failure to recognize it and leaning on her. This certainty and their unacknowledged need for her had seduced Ms. L. to still want to please them. Their united front in denying the trouble in the family, their inability to process painful emotions, and their leaning on her to take care of them, had all combined to undermine their eldest child's confidence in her own perceptions and experience, and had trapped her in this decontamination script. Her struggle to claim her own reality, to feel entitled to her feelings and needs, and to give up her assigned role in the family, had many ramifications that continued for the next several years.

Soon after these meetings we reviewed the results of our six-week evaluation, which included reports from therapy, psychopharmacology, nursing, social work, community, as well as psychological projective testing. The latter indicated a central problem in managing anger and aggression and a fear of losing control, which Ms. L. readily acknowledged. She spoke of being terrified by her father's and her brother's out-of-control anger, and of fearing that her own anger could become lethal. She also realized how these fears had crippled her capacity to defend herself or to speak up when needed, and how they had left her feeling enormously guilty, and suicidal for her own impermissible, rageful, even murderous, wishes, particularly vis-à-vis her collapsed mother. All of these realizations helped her to understand why she needed to stay for longer treatment and not return to school in a few weeks.

When we talked by phone with her parents to relate the findings of our evaluation and our recommendations for a longer stay, they were shocked to learn of her continued suicidal wishes and the depth of her troubles, but quickly focused on their hurt that she had not been able to tell them these things on a recent visit home. Their reaction both reflected their powerful defenses against all suffering and challenged their deep need to believe that this was a loving, accepting, communicative family. Yet during this conversation, it became clear that *this family was unable to communicate whenever any differences that threatened separateness* were expressed. At the hint of disagreement, the father would become angry, loud, and attacking, while the mother would obsess about Ms L.'s medications, and when Ms. L. expressed her annoyance at not being heard, the father harshly criticized her. The father seemed completely unaware of his own anxieties, of their impact on his children, and of how he shut down communication with his anger. These exchanges demonstrated how rigid these defenses were, and how they communicated that *there could only be room for the parents' reality in this family, which was an idealization of how wonderful the family was*.

After this phone call, Ms. L was intensely angry at both her parents and was surprised by the strength of her feelings. During this same period she had two nightmares, one about her father attacking her and being out of control, and the other about him dying as a result of her anger at him, which left her feeling frightened. A few days later she had more nightmares, one in which her father was yelling and hitting her, and another in which he was approaching her sexually and asking her to do things to him. Ms. L. was terrified by the powerful feelings evoked in these dreams, and by her inability to hang onto these feelings when alone. *Her own reality was very shaky.* She knew she needed me to help her articulate these powerful feelings, but this left her feeling weak and in danger that I would then have power over her. These feelings reflected the degree of coercion and intimidation that had occurred in this family.

As she struggled with this intensification of her feelings, she became more suicidal, which resulted in her taking twenty-five pills of Unisom, knowing it was a non-lethal dose, and not telling anyone for two days. She then acknowledged in therapy that the pills were the first step in a suicide plan that included tying herself to the railroad tracks; feeling numb from the pills and thus not fighting to free herself. Here again was her identification with Anna Karenina and her unconscious identification with her mother having been hit by a truck and her murderous rage. It also revealed the depth of her confusion, and helplessness about what she was responsible for, her terror of her anger, and her hopelessness.

At this point in our work, I pressed her hard about her commitment to staying alive and to engaging in this therapeutic work. She spoke about her deepest dilemma, namely how her rage was unacceptable to her because she feared if her parents knew, they could never love her. Thus she was up against an impossible choice, namely *to be real was to lose love*. Her awareness of always having to choose between being known or suppressing herself to get love was now becoming much more available to her. This new awareness allowed her to begin to notice how others managed anger and still cared about each other, and how when I was angry with her (e.g. around her pill taking), I did not yell at her; instead, I had wanted to talk about it and to understand why she wanted to die, which had amazed her. She was embarrassed to say that she was glad to be alive.

Her sexual dream led us to exploring the powerful oedipal configuration in the family, in which her mother's weakness and collapse had strengthened Ms. L.'s own feelings of being the more desirable and better companion for her father. Here is the psychological seduction, namely her belief that she has a special relationship with her father. She spoke of her fantasies that she should dress up and go with him as his date to various dinners, which her mother had no wish to attend. She felt she loved him more than her mother did. These revelations of her love for her father made her very uncomfortable, yet, given the adult role she had had to assume in the family, she was beginning to understand how these feelings were now making sense. We also talked about how her father seemed committed to her mother and had not divorced her all these years. Beginning to put all of these feelings into words at first seemed to bring relief and free her. For the next several days, she felt energized and reported that she was having very sexual dreams about old boyfriends. She also began to have more honest phone calls with her parents, telling them she felt terrible, and how she had learned to deny her feelings in the family. But these positive effects were not to last. We had just scratched the surface of these oedipal fantasies.

In the early fall several events occurred in quick succession. Her family ignored her twenty-first birthday, which she spent alone, feeling angry and unloved. She went through a complicated grieving process about her not being able to return to school, her disillusionment around her father, and her own weakness and lack of courage. She was upset about how she had got into trouble at the hospital. She had felt *unable to say no* to underage peers when they asked her to buy them liquor, afraid she wouldn't be liked, which had temporarily put her treatment in jeopardy. All together these events led to a *painful sadness that was new to her*. It represented a real break with her family's avoidance of sadness and grief. She stated she had lost her way and would have to trust my saying that feeling and bearing sadness was healthy and important and not a sign of weakness. She also reported a dream about people wearing elaborate disguises and then taking them off at night. She experienced herself as one of these people, *but she could not take off the disguise, even when alone*. She felt intense anger at her parents, then immediate guilt, and then a strong need to be hugged by them and reassured, which led to a deep, *heartfelt sobbing as she longed to be a small child again*. She was working very hard to sort out this impossible choice she had struggled with for so long – to be real was to lose love – and to accept reality and grieve the loss of a childhood she had longed for and now could never have.

This new access to her grief, which validated longings that had been deeply suppressed for years, combined with her growing trust in me and in our work, opened up a flood of memories of physical and psychological abuse that had occurred in the family. She now felt her reality strong enough and felt safe enough to describe regular beatings by her father that were terrifying. She described how often her mother would initiate them by blaming the children for something (e.g. they took her pen or spilled something), and then she would threaten with: "Wait until your father comes home!" She remembered how anticipating his arrival was torture. She felt her mother was so dumb that she could sometimes set up her sister to get beaten, so as to avoid it herself. Here is another source of self-disgust and her recurring fear of being like her mother. She described an awful incident when her father had tied her younger brother to the stair rail and left him there all day while the family went out.

At another point, when her younger brother went to school with a handprint on his face, social services were called and they made a home visit. Ms. L. reported that her parents told their children: "You can tell the truth, but if you do, they will take you away and you will never see us again." Under such a threat, the children did not tell the truth. Ms. L. rationalized this failure by saying there were some advantages to staying in such an abusive home; she did get to go to private schools. As we explored the deeper meaning of this event, namely, that her parents seemed to understand the "truth" and the legal consequences of their abusive actions, but made no effort to change their behaviors, or to apologize, or even to acknowledge the impossible situation they were putting their children in of having to choose to continue to be abused or to lose their parents (*to be real is to lose love*). Ms. L. again felt intense anger, fear, and sadness as she slowly took in more of the reality of her experiences in her family.

When we tried to address the beatings in a telephone session with her parents, her father minimized their effects, stating that his having been beaten as a child had never affected him, and his children should realize that he loved them. He was so well defended that he simply could not process the intensity of the intimidation, fear, and helplessness that Ms. L. had experienced as a child and continued to live with, just as earlier in his life he had been deaf to and unable to access his own fear, helplessness, and suffering. This denial of his own suffering and painful experiences, and his own self-loathing for such weakness, had enabled him to project this self-hatred, and anger onto his young, needy, helpless, and allegedly ungrateful children, thereby giving him free rein for his self-righteous, vengeful, abusive rage.

Soon after these revelations, we had a face-to-face family session with Ms. L. and her sister. Beforehand, Ms. L. feared her sister would not validate her experience or would see her as disloyal for speaking about the abuse. Her sister, however, did validate the beatings and their mother's emotional unavailability, but she did not share Ms. L.'s disgust for their mother or her idealization of their father. She seemed to feel no disloyalty; rather her impulse was to get away from her parents. *She clearly had not been seduced* into the polarized world that Ms. L. lived in. Ms. L. felt deeply jealous of her sister's ability to disentangle her own self from the family. For the next several days Ms. L. felt shock and shame at how much gratification she had got from feeling she was better than her sister. She was enraged that her sister understood some things better than she did and recognized in herself a mean streak, remembering that as children, she had been glad when her sister took the beatings. She briefly became suicidal again as she came up against her own sadism and her unwillingness to give up being the best and "the chosen one." *She was now engaged in a deep, painful, and mighty, but now unavoidable struggle, if she was going to find her way out of her polarized internal world of being either the best, the chosen one, or the worst failure, who perhaps should be dead.*

This internal struggle – between clinging to her "special" position in the family versus seeing her parents more realistically and thereby claiming her own limitations, needs, and feelings, including accepting her anger, disgust, and hurt – manifested itself over the next several weeks in massive swings from one side of this polarity to the other. Each trip home would convince her that her father or mother needed her and that she should leave treatment and go back to school. She would then feel a strong need for me, for understanding, for an acceptance of her rage, hurt, and neediness, and for the protection of this treatment. At those moments, she did not want to leave, but then would feel guilty about spending her father's money while revealing his abuse. Exhausted by this struggle, she nevertheless was slowly realizing that her parents could not meet her needs.

Thanksgiving seemed to mark a major step away from her family. She was ambivalent about going home for this holiday, worrying that she might act as if everything was all right. But she did go, partly to alleviate her guilt, partly to get a break from this difficult work, and partly from just wanting to be taken care of. While at home, she initiated a two-hour family talk during which her father reportedly stated that 95 percent of the time, he did not care what his children thought. Yet he was then shocked to hear that they in turn did not feel close to him.

Upon her return, Ms. L. was initially deeply saddened to see how no one in the family seemed to care about anybody but themselves. But shortly after, her deep ambivalence toward her parents and the power of her oedipal struggle soon took over our work. *She could not integrate the abusive, brutal, uncaring father, with the father that she adored, idealized, and had tried so hard to please.* She revealed both more details of his physical and emotional abuse and of her sexual wishes and fantasies about her father. She was deeply repulsed by these wishes, but could not get them out of her mind. Thus her tolerance for her "badness" was slowly increasing, which allowed us to continue to pursue this tangle of feelings.

We reviewed again how her mother's collapse had seduced her into taking up this role, vis-à-vis her father, and how her parents had deferred to her in several important decisions, seducing her to embrace the grandiose belief that she could do anything in the family. This was a heady, all too believable possibility for her. At one point I even wondered if she had felt the family was so corrupt that she could actually marry her father. She acknowledged that she did believe this, and felt angry and spurned by him, recognizing that he seemed to have no interest in this possibility (*he had never approached her sexually*), but she had protected her fantasy by saying that she had never offered herself either. Here we have the other side her repulsion and disgust for her oedipal wishes, namely her grandiose belief that she would have been irresistible to her father. She was also extremely angry at her mother for being so mindless and dysfunctional. It seemed clear to me that she had not been protected in any way by her mother.

These sessions were intensely emotional, and she became increasingly dependent on me, at times wishing I would take her home and mother her. During this same period, she was also becoming more involved with a male peer, with whom she was trying to be more open and honest, and with whom she could share her anger at her parents, as he too shared his anger at his parents. This led to their sharing their sadistic fantasies about torturing their parents. Her deepening trust in our work and in this new relationship with a male peer was allowing her to begin to accept her sadism and anger at her parents as having some basis in the reality of their neglect and abuse of her. She was then able to take the following step. She decided she *could not* go home for Christmas. She felt that given her intense, conflicted feelings towards her parents, she no longer knew how to relate to them. Soon after she communicated her decision to her parents, her father retaliated by announcing that he would not pay for treatment after February.

When we discussed the timing of these two decisions in a telephone session with her parents, the father said he was sad and hurt by her decision but denied that he felt angry. Yet he then proceeded to angrily harangue her for fifteen minutes, stating she "was putting daggers in her parents' hearts." When Ms. L. suggested that he was trying to make her feel guilty, he became insulted and enraged that she should suggest such a thing. He also denied that his limiting the funds for treatment had any connection with her decision not to come home for the holidays. Once again, he could not own his anger, and could neither understand her reasons for not coming home, nor could he accept her reality of her childhood and her life, stating how hurtful it was for him and her mother. This was the last family meeting we attempted.

Her decision not to go home for Christmas was experienced by him as a massive separation threat and betrayal. The vehemence with which he tried to deny her experience and reality brings to mind Shengold's (1989) work on "soul murder". *His reality as the good parent, who was being hurt and abandoned, was the only reality possible in this family.* He therefore felt entitled to use his rage, his lack of interest in who his children were, and his money to try to fight off any threat to his belief that he and his wife had created a loving, happy family, even if it may lead to jeopardizing his daughter's mental health and or crippling her essential core. Ms. L. too had been captured and seduced by this family myth prior to her hospitalization, but she was now in the midst of an intense struggle for her future life, her reality, her mind, her heart, and soul. She could no longer go back to the way things had been.

At this point in our work together, Ms. L. was deeply shocked and upset by her father's actions, but she was now determined to find a way to continue this work. By stepping down to the less expensive programs, she realized she could stretch out the money to cover treatment until early May. But the holidays were extremely difficult for her. She was frightened and lonely, and again begged me and the Riggs nurses to take her home with us or to adopt her. I struggled with but was able to contain my own counter-transference wishes to do something for her for Christmas.

The next four months were extremely difficult. Ms. L. alternated many times between feeling enraged, like a "spoiled brat" who wanted to be taken care of, versus accepting responsibility for herself and doing what she needed to do. She kept coming back to her shock and sudden realization that her parents could act so vengefully, and that they just could not understand what her treatment here was all about. At these moments she could get in touch with deeply painful, hurt feelings and more memories of her mother's failures. She realized that *whenever she had tried to challenge or to complain, she was told she was being bad, selfish, and disrespectful, with the unspoken meaning of: "How dare you have a separate perspective!"* She wanted to escape all of this pain and just do nothing, or only what she wanted to do, but she realized that this was the way her mother lived, namely, numbing her feelings and abdicating her responsibilities. She felt she could not "let herself off the hook," and that she needed to find the courage to struggle against this wish, recognizing that her mother had given up the struggle. Her mother represented a powerful negative identity, and she was now working hard to free herself from its hold on her.

After the holidays, she and her parents got into a standoff about who would visit whom first. When they failed to show up for a weekend visit, Ms. L., for the first time, missed several of our sessions, leaving me a note about her rage, pain, desperation, and her anger at me. When she came back, she talked about how hurt and angry she felt that I had been unable to protect her from her father's retaliation and that I had been unable to change his mind about the money for her treatment. She also stated that I had become the representative of reality and limitations, and that, in spite of her efforts to corrupt me, I had not taken her home with me, and that some part of her *hated that I made sense*. After acknowledging all this, she admitted that she had not given me the Christmas present she had made for me because of her anger. She then confessed that some of her anger at me was because she could not express her anger at her parents; if she did, they would retaliate and make things even worse, and she knew that I would not retaliate.

This was a very powerful and deeply moving session. She had risked acting on her anger by not coming to our sessions, and not giving me the present she had made, and she then found the courage to come in and face me and tell me all about it. After this session, she began to feel that maybe she could get through this, even though she now felt frightened and desperate. She said: "*I can feel a small fragile self beginning to form, a self I can bring here to the therapy, and show sometimes to my boyfriend, but I cannot take home.*" She was now well on her way to really getting better. Our struggles would now involve helping her to grieve her losses and accept realistic limitations of her resources and her abilities, and finally give up her special role.

As part of the plan to lower the cost of her treatment, Ms. L. did find an apartment and even enjoyed spending some time there. Getting a job was much more conflicted for her. It seemed to symbolize a major step in asserting her independence and giving up on the wish to be loved and taken care of by her parents. The core of this conflict meant accepting her reality, namely, how abusive her childhood had been, and bearing all the pain involved in that, as well as giving up her special, favored, fantasized position, including the feeling *that she was now owed something. She felt paralyzed.* Yet as the month dragged on, she got bored with nothing to do, and this helped her to understand that she was really *not* like her mother. She could not sit and watch TV day in and day out. Thus, part of what she seemed to be struggling to sort out had to do with *could she actually be a separate, different kind of person than her mother?* What kind of woman did she want to be? And finally, she was slowly beginning to recognize and own who she was.

During this same, time her relationship with her boyfriend was deepening, and *she realized how frightened she was of real closeness.* She was surprised by how shaky and vulnerable she felt. Her dreams now were about not being able to hold his attention or losing him to another woman. We were now able to connect these worries to her deep hurt in relation to her father and his not choosing her over his wife, and to *her deep sense of inadequacy as a valued person.* She was having trouble differentiating this new love from her father, and found it hard to accept that one could have a love relationship that was not abusive.

During this struggle she also, unilaterally and suddenly, decided to discontinue her medications and then to endure the resulting physical withdrawal symptoms. Her feelings had now intensified without the medication, but she had decided that she wanted to and needed to feel these feelings, thus, she was determined to try to get through this crisis without medication. She also noticed that she was not suicidal, in spite of this intensification of her feelings. This action seemed to have several important meanings for her – an act of defiance against her dependency on us (the hospital staff), a need to take charge of her life, the need to discover that she could bear her pain, and perhaps the most important meaning was that *she needed to begin to trust herself.* She is not the only patient in my experience to make this choice, at a similar point in treatment and for similar reasons.

In the spring, I went on vacation for two weeks. She was not able yet to make use of an interim therapist, and missed having someone to talk to about her deep feelings. Two important events occurred in my absence. She and her boyfriend spent a day in New York City riding the subways, and she reported that she had finally mastered her fear of wanting to leap in front of trains. She also made a trip home, during which she had watched a lot of home movies of her childhood. She said they were awful, full of her mother yelling, and of her being mean to her sister after her mother had been mean to her, which left her feeling very sad. She stated that she never wanted to see them again. *These movies seem to have finally destroyed her fantasy of a happy childhood, which she had long struggled to maintain in the face of physical and verbal abuse.* She now seemed more able to bear this sadness and grief.

My return coincided with the absence of her boyfriend. She felt some relief that I was there so that she could cry and talk through her feelings of vulnerability, jealousy, and her fears of losing him. She missed their deep connection, which felt like a very different kind of loneliness to her. As her missing of him intensified, she experienced intense anger, lasting for several days, which seemed to alternate with her longing. We began to relate this anger, as well as this deep longing to be cared for, to her childhood, and the lack of nurturance and empathy from her parents. She acknowledged that she had spent her life *not letting herself feel this painful longing*. She would always snap herself into a false cheerfulness. Once again her intense sadness made her feel she was getting worse, but again, she was able to accept my saying that it represented a new strength and progress.

After her boyfriend's return, she continued to struggle with episodes of jealousy, and noticed how unstable she felt inside, yet at the same time she felt less labile than ever before. Once again we related her insecurity to her father's rejection of her, but in this context, her belief that men were helpless if women approached them sexually was more prominent. *She continued to believe that if she had approached her father sexually, he would have had sex with her, thus she now could not believe that her boyfriend could be loyal to her if another woman came on to him sexually.* I wondered with her if this was yet a another way of her discounting her own value as a person, as well as her own real experience of the importance of their ability to talk and share feelings with each other, and I also noted that neither of those capacities were part of her relationship with her father. *I suggested that maybe she still could not imagine that outside of therapy, if she showed her true self, she could still be valued and loved for who she is as a person.*

As the time of her discharge got nearer, she began to focus on reapplying to college. She was full of anxieties, some of which were social. She had become more authentic with me and with her boyfriend, but she did not know yet how to deal with the larger world. She could not go into her false, excessively nice mode so easily any more, but she had no other way of being, e.g. she simply did not know how to talk to others about ordinary things. She visited her friends at her college, and it went well, but she again felt intense grief about not graduating with her class.

She was also anxious about being "judged" by the administration, e.g. what would they think of her asking to be taken off medical leave and be readmitted. She went through what had now become a typical sequence for her: *anxiety that if she had needs or desires, she would be attacked or rejected by the other and then forced to comply, then blaming or discounting the other (e.g. a silly and useless requirement), then avoiding the task, then talking through her feelings, then feeling better and calming down, and then finally taking action*. She could recognize her pattern of avoiding hospital staff, fearing they would think badly of her, then turn away or disagree with her, and she would then have to do what they suggested, and could not be real. Such thoughts were so much more conscious now, so it was easy for us to relate these expectations to her experiences in her family, where any disagreement her with parents was equated with separation, with her being a terrible, ungrateful person, and with no possibility of talking through feelings and having one's feelings and needs accepted.

In her treatment here, she had been able to take risks in the two relationships, her therapy, and with her boyfriend, where she felt safest, but she had not yet worked out her difficulties in setting boundaries with her peers for fear of not being liked. Nor had she worked out her fear of staff, as authority figures who she imagined would insist on compliance, without the possibility of a conversation or a negotiation. Thus vis-à-vis the larger world, she could still get stuck in the first part of this sequence: anxiety about being rejected if she was a real person with needs, then blaming the other, and then avoiding.

Before discharging from the hospital, Ms. L. had to negotiate with her family about money issues. Her parents were angry that she had not yet been able to find a job. She reported that, in a three-hour telephone conversation with her parents, she had been direct with them. At one point her father got quite angry and she was able to say, "If you keep yelling at me, I'll hang up," and he stopped. At the end, they thanked her; it was a very different kind of exchange. They were able to agree that she had to get a job and earn money or he would not pay for her college in the fall. He also had agreed to pay for outpatient therapy. He seemed to have softened a little, perhaps because Ms. L. was still talking to him and still needed his support, and perhaps because he was deeply relieved that she was no longer suicidal and sensed that this treatment had helped and that she was better. She had accepted her side of the bargain, but still felt angry at her father for financially threatening her treatment, forcing her to step down, and to leave before she felt ready to do so.

As we processed her impending discharge, she was able to say that she had felt safe in the treatment setting and was frightened to leave it. She was able to say goodbye to the staff and to the patient community, but resented acknowledging the staff's importance to her. *She was still capable of feeling that to need others meant she was weak.* She had also not finished her work in the art department, having pulled away in recent months out of her anger at the Austen Riggs staff for not adopting her or not offering her free treatment. We talked again about her continued difficulty in grieving her losses and in accepting realistic limits. *We related this difficulty to her continuing sense of entitlement that she should be taken care of (one side of the polarity) and to her fears that she was undeserving of help, weak and not ready yet to leave (the other side of the polarity*). She wondered if she would always need therapy. I said that she was able to trust herself more now and was getting stronger and stronger and that as soon as the habit of self-awareness, examining her reactions and her life became dominant and habitual, she would not need it. She agreed that examining her life felt a lot better in the long run than denying and avoiding feelings.

She planned to remain in the area for the summer, and return to college in the fall, so that we could continue our work face-to-face together. She got a job in June as a waitress at a local restaurant, and took a course at the local community college. The job put her in touch with many different kinds of people, and she began to realize that the same approach by her to each customer produced many different results. A grouchy customer was simply grouchy, so it wasn't all about her or her fault. This was one more important step in developing her capacity to see the other accurately, and not through her own projections and fears. She continued to alternate between fearing she was returning to school too soon, versus feeling she was ready to go and maybe didn't need therapy once she left. We did another series of psychological tests to get an in-depth assessment of where she was. The testing indicated she was more open, but that she had not yet integrated her anger. Her IQ had taken a jump (which is not an unusual finding once the mind is freed up) and that she was no longer depressed or suicidal. As she left in September we agreed to two sessions a week, one by telephone, and one face-to-face when she came back weekly to see her boyfriend, who was still in treatment.

Reentry into school was a mixed experience. Socially she was very lonely and isolated; all her friends were gone, and she had not yet developed a new public persona. On the plus side, her approach to work had changed markedly! *She was no longer driven to be the best.* She worked efficiently, with little stress and got eight hours of sleep every night. She seemed both pleased and perplexed, saying, "it's just happening." *She was also less idealizing of her advisor, as she was now able to see some of his limitations*. The September 11 attack left her deeply shaken. It felt terrifying, e.g. it felt random, unfair, leaving people without any recourse, helpless, and terrified; all were elements of the abuse she had experienced at home. It took her weeks to calm down. A medical problem and having to wait for the results of a test felt like the dread of waiting for her father to come home, knowing she would get a beating.

When she went home for thanksgiving, her sister attacked her, angry that Ms. L. had treated her so badly when they were kids and now never called her. Ms. L. was both quite shaken by this and enraged at her sister, feeling undermined and deeply hurt. Once again, she had to face her own sadism, and again, she felt briefly suicidal, which we understood as an exaggerated reaction to her failures and not a serious threat. As she worked through this, she was more able to accept her limitations, and to take care of her needs, first by asking for an extension on a paper, and second by writing a conciliatory letter to her sister. Her letter enabled them to have a better visit together at Christmas. Both of these responses represented more evidence of her continuing recovery.

During the winter break, we had more face-to-face sessions, and Ms. L. cried when it was time to go back to school. This departure felt to her like a real "home-leaving," which was new to her. Over the course of the spring semester, several familiar themes recurred and were reworked in a deeper way. Her unbounded fear could be aroused by hearing coyotes on campus, fearing they would attack her in her room. This fear evoked vivid images of her father's crazed look, with the veins sticking out of his red, angry face. She could even imagine that his teeth were sharp. Making these links helped her calm down. She also began to recognize that she was repeating her family's pattern of taking out her fears and frustrations on her boyfriend by blaming him for things. She did not want to keep doing this, but described how she could get disconnected from her hurt and distress and then become very judgmental and angry at her boyfriend. Recognizing this disconnection in herself, helped her begin to understand more deeply how this had happened with her parents. She then asked a very important question: "If I repeat this, is it my fault or theirs?" I said, given what she now understood and had worked so hard on, that now it was indeed her responsibility not to disconnect and repeat her past. I added that the same responsibility holds for each of us. So, she needed to continue to be open to her grief and to bear what had happened to her. By staying connected to and working through her fears, distresses, and hurts, she was now beginning to understand that it was her parents' unwillingness to bear and grieve their losses that had led to their failure to take responsibility for their own suffering, which in turn had led them to feel entitled to emotionally and physically abuse their children.

The other major theme involved her fears about believing in herself and her capabilities. She was getting pressure from her professor about applying to graduate schools, but she didn't feel ready. She began to question what she was supposed to be doing with her life, and again pulled for me to be more than just her therapist. *She could not yet really believe that things could be OK for her.* She still feared what others thought of her, and wanted them to think she was terrific. We had a very moving session in which I said to her that the worst had already happened in her life, but the threat of attack still lived in her imagination. Could she now believe that the abuse and the need to deny her reality and goals in order to take care of her parents were really over? She began to cry and say it was such a relief to think about that; *it felt weird to make her own decisions and to take up her own life without feeling guilty. She said she could only do it sometimes*. She also said this session had really affected her and that she felt relieved and happy.

In the summer, we had more face-to-face sessions. She had one more semester to complete, and planned to work on her thesis. As she struggled with her guilt around separating from her family, it now took the form of whether or not she could have separate feelings from her boyfriend, for instance could she feel happy if he was depressed. She began to get in touch again with her rage at her parents. Her mother was so depressed and Ms. L. never understood why. She reported revenge dreams in which she told her mother all the ways that her mother had hurt her. She now felt, "How could she have done that!" She recognized all the things she wanted to change before she would have any children of her own. She also became enraged with her father, remembering how she would say, "I'm sorry, I'm sorry, I'm sorry," when she was being beaten, hoping he would stop. And as she reported this, she said, "I'm getting so angry, I can hardly speak!" *She could finally feel that she didn't deserve either her mother's neglect or her father's beatings*, and that sometimes she knew she was not going to take it any more! Yet she could acknowledge that she did not always feel justified in her own anger, feeling that she sometimes overreacted, and was still taking things out on her boyfriend. She still did not feel free in her head, and could not yet say that she loved her life.

Near the end of the summer she had an important telephone conversation with her mother. She told her mother how angry she was at her for setting up the beatings, and that she didn't want apologies, but only that they could speak honestly with each other. She told her mother how she still lived with the consequences of those beatings every day, e.g. her fear of making mistakes and apologizing for everything. Her mother was able to listen and to acknowledge that she had *never* thought about the consequences. The mother's validation of Ms. L.'s reality enabled Ms. L. to feel that *maybe now she could bring the two realities together.*

Ms. L.'s last semester of college soon became fraught with intense anxiety about what to do after college. This anxiety was manifested in several ways: wanting me to be her mentor, wanting her father's advice, and worrying what kind of parent she would be and if her fears would create anxieties in her kids. Throughout these months she continued to work steadily on her thesis, which was a new and positive experience for her. It seemed that her intellectual capacities had truly been liberated and that she could now work freely. Her parents continued to take no interest in her work.

Each new transition increased her anxiety markedly. As graduation neared, she was stressed, afraid, and unable to decide what to do. She again alternated between wanting to take care of her parents, and then feeling rage about the events of her childhood. Her father lost his job, and she was briefly pulled back into believing that she had the power to help him. When I challenged her on this, *she said she wanted to have that power. She felt she was owed a debt, and was finding it hard to let go of that.* She did regain her perspective about helping her parents, who were now pouting about her plans to move farther away. But when she moved in January, *she again resisted getting a job, struggling for five months with accepting the need to support herself.*

The intensity of her anxiety about being on her own had re-evoked her old pattern of blaming and avoiding, and feeling entitled to be taken care of. She did not want a job. She had done so much already and felt her parents owed her a living for graduating, thus she was enraged at the unfairness that she should now have to support herself. She still didn't feel like an adult. She had very little confidence that anyone would want to hire her. As we processed all of these anxieties again, she managed to send out her resume. In the end she found a very good job in her field, and felt excited to be working. Her father belittled the amount of money she was being paid. At Thanksgiving her sister and parents came to visit her. Her father acted badly by isolating himself and pouting much of the time, but she did not let it get to her. *By this time she reported that she felt relatively happy and we ended our work together.*

Two years later, she called and I learned that she had applied to graduate schools, and had got into one of the top programs on the East coast. Each step had been briefly filled with anxiety, as it was her entry into a new social setting. She and her boyfriend were still together and doing very well. She had chosen a female advisor to work with, and was again experiencing her old fear of authority figures, namely, if she tried to get her needs met, she would lose this woman's support. But she was also excited about the research project she had taken on, and was putting in long hours, willingly, without complaint. She seemed to have got past her earlier sense of entitlement, and had made what sounded like a mature commitment to her chosen career, and even spoke about marriage, perhaps a few years from now. She felt she still needed more therapy and support, and had located someone connected with the university's student health department. She was now asking me for reassurance that this need was not weakness or a failure on her part. I encouraged her to get whatever help she needed now, and offered to send this new therapist information about our work together, which she readily agreed to. Several years later, at a chance meeting, I learned from this therapist, that Ms. L. had become financially and to a large extent emotionally free of her parents, and was trying to help her siblings do the same.

Concluding discussion

I have used the case of Ms. L. to demonstrate what I believe to be the affective dynamics involved in the repetition compulsion. This clearly represents a rejection of the death instinct as a viable explanation. Ms. L. was not endlessly driven by a self-destructive motivation. Rather this case represents a *complete acceptance of affect dynamics as the primary factors operating in all psychic illness*. In this case the primary affect was disgust, which in Tomkins' system is the affect that powers the decontamination script. This script, as a conjunction of greed and cowardice, involves a maximizing–minimizing script, which compels the person to engage in repeated cycles of enchantment–disenchantment, namely being seduced to take in something that seemed to be wonderful but turned out to be rotten. As was stated earlier, two opposite extremes cannot be achieved. It is a seduction into believing that the prize can be achieved and that failure can be escaped – "a game that must be played." Ms. L.'s parents hogged all the goodness and projected all the badness onto their ungrateful children. But they had seduced their eldest daughter into a special role, after the mother's collapse, demanding her loyalty to the myth that nothing had untoward had happened. Ms. L. must have been a lively, appealing, and gifted child, an easy target for parental projections of their goodness. This was a heady, confusing place for a young girl to be in.

There was an unconscious, unspoken bargain on both sides. On the parental side: "You take care of us, covering up our weaknesses, anxieties, and abuse, so we never have to suffer, and pretend this is normal, and we will pay for your private schooling and other material needs." On her side:

> I will deny your weaknesses, anxieties and your misuse and abuse of me, and the legitimacy of my emotional needs and my rage at you in exchange for your love and money, so that I can go to good schools, and maybe the chance to win the big prize, namely marrying dad.

Ms. L.'s intense oedipal struggle was evoked by the mother's collapse and then having been put into an adult role. But I want to make clear that an intense oedipal fantasy is not a necessary condition for the formation of a decontamination script, or for the dynamics of a repetition compulsion.

Such an unconscious and unspoken bargain was doomed to fail, because it had all the dynamics of a decontamination script, with its maximizing–minimizing strategy, which compelled Ms. L. to engage in endless repetitions between the two poles of being the "chosen one" or "the worst loser." Caught in such a polarized world, she could never learn that her dependency needs and feelings of distress and anger were normal and that with loving support they could be endured and valued.

The case material detailed Ms. L.'s several repeating cycles of being shocked and then owning her experience and then slipping back into the bargain of being special. She was shocked and disgusted by her father's "sleazy" behavior, later shocked by his vengeance; then shocked at her sister's anger at her, and how her sister had figured out things she had not been able to; then shocked by her own sadism, and her disgust and murderous rage at her mother's dysfunction, and disgusted by her cowardice in being unable to take a stand with peers and authority figures, always needing to please them. Each of these cycles challenged her capacity to hang onto the idealization of being the best and the chosen one in the family, and each challenged her capacity to bear her suffering and to not feel disgusted by her buried dependency needs, her grief about her childhood, and her anger, all of which could cause her to feel weak and that she was getting worse, and thus would lead to a plunge into suicidal thoughts.

The oedipal trap she was caught in seemed to involve her most grandiose fantasies and desires and led us through many repetitions, variations, and deep worries, and to another version of the dilemma inherent in this script, namely: "*can I be real and still be loved.*" This fear could be activated by authority figures and peers, as well as by her relationship with her long-term boyfriend. She was engaged in a deep struggle to believe in this new love, and that *she really could be loved for the person she was and trust in his loyalty and in her own experiences with him.* Her father had jilted her (I must be unworthy in some way). "Maybe my father did not choose me because I had never approached him sexually (perhaps I really am irresistible). Will my boyfriend be vulnerable to such approaches?" *These were deep worries about her self-worth as human being that she had to overcome.*

She also needed to work through her idealizations of me; maybe I would adopt her and meet all of her needs. But as her courage slowly began to grow, she was able to express her rage at me for not protecting her from her father's vengeance or not being able to change his mind, and for not being corruptible and for making sense; she needed to unleash all her rage at me, knowing I would not retaliate, and because she could not rage at her family. The other issue that involved several repetitions had to do with earning money and supporting herself. Each step towards autonomy evoked deep worries about her worth, and she reverted back to her entitlement about feeing she was owed something. At those times, it felt like a betrayal of the *unspoken bargain* she had made (see above). She really did not want to work and felt she should not have to work. This issue was also tangled up in a negative identification with her mother, who had adopted such an entitled stance. It was an important step toward independence for her to realize that she could not just sit around doing nothing, which meant that she was really not like her mother, a belief that enabled her, finally, to have an honest conversation with her mother. With each working through of these repetitions she moved a little closer to accepting limits and reality, which included slowly giving up both the grandiose fantasies of being the "chosen one," as well as being the "worst loser," and most cowardly one.

The final step seemed to involve a genuine acceptance of taking responsibility for her actions, namely, that she would indeed be responsible if she repeated the things her parents had done. She was deeply relieved by the thought that the worst was over. This acceptance of her responsibility seemed to help her to slowly find the strength and courage to grieve her losses and to accept the reality of her family's and her own limitations, and to believe that being able to suffer really did represent strength and progress. She was moving into a mature limitation-remediation script, which included being able to enjoy her life and to work well, without the burden of having to be the best. She was able to say near the end that it felt so much better to be aware and examine one's life.

The last time I heard any news of her, I learned that as each child pulled away and became more autonomous, their parents became more and more isolated, depressed, and uncommunicative, even with each other. They could take no joy in their children's successes, and instead nursed their own hurt at being abandoned, and were still unable to master the pain of separations. Ms. L. had been the most seduced by the family myth of the three children; she had needed and received the most intensive treatment, and perhaps, thereby, achieved the most enlightened, psychological separation from these parents. Her two siblings have had the benefits of some treatment, but have also had more trouble in expressing their needs directly, rather than through explosive rage, and thus are perhaps more at risk for repeating the abuse they received.

I believe that Ms. L. was able to use this treatment as well as she did because she seemed to have had the benefit of a good enough beginning in her early life, perhaps before the birth of her brother, and before her mother's later collapse. Thus I believe she began with a favorable ratio of positive affect over negative affect. Although initially she had moved to an anti-toxic script and felt suicidal, and at times voiced such a wish, after I confronted her early on, and asked about her commitment to our work, it was not a major theme. Given the extent of the neglect and beatings in this family, I was also surprised that my early intervention of strengthening the bond between the siblings led to such a quick change in their behavior toward their parents and an acknowledgment of the two realities in the family. Again, this suggests that all three siblings had had a good enough beginning. She alone had been seduced by her special role in the family, but she could now also share these negative experiences with her siblings, which enabled her to slowly deepen her bonds with them.

Perhaps this good early beginning also enabled her to relatively quickly feel safe and to trust in me and in the therapy. These factors seemed to indicate that she was just waiting for someone to understand her and to take her seriously. She was lost, and needed help to get in touch with her deeper needs, and to bear the pain of her problems, but she did not seem to have built up powerful defenses, except in dealing with her anger, which only slowly emerged. She was aware of and could be open and articulate at times in framing her struggles, e.g. she knew that she was hiding behind a mask, even to herself. Some issues opened up quickly after family sessions, during which the social worker and I were witnesses to her parents' refusals to accept how the family really worked. Once these issues opened up, she was very forthcoming with her fantasies, fears, and her not wanting to let go of her special role, and willing to sort through them and understand them.

She was most vulnerable and scared when she began to feel her very small, beleaguered self emerge, a self that was fragile and needed nurturing, but a self that was there, and had survived it all. I believe this hidden self was another indication of a good enough beginning, resulting in an early favorable balance of positive affects over negative ones. Her primary struggle, which was repeated many times, seemed to be to give up her idealization of her father and her special role in the family, and to join her siblings in their legitimate anger at their parents. This special role made it very hard for her to put the image of the idealized father together with the angry, retaliating father. Given her special role, she had more to grieve than did her siblings, and in the end she was able to grieve her childhood more deeply, to work through her anger at both parents more thoroughly, and to achieve a greater separation from the family patterns and to slowly embrace an acceptance of adult responsibility that, so far, neither of her two siblings appear to have done.

Chapter 8

Trauma and the anti-toxic script

This chapter begins with a definition of trauma and the anti-toxic script. That is followed by a brief discussion of the distinction between the defensive results of trauma that occurs in childhood versus the aftermath of adult-onset trauma. I will then describe the formation of an anti-toxic script in childhood based on the data from the Denver–Boston longitudinal study, and trace the ongoing development of this script through the life course of this individual into his mid-thirties. I chose this case because the adult outcome contained many surprises that were difficult to understand. The psychic organization of this person was then clarified by a deeper understanding of Tomkins' scripting process.

The definition of trauma and the anti-toxic script

I have argued that the two most biologically based essentials in life are the ability to make sense of one's world, leading to psychic coherence, and the ability to be an effective agent in shaping events in one's world. Starting from that premise, I define trauma as an event that is experienced as a major violation of the way the world should be, a betrayal of one's basic trust in one's own and in the community's sacred belief in what is right and wrong. Therefore it is an experience beyond one's capacity to comprehend; at the same time, it renders one completely helpless. It thereby constitutes an attack on both of these two basic essentials of life, and as Bentolila (1996) reminds us, such an event makes it impossible to return to a prior state of innocence; life can never be the same afterwards. Such an event overwhelms the psyche's ability to function, undermining coherence and agency, thereby evoking the toxic affective states of terror and rage, and creating the urgent need to develop the strategies involved in an anti-toxic script.

In Chapter 6, I described the function of an anti-toxic script, as designed to protect the psyche from re-experiencing the terror, helplessness, and incoherent confusion of a trauma. My description was based on my clinical experience of working with patients who had experienced childhood traumas, which had resulted in vertical splits in their psyches. This kind of trauma work is familiar to many clinicians, and involves working through the trauma within the safety of the therapeutic relationship, so as to split off part of the psyche into awareness and begin a healing process. Rather than present a therapy case, in this chapter I will describe the formation of an anti-toxic script based on one of the longitudinal cases for which there is detailed childhood data as well as follow-up data in adulthood in order to demonstrate the formation of such a script.

But first, I would like to go back to the important insights that Ghislaine Boulanger (2007) offers from her work with patients who have experienced adult-onset trauma that I discussed in Chapter 6, to remind the reader of the different implications for treatment in adult-onset cases. My definition of trauma as violating our two most essential needs would still apply, but adult-onset trauma, as Boulanger (2007) describes in her book represents trauma at a much greater magnitude, resulting in a massive assault on an already formed adult psyche, producing symptoms that may represent a much more extreme version of an anti-toxic script, in that one is dealing with a collapsed self. She states that

> rigorous attention to the patient's experience must take precedence over any preexisting theory of mind. Invoking early conflict, developmental arrests or childhood trauma as an explanation for the alienation of adult-onset trauma is tantamount to *blaming the victim*, which is a political position. It should not be a psychoanalytic one.
>
> (p. 180, italics mine)

Boulanger's descriptions of the consequences of such massive trauma occurring in adulthood include the *ongoing suffering* of the survivors that occurs in nightmares and flashbacks that continue to overwhelm the psyche, as if they continue to be frozen in that catastrophic moment. They also experience a deep sense of forever being outside the normal world of others, which includes a despair of ever being able to communicate their experience, for fear of traumatizing others, an experience that continues to feel overwhelming and to be too close to their awareness.

These descriptions of the survivor's suffering from adult-onset trauma indicate the enormity of the assault on the adult psyche, and the multiple, complex effects of such near-death experiences. The defense of splitting off such experiences (as is possible in childhood trauma, when the psyche is not fully formed and can be protected from the threat) seems wholly inadequate in the face of such life-threatening, annihilating trauma. Tomkins' description of the anti-toxic script, therefore, is probably most applicable to cases of childhood trauma, in which the splitting defense is more effective, although some aspects of this script, namely the terror, may still be applicable to catastrophic trauma in adulthood.

What follows, then, is a description of the formation of an anti-toxic script drawn from the longitudinal study mentioned above. This case contains many details of the child's early life, which include home visits, clinic visits, as well as projective testing at various times in childhood and two contacts in adulthood that include interviews and projective testing spaced ten years apart. As clinicians, we do not usually have such complete early data on our patients. Although this individual never became a psychiatric patient, his detailed history provides a unique opportunity to increase our understanding of how this child organized his psyche over time in a less than optimal environment, which resulted in the development of an anti-toxic script, and how it continued to affect his adult experience.

Longitudinal case material

Let me begin by introducing the parents, who we will call Mr. and Mrs. X, and their son, who we will call Eric. At the time of their marriage, Mrs. X is 27, and Mr. X is 44 years old. They both come from somewhat troubled families, with delinquent or disturbed members, and both had engaged in the past in brief phases of delinquency themselves. At the time of their meeting they share, at the very least, a struggle to control their weight and their consumption of alcohol, and a wish to change their life situation – for the mother a chance to escape an intolerable family situation, and for the father a chance to settle down and start a family. They had known each other only a few weeks before getting married; it is her first marriage, and his second, perhaps third marriage. Mrs. X becomes pregnant almost immediately.

During this pregnancy Mr. and Mrs. X become a part of the Boston–Denver Longitudinal Study, which includes an intensive psychological evaluation of Mrs. X. She is experienced by the interviewers and testers as highly anxious, which she expresses through somatic complaints, with confused, fragmented, and concrete thinking, lacking a core identity, but as benign, emotionally warm, but also labile, drifting sort of hopelessly, seeking some kind of safety and protection, with an insatiable need for approval and contact. She has an IQ of 70–80, and tests as more undeveloped than pathological. She experiences herself as stupid or "nuts" and worries that others will see her as crazy. The fathers in this study were not tested, but from interviews this father appears to be well organized, enjoys taking charge, cooks for his wife, is intelligent, with only an eighth-grade education, is hard-working, and has bronchitis. He comes from a background of extreme poverty that included a stern upbringing, and hopes to provide more opportunities for his children than he experienced. After several years in the marines, he got training as a master mechanic, and works nights. He has a temper, yells, threatens violence, and perhaps becomes violent on occasion, then feels guilty and tries to placate.

Mrs. X both idealizes his bigness and smartness and fears his anger, yet provokes him by engaging in activities that are objectionable to him. During the last few months of the pregnancy the couple moved in with Mrs. X's family in order to save money. There is much tension in the household. They will move to an apartment downstairs when the baby is born. The pregnancy and birth are uncomplicated; the baby, a boy, weighs 7 lbs. 15 oz. and is named after the father. The infant is described as having a good healthy constitution, an easy baby temperamentally, appears to have a well-organized nervous system, is easily comforted, and active. Early on he shows a preference for gross motor activity and throughout the first year is more advanced in this area than in others.

Observational data of parental behaviors

The mother's parenting style becomes evident early and is full of contradictions, alternating between anxious hovering and ignoring the baby, between intrusive, provoking, teasing, angry behaviors versus others that are warm, affectionate, and comforting. She is disorganized, indecisive, intolerant of being alone, and unable to get beyond her own impulses, feelings, and fantasies in order to perceive the baby as a distinct separate being. Thus she often misreads his cues, unable to think through a series of behaviors, e.g. she wakes him from a sound sleep for a bath, feeds him when he is not hungry, teases him with the bottle when he is hungry, taps and pokes him when he is calm, causing him to cry, alternates between picking him up and holding him at the slightest whimper, and propping him up for hours at a time, ignoring his cries. She complains that he cries too much, which makes her mad, and, at the same time, says she can't let him cry and holds him constantly. By the time he is 3 months old she is yelling at and slapping him for drooling and crying; a month later she says he has a temper and is fresh. By 5 months she has disrupted his sleep – interfering with his capacity to fall asleep on his own by rocking him to sleep and she takes him to bed with her every night. This inconsistency and disorganization is characteristic of her style throughout Eric's childhood.

The father's parenting style offers a variety of contrasts as well as challenges for Eric. He is more stable, consistent, patient, and responds to Eric's cues with less projection and anxiety. He is proud of his son, enjoys interacting with him, and is invested in teaching him not to be afraid, by using primarily counter-phobic techniques, which are not empathically attuned. He is strict, tolerating no disobedience and is prone to deliver angry, harsh punishments, which are far more effective than the mother's. He feels he is the better parent and criticizes his wife for spoiling and giving in too much, for hitting the child too much, without effect, and for neglecting the child. In the early months, he is a tender, responsive playmate. At around 7 months, when Eric is pulling himself up to stand, and the mother says Eric is afraid of falling, the father takes pride in teaching his son not to be afraid by unhooking his hands from the side of the playpen and pushing him down. The father's style is consistent throughout Eric's childhood. During the first several years, the father is unhappy with the sleeping arrangement that the mother has created, and periodically he forcefully intervenes by insisting that the baby stay in the crib and cry it out, an instance that includes yelling at and spanking the baby or shutting the door and letting the baby cry for hours. This tactic may succeed for a night or two, but the mother always manages to undermine his efforts and get the baby back in bed with her. The father sleeps in a single bed apart from his wife during much of Eric's early life.

How does Eric experience this family?

Let us switch now to Eric, and ask how he manages to organize his psychic life around these two parents. In early infancy he has to make all of the adjustments to his mother – to her intrusions into his efforts to regulate his sleeping, his eating, his states of quiet interest, with her poorly timed, inconsistent, and over stimulating behaviors. At such times he is clearly in a reactive position. He seems to manage fairly well, given his hardy constitution and well-organized nervous system, although he is often described as somewhat tense and irritable. So far, perhaps, her behaviors are just within his capacities to endure without long bouts of crying. He also has to adapt to long periods of being propped up in his crib, without toys, and being ignored. Again, he seems to endure this, and may even profit from being alone, free of his mother's intrusive disruptions, but on occasion he does cry after a while.

Up until around 8 months of age he appears to the longitudinal staff to be developing very well. He is described as smiling, friendly, and quite appealing, manifesting a normal engaging sociability; he can invest interest in his toys, and he is motorically advanced. Several members of the staff have observed his mother's rough and intrusive behaviors, but he is observed to respond with pleasure and excitement. The father has a more modulated, responsive style of interacting with Eric. Thus perhaps the combination of Eric's natural endowments and the father's inputs were enough at this developmental level to override the mother's behaviors. It would seem that for the first seven or eight months of Eric's life, then, that the mother's inconsistent caregiving is not negatively affecting her son's developmental progress. The only area she has disturbed is his own regulation of his sleeping. He cannot fall asleep on his own and if left alone to do so, he cries for hours. Leaving an infant alone to cry "for hours" undermines the infant psyche's capacity to maintain a cohesive state, which may evoke terror. It is not clear how often Eric is left in this state.

Things change at around 8 months

At around 8 months this developmental picture begins to change. As Eric begins to become more active, to develop more initiative, and to become more interested in the world at large, the parents' limitations become more glaring. Near the end of Chapter 2, I briefly described Sander's epigenetic series of developmental issues that needed to be re-negotiated at each level. Eric has now entered the stage of initiative and his behaviors are now more intentional and goal directed, presenting new challenges for his parents. The mother responds to his growing mobility by keeping him in the playpen for hours at a time, without toys, and when he is out of the playpen, she cannot control his behavior. She teases, scolds, yells, and hits, and Eric gradually develops the capacity to ignore her and to pursue his activities. He begins to turn more to his father, greets him with excitement and pleasure when his father comes home, wants to be with him, and cries when he leaves. His father is responsive to Eric. His parents argue about how to discipline him – whether to hit him on the hands or on the bottom. Eric resists his mother's efforts to feed him, but responds when his father feeds him. During this same period, the father again insists that Eric sleep in the crib, and, on one occasion, is described as throwing Eric in the crib, and then feeling so bad about it that the next day, he bought him a new toy. Also, soon after this there is an episode where the father spanks Eric for crawling behind the stove, and Eric stays behind the stove and screams in protest. Perhaps Eric's protest expresses some angry, hurt feelings of a betrayal of trust vis-à-vis his father. From this period on there is a gradual emergence of several trends that continue for the next year or so.

Eric's development begins to take on less favorable aspects. His mother complains that she cannot control him and says how bad he is, but oscillates between yelling at and hitting him and giving him whatever he wants. She believes he is smarter than she is and that she has little to teach him and thus she expects him to learn from his own experience – she leaves him alone for several hours, in the playpen, or tied up outside. In the afternoons they watch TV together, or he pesters her. The father continues to criticize his wife for her neglect of Eric. He intermittently intervenes, buying toys and books, teaching his son not to fear heights by putting him up high on a ladder and leaving him there to climb down on his own, and sometimes he intervenes with a stern punishment.

Eric is left alone to depend on his own resources to entertain himself for several hours at a time. With no one around to participate in his activities and to help him sustain and elaborate on his interests, there is a gradual decline in his investment in his toys, and a greater reliance on gross motor activity. From 15 months on he manifests a short attention span, which becomes characteristic of him. He runs, climbs, gets into everything, but stays with nothing. He also puts many things into his mouth and is eating dirt, sticks, plaster, and drinking from rusty cans. When Eric is about 19 months old, the family moves to the country and buy a dog, which the mother ties up outside because she hates dogs. Eric now spends a lot of unsupervised time outside in the yard with the puppy, relatively unprotected from a variety of dangers. He wanders off in the woods and gets lost; he wanders into a hole filled with water up to his neck, before his mother finds him and his parents finally drain the hole, and he receives a number of cuts, scrapes, and bruises from falling off the roof of the car, off the rock fence, etc. How is Eric experiencing these events? The mother is always afraid of the father's angry reactions to these mishaps. We learn many years later that he beat her for her neglect of the child, and as revenge, she withheld sex from him by keeping Eric in bed with her.

As Eric becomes more invested in his own plans and more self-assertive, he develops elaborate ways of resisting, ignoring, provoking, and defying his mother. These behaviors slowly evolve into a more generalized non-compliant stance, which is observed at the clinic during several consecutive testings. By 16 months of age he seems determined to set himself against his parents. They are using a leather strap to discipline him and they report that he does not cry when they hit him. With some pride they call him a "tough nut." But we must ask how Eric is experiencing this pain – is he suppressing all his feelings of pain, fear, anger, while being hit so as not to give them any satisfaction? Is this an angry struggle for the survival of his psychic self, so that to cry would be to sacrifice his self in some way? If so, it speaks to an impressive capacity to withstand, endure, and survive, even if only in opposition and without a clear sense of a positive goal. When the father was asked twenty-five years later how he would characterize his son, he said, without hesitation, "persistent." Perhaps his impression dates from this early stubborn stance by his young son. It must be remembered that these beatings are occurring during the same period when Eric is happily sleeping with his mother every night, times that the mother describes as full of kissing and hugging. How is Eric putting his daytime defiance together with his nighttime affectionate embrace of his mother?

Data from the play sessions at the clinic

Near the end of Eric's second year and the beginning of his third, the longitudinal study had him come in for a series of play sessions, which was standard procedure for all of the families in the study. Over the course of these sessions Eric seemed restrained and controlled. He went from toy to toy, spending a few minutes with each, but never developing fantasy themes or play; indeed he did not seem to know how to play. He accepted limits easily, but did not develop a relationship with the staff person. He spent most of the time feeling surfaces, textures of objects, filling and emptying crayons and beads, and showed some interest in sucking the baby bottle. The mother then called him a sissy, saying she had removed the bottle several months before. He left the room easily with the play person to go get milk and cookies, which surprised the mother, who claimed that he won't leave her side at home. He became engrossed in pouring the milk from cup to cup, spilling it all over the table and floor, and he wanted the cookies all for himself.

The staff were surprised by and impressed with Eric's control, although they had observed him at home to go off and sit quietly looking at books. In the final session, Eric asked the play person several times if something was okay or alright? The father had been home recently, because of a strike at work and the research staff wondered if Eric was beginning to get more structure and control over his impulses vis-à-vis his father, something they felt he never gets from his mother. They also noted that Eric held onto objects tenaciously, perhaps the result of the mother's intrusiveness, and that he could not seem to let himself be aware of the prospect of milk and cookies, but when they arrived he smiled with eager anticipation, again enjoyed pouring and spilling, but then put everything away before it was required to do so. Is this a way of protecting himself against the interruption of others, by controlling the beginning and ending of activities, or does it represent an effort to modulate his hopes, excitement, and enjoyment in order to protect himself from the sudden deflation of such states? Is his spilling the milk a way to explore something he could never get away with at home, or testing the limits at the clinic, or is it a defiant spoiling of a good thing?

There is a break in our data at this point. In the last interview with the mother, she is full of worry about Eric, and about the criticism of relatives on both sides, who are predicting big trouble in the future because Eric is so wild and uncontrolled; others in the family who acted like this when young ended badly. There are easily available negative identities that continually haunt this family, and the mother doesn't know what to believe. If we try to project Eric's future development from this point in time (as we did try to do in this longitudinal study), the prognosis is not very hopeful. Fantasy play is not available to him; he is restricting his interests to short explorations, and he is restricting his affects, e.g. he is unable to anticipate positive events; thus his inner life seems somewhat impoverished. He is not focused on interpersonal relationships and relies heavily on gross motor activity. He remains unprotected and unsupervised, and is isolated from peers most mornings, at other times he has to deal with his disorganized, vacillating mother and his more structured but also more frightening father, with negative family identities more available than positive ones. The defenses and inhibitions that seem to be developing are all aspects of an anti-toxic script.

On the other side of the ledger, Eric seems to manifest some strength. He has the ability to resist and oppose his mother, at least during the daytime, although she does hit him, when she can catches him. He can differentiate situations and people, and respond with more control in the presence of an attentive other, e.g. the play person at the clinic and at times his father. He watches TV, which might be a source of learning he cannot get from his mother. Finally, there may be some strength in his capacity simply to survive; the research staff felt there was some irrepressible quality in him and that somehow he would find a way. Is he in a holding pattern then, just waiting for more promising circumstances? Or is he gradually shutting down and closing off avenues for future growth?

Three-yearly assessments

Ordinarily, as with other families in this study, this family would not have been seen again until Eric entered the first grade, but perhaps because the research staff was concerned about this child, this family was contacted yearly between the ages of 3½, and 6½ when Eric finally entered school.

A year later, when Eric is 3½, the mother's complaints are the same. Eric is so wild she cannot control him; he doesn't stay interested in anything and breaks all his toys; she gets so angry she hits him all the time; he's so smart he talks in complete sentences; he's got lost in the woods again and in the streets of Boston during a visit with relatives. During his visit to the clinic, Eric dives into the toys in a greedy way and would have made a mess of the whole room if he had had the time. When it was time to leave, he nearly threw a tantrum and ran away from his mother, who was trying to drag him off. But there are some new elements. The mother is now pregnant again and she teases Eric that he will have to share all his toys with the new baby. The father decided, at some point, that since Eric can't sleep alone, he should sleep with his father. So now Eric plays outside most of the day, has no nap, falls asleep in front of the TV, is put to bed, then when the father comes home at midnight, Eric wakes up, has a snack with his father, tells him about the day's events, including the things he got punished for, and then they go to bed together.

Eric now has a playmate, a little girl, who he calls his sweetheart; he kisses and hugs her a lot. He doesn't share his toys with his cousins. He has a stuffed bunny, which he takes to bed with him and talks to, when he thinks no one is listening, e.g. "I like you. Do you like me?" Eric is mean to animals, e.g. the chickens and a kitten that he pulled and threw. He has begun to threaten to hit his parents back when they hit him with the strap. His mother reports that she sneaks up on him, to catch him by surprise and lets him have it, otherwise he is not afraid of her and won't stop what he is doing. She tries to scare him with stories of the bogeyman to keep him out of the woods, and says he has two favorite books, *The Three Bears*, which he knows by heart, but she can't remember the name of the other one. Sometimes he tries to help her gather eggs, or with cooking, but she says he just gets in her way.

Soon after the new baby is born (another boy) a home visit is made to the family. It is a very distressing visit. The paternal grandfather is living with them and he and Eric do not get along at all, and he predicts disaster for Eric. The mother is yelling and going after Eric with the strap every two minutes. His speech is infantile. The mother reports that since the baby's birth, Eric won't go out and play. He sleeps in his own bed now. She says the baby is so wonderful, no trouble – whereas Eric has always been trouble. The visitor leaves wondering how Eric could not escape having a negative image of himself as a bad boy.

Almost a year later, when Eric is about 4½, the family is seen again. There is less tension in the family since the father had to put the paternal grandfather in a nursing home, after he hit Eric over the head with a beer can, but the old themes with the mother are still there. Eric is still uncontrolled; he has broken the windows in the tool shed and in the chicken coop, and hears several times a day how bad he is and how good his little brother is. The father has had an operation and is home recuperating. He talks quietly to Eric and explains things to him and Eric listens, and comes to his father. Eric's speech is slow, slurred, and somewhat infantile. The maternal grandmother is there for a brief visit and she seems warm and nurturing, adding a positive atmosphere.

A few months later, the mother and Eric come to the clinic for a series of play sessions, cognitive and projective testing, and an interview with the mother. We learn that the father continues to have an undiagnosed stomach problem, that the baby got quite sick with bronchitis, and that the mother was briefly hospitalized for a miscarriage. Eric, once again, separates easily from his mother; he is shy, with his head bowed and an averted gaze. He has an awkward walk and odd speech, with a high pitch, infantile voice and poor articulation, but he is easy to relate to, and cooperative, yet the staff feel that if he is not intimidated, he may become aggressive. On the Stanford Binet he scores a year ahead of his chronological age. He is uncomfortable with the projective test; he tries to avoid the images on the first three Rorschach cards by calling them maps and focusing on the spaces, seeing them as houses where boys and chickens live. He sees card 4 as a big gorilla with sharp teeth, and card 5 as a giant monster bird, like the monsters that come out at night (is he having nightmares?). At this point he says that he has monster cards at home, but they are only cards. "These pictures have bigger monsters and they scare me." He sees monsters on all the other cards. On the first card of the CAT he sees baby chickens spilling their food all over the floor and the mother hitting them, but after that he sees only monsters. Here we see clear evidence of the fear/terror Eric is experiencing; although displaced onto monsters, it is very close to the surface. Eric is unable initially to draw a person; he draws a duck instead. He then tries to draw a girl, saying, "I don't know how to draw a boy." In the second session he does draw a boy – an elongated stick figure with large hands and feet, suggesting a child who feels his enormity and frailty at the same time and the importance of experiential contact.

In the play sessions, he spends the most time with the dart gun, and the hammers and saws. He tries hard to hammer nails into a board; his fine motor coordination is not good, but he is patient and persistent and finally succeeds. He tries hard not to spill the milk and takes all the milk and cookies for himself, without a thought of sharing (so hungry). By the third session his high-pitched voice is gone and he seems more subdued and related. He finally gets into some fantasy play with the doll house, in which he puts various family members to bed and then covers them with objects as if to bury them; he even says, "he is dead" but then takes it back and says, "he is sleeping." He seems to have been aware of all the family illnesses and has been frightened by them.

Throughout these sessions, his expression is placid – no exuberance, very matter-of-fact. The staff felt that if he could come back for more play sessions he would be ready to begin to work on some of his struggles. He seemed to be trying to figure things out by using his imagination. He is seen as vulnerable, denying his worries about his father, frightened of his own aggression and the aggression of others, not always able to separate fantasy from reality, and a little concrete, e.g. will not use a cowboy hat on a fire truck in the play session. His self-concept seems shaky. The staff wonder if he is struggling with the difference between a baby and a little boy, given the mother's preference for dealing with him as a dependent baby; she still dresses him, tries to bind him to her; babies are good, boys are bad and uncontrollable.

About a year later, when Eric is 5½, there is a home visit. The father has had another operation, several infections, with draining still going on; he has four holes in his stomach. Eric is alone much of the day; his playmate is no longer available. His mother says that Eric minds pretty well now since her husband "finally did something about it," but the interviewer is unable to find out what the father did. In the interview data collected at the twenty-five-year follow-up, the father recounts "the only beating he ever gave to his son" as happening out in the yard, with some wire from the fence, because Eric had been letting the chickens out and breaking eggs. He imagined that his son probably still remembers that beating. It is likely this is what the mother was referring to. At any rate, Eric is now more disciplined and acts respectfully toward his father. He has four chicks of his own to take care of, and he helps collect the eggs that the family sells. The father feels that Eric is bright – he can already do some figures, and knows some letters, but expresses disappointment that Eric won't stay with anything for more than fifteen minutes, even though the father bought him "many kinds of things" for Christmas, e.g. building blocks, a blackboard, a paint set, and a magnetic set.

The interviewer noticed that Eric wrote letters on his blackboard from right to left, and when she explained that "we write in the other direction," he quickly did so, without errors. She assumed that clearly no one had bothered to explain, and that his parents seem to expect Eric to do it all on his own. We also learn that Eric can be quite malicious to his sibling, but he is afraid of his father, and so keeps his impulses under control, so at times the two boys "can play together okay." The younger child is now 2 years old, and the mother reports that he has a terrible temper, compared to Eric, who was "never like that." The interviewer finds Eric easy to talk to, charming, winning, and puckish, but still manifesting infantile speech and motor restlessness. She feels his mind is ready and he needs to start school, and have peer interaction, but given his date of birth, he has to wait another year. Arrangements are made for another clinic visit with play sessions and testing.

Eric seems shy and almost scared at the beginning of each play session, but relaxes fairly quickly, becoming talkative, almost entertaining, with speech and gestures designed to create a dramatic effect, although his speech is poorly articulated and hard to understand. He mentions his father's stomach problems several times, his brother's naughtiness, saying, "I think God put the devil in him," and says how hungry he is as he eagerly goes for the milk and cookies, recalling how he used to spill the milk. At one point he says his cookie wants to slip out of his hand to get milk all over the table. When the play person asks why, he says, "'cause he's crazy." He is concerned about putting things back after he uses them, about transgression and punishment, about alligators and bulls, and how they can hurt you. The cognitive testing shows him to have an IQ of 107, with an uneven performance; he is particularly low on information and shows poor social judgment for his age. Fatigue seemed to interfere with his performance on the block design, thus his IQ may be slightly higher.

The projective tests revealed that he is much more able to integrate fantasy, affect, and reality than a year ago. He sees gorillas on cards 1 and 4, vultures on cards 2 and 5, and sees stomachs on several cards (indicating an awareness of his father's problems), but produces well-integrated responses on the other cards, with a lot of movement responses, suggesting that he may feel most comfortable in active engagement with the environment. This is consistent with his earlier need to be in physical contact with surfaces. His responses to the CAT pictures reveal several attitudes toward his parents. The father is seen as strong and frightening, and at other times as old, weak, and someone who can be outwitted. The mother is seen as protection against monsters, but also as someone to be resisted. The boy wants to go with the father, but is also afraid of injury from the football, nails, etc. He draws well-articulated boy and girl figures; they are facing forward, smiling, and reaching out, but are floating at in angle in the air. He is still not quite grounded and safe, although things have changed since the previous year and he is better organized. He seems to be struggling with his ambivalent identifications toward both parents, and perhaps also with omnipotent fantasies and fears of injury and punishment.

Assessments before, during, and after the first grade

A year later, several months before Eric enters the first grade, another home visit and clinic visit are scheduled (an assessment, before, during, and after the first grade was done for all subjects in this longitudinal study). The picture is somewhat mixed. The father is still sick, with an unclear diagnosis, as his stomach continues to drain. He seems somewhat depressed, has been unable to work, and the family is struggling financially. Eric can settle down and work on two puzzles with the visitor for forty minutes, and impresses her with his ability to concentrate and work. We learn that Eric has wandered off again and was bought back by the police. We must ask what goes on inside of Eric when he wanders off and gets lost. Does he need to keep moving all the time?

At the clinic, during the play sessions, several interesting themes emerge. He continues to be concerned about putting things back, but now it is clearer (and reminiscent of his behavior several years earlier), that he *interrupts his pleasurable play* and starts putting things away before the play is really over. He shows the same interruption pattern with hand puppets, as if he cannot really let himself get into the fun of playing. Even when the play person now persists, and is able to evoke a few smiles, he does not sustain the play, and moves onto something else. Another striking theme is his explicit identification and alliance with his father. How his father bought him new clothes and his mother didn't know about it. How his father can drive and how he is going to go to college, and be a marine and a machinist like his dad. He also talks about his father's health problems, the pus that comes out of hole in his father's stomach, and about injury. Several times he looks at the window and says, "If I tipped out, I would get killed or hurt." He is very careful with his milk and cookies and does not want to share them with his brother.

His IQ is a little higher this year, at 115, but his speech is still not very clear. He is aware of his lack of school learning and worries about getting along with other kids. He appears somewhat solemn, even pedantic at times, and has a tendency to perceive reality and then veer off into fantasy that he represents as reality. On the Rorschach, he cannot maintain a separation between two images. On card 1 he sees the sides of a gorilla and the middle as a frog, calling it a gorilla frog. On card 8 he sees a skeleton and then a cliff, calling it a skeleton mountain, and on card 5 he sees a Martian and bird, calling it "a Martian monster bird." Some of his fantasies are openly destructive and frightening. On card 3 he sees a monster head, which the monkeys are fighting over and its going to break in two. On card 10 he describes someone stuck in a clam and a devilfish electrocutes the clam to open its mouth so the person can swim out. On card 4 he sees a giant with a big "pin club" (a club with pins in it) that clobbers people when they come to his castle in the sky. On the CAT, on cards with food there is a lot of spilling and misbehavior. These stories seem to involve anger at the mother. Eric aligns himself with the father against the mother, but is not really convinced that the two of them are a match for her. Parental roles are confused; he calls the figure on card 1 a mother rooster. His drawing of a boy has strange, ghost-like qualities, creating a wispy, nebulous effect, looking starved with an insubstantial quality. The arms and legs are sticks, with a wobbly, maimed quality to the right arm.

Although his fantasy life is very active and freely expressed, it is full of frightening images. His emotional expression is restricted. The tester feels he does not have much stamina under stress and tires easily. I would add that given his father's weak condition, Eric's terror is closer to the surface and perhaps can overwhelm him at times; thus he is struggling to hold himself together. So as he is about to enter the first grade, he appears to be on very shaky ground. He is holding onto his father for support in taking this next step, but is not at all sure he will make it.

All of these contacts beginning at age 3½, until Eric entered school, were not part of the regular protocol for the subjects of this longitudinal study, but as was stated earlier, the staff were concerned about Eric and his family. Upon entering the first grade, he now receives the same attention as all the other subjects. This entails the assessment before entering the first grade, being observed several times in school, interviewing his teacher, and more home visits and testing at the end of the school year. So, how does Eric manage this major transition?

Surprisingly he does well in school. He is shy at first, but gradually warms up to the teacher and begins to make friends, even though he is somewhat of a loner, keeping his head in his work rather than socializing. He is awkward and a little bigger than most of the children (and probably slightly older). He does well on his school work, concentrates on it, and works quickly, getting stars on most of his papers. He enjoys learning to read and moves up to the top reading group. He is not a trouble maker. The teacher is clearly invested in him, works hard on his shyness, and thinks he has come a long way, even laughing sometimes.

She worried when he missed several weeks of school, and when, at times he came in looking dirty and disheveled. From the home visits we learn that the father continues to be sick and was hospitalized again (perhaps this is when Eric missed days of school). We also learn that Eric loves school and his teacher, how hungry he seems for contact with the visitor, not wanting her to leave, showing her one thing after another that he has made at school. Some new families have moved into the area, so Eric now has playmates in the neighborhood. The mother is still critical of him; she expected trouble at school; this success will not last. Even during the last home visit, at the end of the school year, when Eric has received almost all As and is very proud of his school work, the mother and maternal grandmother continually undercut him with comments about how he hadn't got to the second grade yet and how they can't understand how he sits still in school, and are predicting a gloomy future.

In the final testing done that summer, Eric is much toned down; the vivid fantasies of a year ago seem to be contained. The giant's pin club used to clobber people now becomes a club with points on it. The Martian monster bird has become a bat. He still has a penchant for details on the Rorschach, but no longer tries to relate them to a larger image. He lets them stand on their own. On the CAT, on card 1 he now sees a mother chicken. He shows more open involvement with his brother, but still retains some sadistic fantasies towards him, and perhaps some jealousy of his brother's closeness to his mother, which he wants to disrupt, even it that involves punishment. Male figures are now less frightening and destructive. His drawing of a boy is much better – a secure definite figure, but drawn in profile. He says he has taken drawing lessons at school. His IQ is now at 123, with a steady performance, which lacked the pedantic answers of the previous year. His answers were to the point and reality oriented.

Our data end here until our subject is followed up in young adulthood. How would we project Eric into the future? He has consistently shown the capacity to make good use of supportive, responsive environments, e.g. the play sessions and school, although in both settings he has remained emotionally restricted and restrained. He is most free motorically and cognitively. He has profound ambivalence toward both parents, which seems unlikely to change, and has an easily available negative identity and no clear positive one. His terrifying fantasies have, for the moment, gone underground, and he continues to be somewhat cautious around peers, indicating the continuing presence of an anti-toxic script, which, nevertheless, has enabled him so far to concentrate on his work at school. His parents seem unable to consistently support his growth and development. The mother's lability, disorganization, and ambivalence are pervasive, and the father expects great things and threatens punishment, but is unable to supply the day-to-day interactive support his son needs.

Twenty-five-year follow-up

When the family is contacted again, roughly seventeen years later, their situation has not changed much. After a heart attack, the father has retired; the mother has been working in a factory. Both are somewhat depressed and dissatisfied with their lives. Their younger son has dropped out of high school, and has been in trouble with the law, once for assault and once for attempted rape. He uses pot and cocaine and lies to and steals from his parents. He has no regular job and is trying to succeed as a musician in a band. Given what we know of this family, such an outcome is not surprising. Indeed it is what our theories can make sense of. But what has become of our subject Eric, now 25 years old? Where is he? What has happened to him since the first grade?

The follow-up part of this longitudinal study involved locating the original subjects, who were now all 25 years old. It succeeded in finding and obtaining permission from twenty-eight of the original thirty subjects, who agreed to participate in several psychiatric interviews, conducted by a male investigator, as well as projective testing carried out by a female investigator.

At the time of the follow-up, Eric was working toward a doctorate degree in the sciences in one the top science programs in the country, having graduated from an Ivy League college with a 3.6 GPA. He has a regular girlfriend and expected to be engaged soon. How has he got there? What is he like as a person?

In the interviews, Eric describes how he was excited by school, although was bored by the repetition in the early grades. He loved reading and was a voracious reader by the fourth grade, taking a book out of the library after school and finishing it before dinner. He also spent a lot of time playing sports. What he does not say explicitly is that through his reading and his sports he effectively removed himself from the family scene. In the summers he did sports, played with friends in the woods, and climbed trees with fantasies of Tarzan. By high school, his life began to take on its adult shape. He really got into abstract thinking, chose science rather than the humanities, played football, and loved being both an athlete and a student.

He chose an Ivy League school over a football school, and worried about whether he could succeed academically. But he worked hard, did well, and played second string football, and intramural sports. He is excited by the challenges of new places, but is also anxious and needs some caretaking. *He had a dog with him all through college*. The person he remembers most warmly is his maternal grandmother, because she pampered him. He wants to appear friendly, *but is anxious in interpersonal situations*. He describes his achievements, his enjoyment of work, and his need for novelty, change, and activity. He loves working in the lab where he can bring action and thought together in the concrete task of making things work. He is not interested in theory or teaching; he prefers applied science. He plans to work as an applied engineer for a while and then get into the business aspects of it. He expects to move around a lot. He does not describe any individuals or relationships. He has clutched on tests all his life; blocked by anxiety – his thinking gets muddled, otherwise he can work well. He acknowledges some anger at his father, for the effect his heart attack had on the whole family, and his failure to take care of himself properly. He denies other negative feelings about his family, and denies his brother's difficulty. He sees his mother as long-suffering. His affect is present but not expressed.

On the TAT he shows a pattern of perceiving affect accurately and then distancing himself from it by denying its importance or its long-term consequences. Father figures are given grudging respect, and maternal figures evoke tension and discomfort. He prefers to keep his distance. He does not seem to know what his problem with his mother is; it remains unintegrated, unmastered, and unarticulated. On the Rorchach he gives only one whole response, and that is card 5, which he sees as a bat. His array of detailed responses contain several small details, references to space and shading and several with poor form. He is able to integrate color and movement responses into some of the detail responses. He has only one human response on card 3, but here he only describes one of the two figures; he does not see two figures in interaction, but he does see two bird heads squawking at each other on card 2. In testing the limits, he does not see two people in card 2, although he could imagine two bears. On card 4, when asked if it could be a monster, he initially says yes and points to all the parts, but then decides it really doesn't look like that to him. *He cannot put two people together.* He clearly is well defended against the monsters of his childhood, and although this defense does not look like mastery, the anti-toxic script works well enough for him. In the Cole Animal Test he would most like to be a bear "because they're free to do what they want and large enough so nothing else can hurt them, but peaceful. They only fight in self-defense and live an uncontroversial life style." He would least like to be a rat, "because they are shunned by people, preyed on by other animals, and don't have much control over their lives." Staying out of trouble, not being victimized, and being in control and free to do what you want are very important to him.

In summary, this outcome, while surprising in the degree of success he has achieved, is not surprising in other respects. He still needs change and novelty, and to be active. He has used available environments well, but he remains emotionally restricted. He has not resolved his ambivalence toward his family; he has just distanced himself from it. His test anxiety seems to contain some of his deeper fears. He does not know himself very well, nor is he comfortable in interpersonal situations. Yet, he has fashioned all of this into a uniquely adaptive mode of functioning, the success of which we could not have thought possible, and could not predict. There are several signs that the anti-toxic script is still present in his adult personality, evident in his emotional constriction, in his inability to see two people together, in his meager human responses on the Rorchach, and in his test anxiety. His response to card 16 in the TAT is relevant here. Card 16 is the blank card and its function in the context of the entire set of cards is to evoke the ideal scene – the scene the respondent most longs for. Here is Eric's response to the blank card:

> What it would feel like if you were lying under a sheet with the sheet pulled up over your head, a white sheet of course. And there

> are bright lights in the room. It's pretty relaxing. It's pretty much isolated from its surroundings.

At this point the tester asks what led up to this scene. Eric says, "Lying in bed, maybe feeling somewhat tense, kind of relaxing, like if you cover your head and face with a sheet." The tester asks how it will end. He says, "Probably fall asleep that way. Wake up the next morning and the sheet's gone. The picture would be different then." Hiding and finding peace is very important to him.

We need to ask why the anti-toxic script is still so dominant in his psyche. What has maintained it all these years? In Tomkins' model, which is consistent with dynamic systems theory, in order for trauma to be traumatizing in the long run, events must continue to feel traumatizing. In Tomkins' model, psychological experience has to continue to be magnified in the context of ongoing events. One's mini-theories and strategies have to continue to be tested and to fail, and be reworked and strengthened. We only have a few clues about the continuing sources of fear and anger in Eric's life. We know that new situations, interpersonal situations, and tests evoke anxiety in him. And we learn from an interview that Lou Sander completed, roughly ten years after the twenty-five-year follow-up, that throughout grammar school and high school his parents fought a lot, which made him anxious and tense. He recalled a fascinating detail, which resonates with his response to card 16 ten years earlier. He tells us that his bedroom was next to the kitchen, and in the mornings his parents would get up early to go to work, and he would often wake up to the sounds of their yelling and fighting. He can remember lying in bed feeling anxious and tense. This is clearly one source of continued anxiety. We also know that his younger brother was getting into a lot of trouble, which must have been another source of anxiety for the entire family.

Discussion and a consultation with Silvan Tomkins

Given that the anti-toxic script is still dominant for Eric, we are still left with the puzzle of how he has been so successful. This script usually crowds out the possibility of other scripts. What is so unusual in Eric's case is that in spite of the presence of an anti-toxic script, there is evidence of the development of other scripts, such as affluent scripts, namely his work is a source of positive affect for him, and earlier in his life, sports was also a source of positive affect. There were still several unanswered questions in my mind. How did Eric manage his nighttime affectionate exchanges with his mother and his resolute daytime defiance of her? Why didn't he transfer this defiance to his female teachers in school? Or to phrase it differently, what enabled Eric to make such good use of others? It was at this point that I decided to consult directly with Silvan Tomkins. Without giving him any other data, I sent him the child CAT and the adult TAT materials to work with. Tomkins had written a book on TAT analysis, and had explored TAT responses exhaustively in volume 3 of *Affect, Imagery, and Consciousness* (Tomkins, 1991). Given only the tests results I had sent him, he produced a formulation about Eric that was a remarkable fit with all the data we had collected. Only then, did I send him the case material I had written up on Eric and followed that up with a visit. We went over the projective material together for a second time, which did not essentially change his first formulation but did amend it slightly.

Tomkins' formulation

In Tomkins' analysis of the CAT and TAT material there was evidence for the following. Eric can receive positive affect from others, but he does not seek it nor does he initiate it. Thus he *did not* integrate his nighttime experiences with his mother; he seems to have accepted his mother's nighttime affections as *islands of positive experience*. He also found evidence of a limitation-remediation script. Eric differentiates between (1) transient distress; (2) more enduring distress, which is part of a limitation-remediation script; and (3) distress that leads to fear, which is part of an anti-toxic script. But he found *no evidence* of a damage-repair script, which is based on the affect shame, and entails the *desire to reestablish a valued positive relationship*. He does not try to repair damage; instead damage evokes distress and escape, again aspects of an anti-toxic script. His record is devoid of shame responses, suggesting the *absence of strong positive bonds with humans or attachments with humans*. Finally, there is evidence of a decontamination script, which attempts to purify deeply ambivalent scenes.

How has he managed to moderate the effect of his fears to enable these other scripts to develop? Both parents used fear in order to gain compliance from their son. And both parents were also the source of some positive affects for him. But in Tomkins' formulation, they presented very different challenges for Eric. Thus it is necessary to examine his relationship to each of them separately in order to understand how Eric organized his responses to cope with each parent. Let us begin with his mother.

Because his mother was relatively ineffective in her punishments, Eric was able to develop several responses to her attempts to intimidate him. This subdivision tends to modify the mother's toxicity, because each response limits the degree to which any of the responses can be magnified. First of all, he can escape from her. This limits his need to develop anticipatory strategies in order to avoid her. He can relax a little, and not tie up psychic resources, and let something begin to happen and then escape. Second, he can counteract his mother through teasing, resisting, and defying. *This limits the development of brooding fantasies of persecution and revenge typical of anti-toxic* scripts. Both his ability to escape and to fight back tended to *magnify action as a response to dense negative affect* (perhaps this is why Eric wandered off so often in his childhood). Third, when he cannot escape or counteract, he has to submit and endure her punishments. Then he suffers the effects of fear and anger and has to devote psychic effort to develop strategies of avoidance of such toxic experiences, as in an anti-toxic script.

The mother's disorganization and affective lability also set limits to her power as a source of fear and of love for Eric. However terrifying she could be at any moment, it would be over quickly. She did not hold grudges. And however warm and affectionate she could be at any moment that too would be over quickly. She did not sustain it. Often Eric did not have to do anything to receive either affection or punishment. Things happened for no rhyme or reason. She created what Tomkins called *plurivalent turbulence*. Eric did not know what to expect at any time from her; he was stimulated in too many different ways. *This led him to segregate his experiences with her. Taking each scene as it came, without trying to connect it to other scenes either before or after, reducing his ability to magnify the toxicity of his experience with her, for psychological magnification requires an active connecting of scenes*. The result of segregating scenes is disconnected islands of experience. Indeed in the interview with Lou Sander that occurred ten years after the twenty-five-year follow-up, Eric was *unable to produce any distinct memories of his mother*, e.g. he could remember getting hugged, but he could not connect it with any event or situation.

The turbulence she created produced a great uncertainty and ambivalence about the affective valence of any scene. *What Eric seems to have magnified out of all this turbulence is uncertainty.* This led to the creation of strategies that involve caution, delay, and vacillation until he can determine what kind of scene it is. In his early years we saw this caution and hesitancy at the clinic. In his adult TAT it shows up on several different cards as caution and indecisiveness, as he envisions a number of possibilities of what the scene is all about, and several possible things to do about it. Such responses are often seen as obsessional defenses or undoing. Here they provide a solution to his mother's turbulent interactive style, but once he has determined that a scene is good or safe, he can then enter it, take action, and work hard, as in the science lab, which he loves. Only when confronted with ambivalent scenes does he look obsessional. Here we see the usefulness of if-then propositions, as in dynamic systems thinking. *His action is conditional on the level of uncertainty in the scene and his ability to sort out what kind of scene it is.*

His father is far more consistent and effective as a disciplinarian, thus he is a more powerful source of fear and anger for Eric. Eric cannot successfully escape or counteract his father. *His efforts focused primarily on compliance toward his father and on the development of avoidance strategies, so characteristic of anti-toxic scripts*. Eric seems to have been deeply afraid of his father, but this fear was modulated in several ways. First of all, because the father's beatings and threats were so effective, he did not have to use them very often. Thus, overall, Eric probably received less aggression from his father than from his mother. Also, the more Eric succeeded in avoiding a beating, the more he could contain his fear. Second, his father was the source of several kinds of positive affect. He was invested in his son's future, he gave him positive goals of education and hard work, he provided counter-phobic instruction, and an ideology of relying on oneself. *These were not empathically attuned responses to Eric, but they were guidelines that Eric could use and identify with, so they seem to have moderated the indefinite growth of fear. They may have even protected Eric from being consciously aware of his fear of his father, for his fear seems to have taken more remote forms, such as the monsters of his childhood, or his inability to remember as an adult the beatings he received as a child.* Third, the father's illnesses undercut his image as a powerful and frightening figure, and suggested an image of an old, weak man who can be outwitted. *This latter image may have modulated both Eric's fear and his identification with his father.* For by early adulthood, Eric shows a grudging respect for his father, but rejects him as a figure for identification. He has surpassed his father. All of these factors would modify the dominance of the anti-toxic script and would leave room for other possibilities.

In conclusion, I have tried to demonstrate how Tomkins' script theory represents a conceptualization of rules, which can provide us with more precise and articulated ways of understanding the psychological dynamics in a case like Eric's; how his anti-toxic script, based on his fear and anger, was modified and how that enabled him to use the meager supports he received from his family to develop his capacities so successfully; and finally how idiosyncratic the formation of scripts can be. Other factors also contributed to his outcome, such as his high intelligence, his hardy constitution and his preference for action (as in his love of sports). These factors also play into his major symptom, namely test anxiety. In a test one has to sit still; tests also contain some uncertainty about contents and one's abilities, when combined with his investment in achievement, they evoke anxiety in him. Given the presence of other scripts in Eric's psychological organization, Tomkins' theory also suggests that in subsequent years this balance could shift, depending on what happens in the future and how those experiences are differentially magnified.

Final contact with Eric at age 35

The last contact with Eric was the interview with Lou Sander, when Eric was in his mid-thirties, which also involved another set of projective tests. We learn that Eric is now married and has a young daughter, and that his father had died a few months earlier. I listened to a tape recording of this interview, so after years of working on these data, I was able to hear Eric's voice for the first time. His voice is strong and steady, but it lacks affective modulation, except at two points in the interview. His voice softened when he spoke of his father's recent death, and it conveyed excitement when he talked about his future plans. There are many familiar themes in the content of the interview, yet there are also indications that he has moved slightly beyond where he was at our earlier assessment.

In the earlier assessment, Eric did not spontaneously speak about any people in his life. He had to be asked directly, and his responses were meager. In this interview he is a little more forthcoming. He can acknowledge some respect for his father, stating that his father did the best he could. He could also produce memories of his father, e.g. going to ball games, sitting at his feet while watching TV, and his father rubbing his head. Other than that, he does not remember much interaction in the family; he felt he was pretty much on his own. When asked about his wandering off, he said he has an image of himself sitting on a rock and crying, but he didn't know if he was just told about that. He said his father was the disciplinarian, and remembers only four or five times being hit with the leather strap – like the time when he broke a window. But his father was also the one who set goals for him, e.g. achieve in school and get a college education. By his high school years, he felt that both parents thought he was special, because he was smart. In high school, he said he hated making mistakes, "I was a perfectionist." But in college, the bar was higher; "I was caught by surprise." He said he adapted, and had to work a lot harder and had to accept that "he would not always score 100." As was stated earlier, *he had no distinct memories of his mother.* Now, when asked about her, there were long pauses in the tape. He remembered some hugs and some scolding but could not connect them to any events. He felt he could get away with things with her, but also felt she lied to him, which he did not like at all. The one clear memory he has of her is the time when she came home from the hospital with his younger brother. The meaning of this event for him is not explained.

What seemed new in this last tape is that he was acknowledging more affect. In the initial follow-up at age 25, he denied his brother's difficulties. Now he accepts them, and speaks of his worry about him. He said "his folks" didn't give his brother a goal like college, and made a lot of comparisons between to two of them. He wonders if his brother's behaviors were a backlash, causing him to feel that he had to be different. He talked about his anger at him as well as his unhappiness that his brother's behaviors had upset his parents.

He speaks for the first time about his own earlier experiences, namely the anxiety he felt at the beginning of junior high school. Would he be accepted by peers? He "didn't dress right" and was seen as a nerd or a fag, and was teased. His grades dropped and he fooled around a lot. But by the end of the year, through sports, he had made some friends, changed his style of dressing, and felt accepted. His father died a few months before this interview, and he acknowledged a sense of loss. He was surprised by this because he said they were not close emotionally, and also because his father had been ill for so long, but it was still a surprise. He remembered his parents fighting, and a lot of conflict every day, which made him feel anxious, and his father's temper got worse as he got older.

He is still married, although we know little about his relationship to his wife. He does not speak about her, and at both home visits, she was silent. Lou Sander felt no connection to her. Eric does speak of some enjoyment in parenting his one daughter, who was at that time 9 years old. He takes pride in her athletic activities and is able to enjoy some hugs with her, and says he would enjoy having another child, but at this time he said that feels selfish. Things are financially difficult now, but he hopes to have his own business some day, in the high-tech area; the exact product hasn't crystallized yet.

Thus, at least in his outward behavior Eric seems to have more capacity to talk about his family and to acknowledge some affect towards them. These may represent *islands of positive experience*, for there is little change in the projective testing material. The testing shows that he is still well defended against deeper anxieties, with stilted affect expression. He uses obsessional defenses, with constricted and isolated affect; the caution and vacillation are still there. He is mildly oppositional, and quite guarded around his aggression, e.g. it sneaks out in many places, and he is concerned about his masculinity. He also shows a trend toward suspiciousness, e.g. he fears sneak attacks (a residue from his mother's sneak attacks?). His primary defenses are undoing, reaction formation, devaluation, and idealization. Again, there are few human figures in the Rorschach and very little pairing. Rather he sees part object representations in isolation. Here are the segmented experiences of his earlier testings, which reduces their affective impact. On the male card, he manifests latent anxiety, provoking a longing for affection. Perhaps this reflects his ambivalence toward his father, which since his recent death, Eric seems to have more access to. The paucity of human figures is also seen in the Rorschach of psychopaths. What distinguishes Eric's responses from that of a psychopath is that there is evidence of anxiety around aggression and around longing for affection from a male.

On card 16 (the blank card) of the TAT, Eric initially makes a joke that, "This is a polar bear eating a marshmallow in the snow." He then says, "You can put anything you want in this. It's a totally blank slate." Finally, he says, "It's a pure white snowfield and sometime soon an animal is going to walk across it and mar it with its tracks." Perhaps this is the best statement of where Eric was in his life at that time. There were still indications of the anti-toxic script, namely in the avoidance of pairings, the isolation of affects, the isolation in the pure white snowfield and in the absence of human beings. Tomkins said, in my earlier consultation with him about Eric's CAT and TAT responses, that "Eric will live with trouble all his life." In this last response, in his mid-thirties, he seemed to be trying to allow for some liveliness to enter in the form of an animal that will walk across the snowfield. However, the result is that the snow will be marred by the animal's tracks. This has the feel of a typical decontamination script, which deals with enduring ambivalences and spoiling. Initially he described an idealized paradise, in which a bear, the animal he most wants to be, was eating a marshmallow alone in a snowfield, and where perhaps he could imagine finding peace, as an escape from his anxieties. But he ends with how this paradise has now become contaminated by some animal marring it with its tracks. A decontamination script would be the next step away from an anti-toxic script. So perhaps he has moved into a better place, but where he has not yet found a way to resolve his deep ambivalences.

Concluding comments

This chapter will summarize the ideas presented in the book. It begins with the various ways my early training in infancy has shaped my clinical perspective, with particular emphasis on the experience of "being with" the other, and my use of the acronym of AIM. It will then discuss the value of taking a biopsychosocial perspective, which involves adopting a dynamic systems perspective and the two most essential needs, namely for psychic coherence and being an active agent in our lives. I then review the capacities of the newborn infant, and earlier denials of such capacities, and the importance of taking a good history, and looking for islands of positive experience. I then focus on Tomkins' emphasis on the idiosyncratic process of making sense of one's experience, and use the example of why my patients ended up in the hospital when their siblings did not. I review the process of script formation, and describe the important advance in Tomkins' formulation of affects, his polarity theory, and his script theory, and the need to finally give up drive theory. I end by urging us to take a humanistic stance toward our patients and always ask ourselves: how is the patient right?

As stated in the Introduction, the organization of this book follows the evolution of my professional life which began with training in human development, followed by an immersion in Tomkins' affect theory, training in psychoanalysis, involvement in organizing the extensive early data from the Boston–Denver longitudinal study, interspersed with over forty years of clinical work in both child and adult hospitals and in private practice. After all these years I have come to believe that my deep understanding of the competence of the human neonate, who, as the result of our evolutionary history, is equipped with a highly complex brain and a readiness to enter into transactions with caregivers, has profoundly influenced my clinical work in several important ways.

First, I would suggest that the early mother–infant transactions, so beautifully described by Beebe, Lachmann, and Jaffe (1997) in which mother and infant jointly create experiences of "being with," can serve as a paradigm for what we are trying to achieve in our work with our patients. Sander (1995) describes such moments as "now moments" that involve specificities of timing and of affective matching, which when achieved create the vitalizing feeling of being known in the other. He describes working with a mother in the 1950s, a time when it was common to believe that infants could not see for many weeks after delivery. The mother reported that her baby had been eating and sleeping poorly and was crying a lot. During her description, Sander was holding the baby and trying to make eye contact. Then, as he describes, the following events happened. "Suddenly our eyes met. The infant threw out its arms, kicked out with both feet and broke into a beautiful engaging smile." The mother gasped in astonishment – "He can see!" she exclaimed. Sander said, "Oh yes, he sure can see." "Oh," she replied, "Now I know he will know who is being good to him." Sander then goes on to say that such a moment of specificity functions as "a window opening a new wholeness, a new inclusiveness of shared awareness: *a sense of being known*" (italics mine). In this instance, the being known refers both to the mother's experience of her infant and to the infant's experience of awareness of her. Sander reports that her baby's functioning improved markedly after this meeting. Other infant investigators have found that young infants choose to look at their mother's eyes. Haith, Bergman, and Moore (1977) reported that 4-week-old infants spent 30 percent of face-to-face time looking at their mother's eyes, and by 8 weeks of age they spent 60 percent of their time looking at their mother's eyes. Thus young infants are actively seeking eye-to-eye contact.

I have used the acronym AIM to describe such vitalizing moments of meeting from the infant's experience, which I described as an awareness, coming together in the infant's psyche of (1) an affect, (2) an intention to act in some way, and (3) mobilizing a response. I suggested that when a caregiver can respond at that specific moment with a specifically matched response, it creates the vitalizing experience of having the meaning of one's inner experience understood, as well as the success of having one's actions achieve a desired result. Such experiences lead to a trust of one's affects, which then supports the use of one's inner cues and understandings to guide one's behaviors and goals. Many of our patients have had too few experiences of such mutually shared vitalizing moments. As a result, they seem to have lost contact with the most vital parts of themselves, namely their own thoughts and feelings about events in their lives or in the world, and their own wishes and desires. Many have lost the belief that anyone would care enough to want to know about them and thus these vital, affectively powered inner cues have become deeply hidden. Or their experiences when alone or when with another have become too confusing and/or too terrifying and have been split off and become unavailable, and/or alien to them. In all of these cases, their emotionally vital inner cues no longer guide their thoughts, behaviors, and goals. Without such inner guidance, patients may feel lost without direction in their lives, or strive to please others, project their alien states onto others, or look to others for direction and goals, which may never feel like their own.

It is our job as clinicians, then, to create an atmosphere of attentive, non-judgmental safety that will slowly allow our patients to risk letting us know what has happened to them, the kinds of early socialization failures or hurts that have brought them to this point in their lives, and the resulting confusions and feelings that are going on inside of them. And through all of this we need to be alert to opportunities for joining in specific moments of "being with," which requires a specificity of both timing and a matching of affective tone. Only then will our patients begin to feel those vitalizing moments of being recognized and met and imagine that "maybe, just maybe, someone will finally value who I am and help me." Patients seem to know when and if someone is really listening and is willing to believe and to bear witness to the troubles that have been so deeply buried inside. We need to be prepared to listen, help them finds words, and be able to bear whatever they need to tell us, so that together, we can help them develop ways to work through their troubles.

When working with trauma, I as well as others believe the patient needs, when it feels safe in the room, to both feel the terror and to put their experience into words. Only then will they be able to integrate these experiences and to rejoin the larger human community through language. Such a process might entail the person writing out the details of their trauma, or even the therapist and patient jointly writing out what happened to them, little by little.

Another way in which my clinical work has been influenced by my history of training is the need to embrace a biopsychosocial perspective, which embodies a dynamic systems perspective. The two are intrinsically entwined. In our biological givens, we are all products of a long evolutionary history, which is the result of a continual dynamic process of reorganization in the face of changing environments. To repeat a basic evolutionary rule stated in the concluding remarks in Chapter 2: the more capable a species is in adulthood, the more capable is the newborn of the species. Every healthy newborn, therefore, has a highly complex human brain that begins even in utero to organize and reorganize its experience in the world. We share with all other animals the basic need for a coherent understanding of our world and the need to be active agents in meeting our needs. As humans we all go through several different phases of development, which require a continual dynamic process of reorganization, which both retains some continuity as well as transforms what went before.

This perspective became essential as I and several other infant researchers tried to deal with the data from the Boston–Denver longitudinal study. Sander's outline of issues that arise in the first three years of life, described in the first section of this book, helped us to understand the complexities of this process, and how difficult it was to project it into the future, while, by contrast, when looking backwards in time events can feel preordained. Sander's issues may help us locate the beginnings of some of the problems in a person's life, such as when mutuality may have broken down in the family. We need to be asking how well the family was able to continually adapt to the ever-growing initiatives of this new agent in their midst, as well as how the family responded to the affective expressions of the infant and the developing child. Tomkins' polarity theory is useful here, in asking was the socialization primarily accepting and humanistic or obedience-driven and normative? Equally important, we need to understand how the growing child was able to function and how each person made sense of what was happening to them and others in the family. I will come back to this issue below, when discussing script formation. Here we are in the realm of the psychic and social aspects of our existence.

This mutual adaptation begins early. No matter how well endowed, the infant is particularly vulnerable to overstimulation, a situation that if not contained, can interfere with the infant's ability to maintain coherent states. For example, if infants are left to cry for too long, more than just occasionally, they may develop a fault line in their psyches, which leaves them vulnerable to disorganization under stress later on. It has taken us a long time to understand the competence and sensory capabilities, as well as the limits of the self-regulatory capacities of the newborn. We saw with infants in institutions, in the 1950s, in which letting infants cry was a daily experience, how these infants seemed to shut down, and did not attach when later adopted. In first part of the twentieth century, when it was very difficult to determine the appropriate dosage of anesthesia for neonates, some doctors did not believe that infants experienced pain, and performed some medical procedures without anesthesia, ignoring the infant's cries. Even now some do not believe that infants experience affects directly, but need to see the affect reflected in the face of the caregiver before they can feel it (see Watson, 1994). These are extreme examples.

In other cases, mothers may be uncomfortable with infants, feeling anxious or reluctant to look directly into their eyes and create mutual gazing and smiling routines, as we saw in the longitudinal case of Cathy, in Chapter 3. In one of the longitudinal cases, the mother put her 3-month-old infant outside in a carriage, fearing she would become controlled by her infant. Eye-to-eye communication is powerfully intimate. Cathy's mother verbalized her discomfort by stating that Cathy was "bored" when Cathy looked into her face, suggesting the mother's sense of her own inadequacy at such times. This stood in stark contrast to the times when she was nursing Cathy, which she described at the most wonderful times they had together.

The lack of experiences of "being with" impoverishes the infant's inner life, creating future vulnerabilities, or, as in Cathy's case, an inability to self-sooth and achieve an inner coherence, an increasing passivity, and a decline in her agency. By contrast, a good beginning with responsive caregivers can become a source of an enlivening engagement with the world and resiliency in the face of later challenges.

Obtaining a detailed early history whenever possible can help assess a patient's strengths and vulnerabilities. This was easier to do while working in a hospital, where we could bring the family in and interview the parents. It is much harder to obtain when working with a patient, in private practice, but nevertheless, making the effort is always informative.

If early failures in interactive patterns continue and become strong enough, they often constrict later possibilities in the growing child, and thus become recognizable and open to rediscovery in therapy. Such people may present as deeply undeveloped without an awareness of their feelings or needs. Or they may have failed repeatedly in establishing relationships or in sustaining work situations. But, even when early interactive failures occur in the family, later opportunities in childhood can offer correctives, e.g. entrance into school, which may provide a gifted teacher who knows how to reach inhibited or troubled children, and/or interactions with a wider range of other children that provide new experiences or perspectives. Sullivan (1953) wrote about the possible corrective influence of school on a child's development, and as we saw in Eric's case in the previous chapter, entering school allowed him both to engage in team sports and to develop his mind, although the underlying anti-toxic script remained in place. Moving to a new town may also open up new possibilities and shift the dynamics in the family in a more favorable way. Erikson (1950) wrote about the impact of the larger social context on families or individuals, which included factors such as financial pressures, religious beliefs, and/or ethnic and racial prejudices. In one case that I treated, in which both the family and school atmospheres were quite difficult, contact with a neighbor opened up a kind and gentle world to this very sad little child. These encounters remained as islands of positive experiences in this deeply troubled person. Looking for such islands of positive experience can be helpful in assessing a person's capacity to make use of treatment.

Working in a children's mental hospital, which treated children from ages 6 to 12, taught me how important a regular, expectable environment can be in calming and in organizing a young child's psyche. Just providing three meals a day at a predictable time had a noticeable organizing effect. And when things began to get too overstimulating, providing non-punitive physical containment or some time-out in the quiet room, also helped these children stay organized and open to finding words, enabling them to continue to work on their issues. Again looking for regularities or helpful others in a patient's history can help assess areas of strength.

Adolescence is another huge dynamic shift, physically, psychologically, and socially. Mental capacities are expanding very rapidly during this period. Heavy drug use at this time usually indicates serious underlying vulnerabilities. Leaving home often occurs during this period as well, and offers a number of important challenges. How a person navigates this period can either enlarge his or her world, or reveal earlier fault lines and unresolved issues. As we saw in the case of Ms. L. in Chapter 7, the challenges in leaving home and entering college, revealed the flaws of the old strategies for coping, and caused things to come apart for this young woman. Often the first breakdown in functioning occurs in college, or when attempting to engage in a serious relationship, or in making a commitment to a career. Each of these steps forward will challenge whatever adaptation one has achieved up to that point. Healthy development involves a continual re-adaptation and growth. When that process gets stuck, some vitality is lost, but life may go on. If the early trouble is serious enough or a traumatic experience occurs, some kind of a breakdown is likely to occur, or suicide may become an option.

How young people deal with past troubles depends on how they function and make sense of their experiences in the family as well as in the world around them. When working at the Austen Riggs Center, we brought the whole family in as part of the initial evaluation process, and I often wondered why my patient ended up in the hospital when their siblings did not. Sitting with a family, one could feel the dominant defensive pattern in the family operating in the room, and how the patient's siblings all seemed to be able to adopt these same defenses. Why was my patient unable to do so? I came to believe that this person, and other hospitalized patients like them, were more deeply sensitive to the unspoken, underlying pain in the family, and/or were emotionally more attuned to, or identified with the hurt of one of the parents. But since no one else in the family seemed able to acknowledge the "problems," my patient's experience could not be validated within the family. Thus my patient could neither take on the defensive armor of the family, nor escape this intolerable situation; they began to doubt their reality, and had become disconnected from their inner vitality, which had made them ill and needing hospitalization. In terms of sensitivity, the analogy of the canary in the mine shaft who senses the lack of oxygen long before the miners, seems apt here. Or in the case of Ms. L., she alone among her siblings had been seduced into a special role in the family, which could no longer be sustained in the more challenging world of college.

This last example, of one sibling needing hospitalization while the other siblings were managing without such an intervention, as well as in the longitudinal case of Eric described earlier, are at the heart this important issue, namely *what sense does each child make of its environment.* It is here that Tomkins' affect theory, combined with his script theory, provides a systematic way of understanding individuality and the specificity of experience. In Tomkins' theory, any affective moment is brief and in order for it to become enduring and meaningful it must become linked to other moments *perceived by the individual* as similar, a process that Tomkins has called affect magnification, which leads to the formation of scripts that are time binding. "Any gratuity must be built upon to reward in the long run; any threat must be elaborated by further action to become traumatic" (Demos, 1995, p. 341). *Script formation is a very idiosyncratic process*, as was illustrated in the example of Laura, who had been hospitalized as a young child (described in Chapter 6) to illustrate the process of script formation. There was no way to predict what aspect of the changing scenes in her life would feel most affectively salient and linked and thereby become magnified. Just as in the case of Eric, whose childhood was filled with less than optimal events, we could not predict either his differential magnification of his experiences with his mother and his father or his outcome. Whereas in the case of my hospitalized patients, given their particular sensitivities, their experiences in their families were unique; either they were seduced into a special role, or they alone seemed to have magnified the unspoken pain, a sensitivity that isolated and confused them and made them ill.

I also want to emphasize the important contributions that Tomkins' affect theory, script theory, and polarity theory represent. His affect theory provides a clear and important distinction between the primary affects of enjoyment/joy and interest/excitement. Both are independent of sexual arousal or libido in the Freudian system. Interest/excitement is hardly neutral. It can be finely tuned in its motivating capacities and thereby is essential in sustaining any long-term engagement in endeavors of any kind. In the ebb and flow of such efforts it is often combined with enjoyment/joy, as one experiences moments of success. But enjoyment/joy, in its savoring responses, can also amplify a wide variety of more passive experiences and events, independent of physical contact. The developmental cases of Donna and Cathy, presented in Chapter 3, were chosen partially to illustrate the importance of the differential socialization of these two positive affects. By chance, the two families we contacted during the pregnancies of the mothers, and videotaped to help us develop categories for our analysis of the larger developmental study, turned out to provide several instructive contrasts. Though Cathy's family could not be defined as abusive or neglectful by any legal definition, yet this child's capacity for developing the two most important human essentials, namely her agency and her ability to achieve coherent states, were not being fostered. We do not know the later outcomes of these two young children, but the trends in their psychic development were moving in quite different directions during this period of their lives.

Tomkins has also understood shame differently, as the incomplete reduction of interest/excitement and thereby closely related to this positive affect. It is based on a deep wish to be reconnected with a valued other, thus it is an affiliative affect. He also argues that shyness, shame, and guilt are identical affects – shyness is about the strangeness of the other, shame is about inferiority, and guilt is about moral transgression, but the experience of a barrier to the continuation of interest/excitement is the same in all three situations. If one has not experienced valued positive connections with others, one will not experience shame at an interruption of a connection. We saw the absence of shame in Eric's responses, and the paucity of human figures in his projective tests. Thus shame is different from other negative affective responses, such as dissmell and disgust, both of which motivate the desire to distance oneself from the other, or anger, which might lead to an attack on others.

Tomkins' clear articulation of the characteristics of each of the negative affects of startle/surprise, distress/anguish, dissmell, disgust, anger/rage, and fear/terror is an important advance in our understanding of the distinct differences in these experiences, versus simply lumping them all together into a category of aversive, negative experiences, or simply as different forms of anxiety. Each of these distinct experiences in their moderate form contain important information, which can motivate a person to take some action to improve the situation. Tomkins' distinction between distress and fear is vitally important, and related to taking an evolutionary perspective. He argued that given our superior cognitive powers of anticipation, it was necessary to experience a less toxic, but still negative affect, in order to motivate humans to persist in solving important problems. Thus the capacity to bear suffering is an important asset, without it, the over use of substances becomes highly likely, leading to addictions. All the negative affects are an essential part of our evolutionary inheritance, thus the more articulate we can be about their distinctive characteristics, the greater the possibility of our finding ways to help our patients and to work constructively with them.

Tomkins' script theory can help us to be alert to the idiosyncratic ways that people have organized their experiences into affect-powered scripts. His studies of the gradual steps leading to addiction is one example of how mild discomfort can become magnified into an anti-toxic script driven by fear (see Tomkins, 1966, 1967, 1968). Clinically, the more we understand the different qualities and dangers of each negative affect as well as the idiosyncratic meanings they engender and the variety of ways they can be organized and manifested in more enduring scripts, the more effective we can be in our treatments. Most serious illnesses involve decontamination scripts or anti-toxic scripts, and may require hospitalization. If damage-reparation scripts powered by excessive shame have become problematic, and limitation-remediation scripts powered by distress are problematic, they can often be dealt with in outpatient therapy or analysis.

Tomkins' script theory is a major advance in our understanding of how personality develops over time. As Brewster Smith (1995) stated in the introduction of my edited volume of Tomkins' writings:

> It is based on human universals – the affects and the scripting process – but readily accommodates cultural and individual specificity of scenes and sequences. It therefore immediately escapes the culture – boundedness of all standard personality theories ... It is committed neither to unity nor to fragmentation in personality

> organization, neither to inner-directed nor to other-directed role – playing versions of personality. It is truly general in its applications and claims ... There are better and worse ways of being a person and Tomkins' theory can be articulate about them.
>
> (pp. 9–10)

This last statement, is directly related to Tomkins' polarity theory (see Chapter 5 of this volume), which evolved out of his study of ideology, and that embodies another major contribution by directing our attention to the importance of the socialization of affect in childhood. He described the differences in a humanistic socialization in which the child's affects are accepted, and guided toward understanding and solving problems, versus a normative socialization in which obedience to a norm of behavior is the highest priority. As Tomkins stated:

> The issues are simple enough. Is man the measure, and end in himself, an active, creative, thinking, desiring, loving force in nature? Or must man realize himself, attain his full stature only through struggle toward, participation in, conformity to a norm, a measure, an ideal essence basically prior to and independent of man?
>
> (Demos, 1995, p. 117)

This polarity is being played out every day in our homes, in our schools, in our national politics, and around the world. Tomkins was clearly a humanist. If we are to help our patients, we too must put understanding and helping above an obedience to any orthodoxy, and in each case we must always ask: *How is the patient right*? *What are they trying to tell us?* We must also accept theories that are in agreement with the latest findings of science, as well as be open to all new findings. Thus we must finally put drive theory to rest!

Lastly, Tomkins' script theory, with its emphasis on the role of the individual in perceiving the personal relevance of affective moments and magnifying their meaning by linking them together into scripts, makes it particularly compatible with the psychoanalytic method, which is designed to detect and uncover idiosyncratic meanings of psychic events and experiences. At long last we are now in the position to combine current neuroscience findings with Tomkins' contributions and fully embrace an affect theory of motivation. Perhaps many clinicians have already done so, but I hope, by presenting Tomkins' work in more detail, to enrich their understanding of specific affect dynamics, and how the formation of each script is both rule-bound and determined by idiosyncratic sensitivities and meanings. These processes begin early, so I also hope that the first part of this book, with its focus on: (1) the infant's capabilities and limitations; (2) the fate of the two biologically based priorities of life, namely maintaining psychic cohesion and being an active agent in effecting events; and (3) the socialization of affects in early childhood, will also enrich the clinician's understanding of the impact that these experiences may have on psychological development. Such understandings may not shorten the therapeutic process, indeed, I do not imagine there are any shortcuts to in-depth psychoanalytic explorations, but perhaps they might inform as well as influence the way one both listens to and responds to the patient's communications.

Afterword

It is necessary to respond to Ruth Leys' recent book entitled *The Ascent of Affect: Genealogy and Critique* (2017) in order to correct the many misunderstandings and distortions of Silvan Tomkins' theory of affect, and her dismissal of Panksepp's contributions in neuroscience as dealing with non-human animals, such as rats. Throughout her book, she presents issues in their most extreme form, such as affect is completely separate from cognition and the two systems do not interact, or that affect always requires cognition to be experienced, or that affect is only facial behavior, or that affect is determined by the situation and is cognitive through and through, or that affects are nonconscious, or that affect has no bearing on intentions, or that there can never be a disjunction between the "real" causes of affect and the individual's own interpretation of these causes, or if one considers affect represents a relative indifference to the role of ideas. Leys (2017) says:

> The fact that a novel or painting makes me feel or think a certain way may be a significant aspect of my response to the work, but simply as my response, it has no standing as an interpretation of it. (p. 323)

Clearly, for Leys (2017) cognition is the only source of meaning, and is therefore far more important. Here is her reading of Tomkins' and Ekman's Basic Emotion Theory and as adopted by Damasio:

> For them, the appeal of the Basic Emotion Theory is that it provided a picture of the emotions as inherently independent of intentions in that the affects are held to be a set of innate, automatically triggered brain-body behaviors and expression operating outside the domain of consciousness and intentional action.
>
> (p. 335)

Since none of these statements about Tomkins' Basic Emotion Theory are correct, one has to wonder if she has really read Tomkins' or Panksepp's work.

Tomkins has argued that human beings have evolved as a multi-mechanism organism comprised of the affect system, the sensory system, the memory system, the cognitive system, and the drive system. Each of these mechanisms contributes something unique and important to our functioning, and each is capable of acting *independently, dependently, and interdependently* with any or with all of them. Both Panksepp and Tomkins have argued that *affect is embodied and functions as an analogue.* Fifty years before Panksepp, Tomkins argued that affect functions as an *analogue amplifier* of differing patterns of stimulation impinging on the organism, and is comprised of a *correlated set of bodily responses that include facial muscles, vocal respiratory, blood flow changes and heightened skin receptivity and other autonomic responses*. The evolutionary value of these correlated responses in that they combine urgency, abstractness, and generality (e.g. a sense of "too much" or "too fast," or "just right"), which is experienced as a qualitative affect state, designed to both (1) capture consciousness, thereby causing the organism to care about what is happening, and with their specific qualitative valance to (2) inform the organism so as to fashion and facilitate a response.

Panksepp is clearly speaking of the human brain when he states that affects are represented in the brain including integrating primitive sub-limbic systems with limbic and higher-order systems, as well as hormonal parameters that modulate circuit sensitivities and forms of neuropeptidergic coding. He also organized a symposium involving psychoanalysts in order to inform them that there is nothing in the human brain that corresponds to Freud's notion of drives. The proceedings of this symposium were published in 1999 in the journal of *Neuropsychoanalysis* (Panksepp, 1999a, 1999b). I would urge Ruth Leys to read this article. Both Tomkins and Panksepp argue that *no effort can be sustained without the involvement of affects.*

Leys' heavy cognitive bias cannot account for the flexibility and complexity of what she calls the Basic Emotion Theory. If sometimes we are not aware of our "real" motives, for Leys that *must* mean that cognition is irrelevant. Again and again she presents either/or thinking. But if we were *always* aware of our real motives, the entire psychotherapeutic enterprise would never need to exist. Psychological defenses are necessary to protect us from knowing things we cannot bear to know because we do not know how to manage the affects that are involved. Such defenses can arise through the socialization of affects in families, so that some affects, such as distress and fear, particularly in young boys, or anger in either sex are not permitted expression and therefore have become unacceptable, alien psychic entities that have needed to become cut off from awareness. Tomkins wrote a lot about the differences between a normative socialization of affects, in which the highest priority is obedience to a norm and thus the child is required to stifle all other responses, versus a humanistic socialization of affects in which all affects are acceptable and the child is offered help and understanding to manage negative affects, which enhances the capacity in the child to suffer and endure difficulties. The United States is currently experiencing an epidemic in opioid addictions and suicides. Such addictions and solutions are efforts to escape unbearable affective states, such as PTSD, or content-less anxieties. Leys' heavily cognitive bias cannot account for such experiences. Tomkins also wrote a lot about ideology and supported it with research using his polarity scale, which demonstrated how these affective socializations create affect resonances toward a normative or a humanistic ideology (see Chapter 6 of this volume).

Also Leys' approach cannot account for infant behavior. The hungry neonate neither knows why he or she is in distress from the increased level of the ongoing stimulus of hunger that is amplified by the rhythmical cry of distress, nor does the infant know whether anyone will respond. *But the infant is aware of wanting this distressed state to end.* Without such an affect mechanism built into the human infant, which results in an auditory signal, the caregiver would not know when to feed or attend to the newborn. We could not have survived as a species without such a mechanism. After many repetitions of the caregiver responding in a timely manner, the infant will come to expect to be fed. But, even so the infant is not in control of the crying response when hungry, thus, in that sense it is not completely an intentional signal, but the infant clearly wants this state to end, even though it cannot regulate the intensity of the cry.

In my home observations of one infant–mother pair, when the child was 3 months old, and hungry, the mother had put her in an infant seat while she prepared dinner for the family. The infant began to cry in response to both her ongoing hunger and her no longer being held in her mother's arms. However she repeatedly alternated this basic distress cry with a brief angry, more intense "protest" cry, which was combined with a turn towards and a direct look at her mother, followed by a brief pause, as if waiting for a response, before she turned away and resumed her basic distress cry. This cycle was repeated several times. Her mother spoke to her throughout. Here is an example of an intentional protest cry. Also in both families that I observed and filmed in their homes, both infants when alone and mildly fussing, attempted to decrease their discomfort by distracting themselves by looking at a nearby object intently; thereby they both intentionally used the affect of interest to offset their mild distress. This was only a temporary solution, for as their distress increased they could no longer offset it. I have used the acronym AIM to describe the internal processes involved, namely that the infant will become aware of a distress affect state (A), will experience an intention to end it or decrease it (I), and will begin to mobilize a response (M). This represents the *dynamic coming together* within the infant's psyche of an optimal level of *affective arousal* with whatever *memory of past experiences* of connecting the antecedents and consequences of previous similar states of coherency, which results in the emergence of an *intention or a goal* and the *mobilizing of an action* to achieve that goal. There is no either/or to describe the internal processes involved, namely that the infant will become aware of a distress affect state (A), and will experience an intention to end it or decrease it.

Leys also only tells half the story of Tomkins' study of the recognition of facial expressions that was rejected by a leading psychological journal, which had claimed that the results were not significant, and his statement that it was rejected because of a heavily cognitive bias at that time. Her version is true as far as it goes. In fact Tomkins' study reported a highly significant finding of an intercorrelation of .86 between faces posed representing affects based on his theory and the judgments of untrained judges, and that this was the first such study ever to find such a consensus. Therefore the journal's rejection did indeed represent a cognitive bias. The study finally appeared in the journal *Perceptual and Motor Skills* (Tomkins & McCarter, 1964), which was an unlikely place to be read by psychologists. This article contains many insights about affects, and again I urge Leys to read it.

Leys' claim that the Basic Emotion Theory says that affect is *only* facial behavior is also false. Tomkins wrote that the face has priority over the visceral changes, which he said were important, but that he considered to be of secondary importance, because the facial response is faster, more precise, and both informs the person and is visible to others. Here in Tomkins' words is a fuller description of the relationship between the face and the viscera:

> We regard the relationship between the face the viscera as analogous to that between the fingers, forearm, upper arm, shoulders and body. The finger does not "express" what is in the forearm, or shoulder, or trunk. It rather leads than follows the movements in these organs to which it is an extension. Just as the fingers respond more rapidly, with both more precision and complexity than the grosser and slower moving arm to which they are attached, so the face expresses affect both to others and to the self via feedback, which is more rapid and more complex than any stimulation of which the slower moving visceral organs are capable. There is, further, a division of labor between the face and the inner organs of affective expression similar to that between the fingers and the arm. It is the very gross and slower moving characteristic of the inner organ system which provides the counterpoint for the melody expressed by the facial solo.
>
> (Tomkins & McCarter, 1964, p. 120)

In this same article Tomkins described the many possibilities that can result from the socialization of affect. He stated that the combinations of affect and the varieties of mixtures that can be learned are limitless. Parents use affects to socialize other affects. One can learn that one's excitement leads to parental shaming, or one's distress can lead to parental punishment, disappointment, or contempt, or if one's anger is punished, it will lead to fear. When any of these feelings are met with parental punishment or disapproval, Tomkins argues that the information from one's face will then be defended against and lost and the awareness of such expressions in others will also be defended against. In other words, "the skills of receiving and sending are intimately interdependent because the face one sees is not so different from the face one lives behind" (p. 130). The socialization of affects in childhood is where it all begins.

Leys is also probably not aware of the full story of Tomkins' involvement in Ekman's cross-cultural study of two tribes in New Guinea. Ekman had asked Tomkins to look only at the facial expressions of these two tribes to check on his own reading of these expressions, which might have been contaminated by the context in which he had seen them. Tomkins gave the same reading of the faces, and pointed out each clue on the face that led to his naming of each affect. Ekman then asked Tomkins what his impression of the two cultures was, and states that "he performed what seemed almost an act of magic" (Demos, 1995, p. 214). He described one group as "quite friendly," and the other as "explosive in anger, highly suspicious if not paranoid in character and homosexual." These were highly accurate descriptions of these two groups. This ability may have seemed like magic, but Tomkins was a master at reading faces and has argued that the history of our affective lives is written on our faces, because the most characteristic expressions will shape the muscles of our faces. He used to turn off the sound during political debates so as to see the rapid movement of affects as they flickered over the faces of the speakers. He could, in this way, more easily pick up a more positive affect, rapidly cover another more unacceptable affect, and could perceive the more habitual expression.

These are just a few of the examples to illustrate how inadequate, the either/or stance and purely cognitive/situational approach to our emotions is, and how out of sync it is with current neuroscience. Leys' distorted, false descriptions of both Tomkins' and Panksepp's work do her no credit.

Bibliography

Angyal, A. (1941). *Foundations for a Science of Personality*. New York: Commonwealth Fund.

Arlow, J. A. (1977). Affects and the psychoanalytic situation. *Journal of Psychoanalysis*, 58: 157–170.

Baillargeon, R. (1990). Young infants' physical knowledge. Paper presented at the 98th Annual Convention of the American Psychological Association, Boston, MA.

Balant, M. (1968). *The Basic Fault: Therapeutic Aspects of Regression*. London: Tavistock.

Beebe, B., Lachmann, F. M., & Jaffe, J. (1997). Mother–infant interaction structures and presymbolic self and object representations. *Psychoanalytic Dialogues*, 7: 133–182.

Begley, S. (2010). The depressing news about antidepressants. *Newsweek*, January 29.

Bentolila, D. (1996). The enigma of the death drive: A revisiting. *Psychoanalysis and Contemporary Thought*, 19(1): 9–11.

Berlyne, D. E. (1958). The present status of research on exploratory and related behavior. *Journal of Individual Psychology*, 14: 121–126.

Bertalanffy, L. von. (1952). *Problems of Life: An Evaluation of Modern Biological Thought*. London: Watts.

Bion, W. R. (1967). *Second Thoughts: Selected Papers on Psycho-Analysis*. London: William Heinemann Medical Books.

Blass, E. M. (2010). The ontogeny of human infant face recognition: Orogustatory, visual and social influences. In: *Early Social Cognition*, ed. P Rochat. New York: Psychology Press, pp. 35–65.

Blass, E. M., Ganchrow, J. R., & Steiner, J. E. (1984). Classical conditioning in newborn humans 2–48 hours of age. *Infant Behavior and Development*, 7: 223–235.

Blatt, S. (2004). Developmental origins (distal antecedents). In: *Experiences of Depression: Clinical and Research Perspectives*. Washington, DC: American Psychological Association, pp. 187–229. DevelDe

Boukydis, C. F. Z. (1979). Adult response to infant cries. Unpublished doctoral dissertation, Pennsylvania State University.

Boulanger, G. (2007). *Wounded by Reality: Understanding and Treating Adult-Onset Trauma*. New York: Analytic Press.

Bower, T. G. R. (1977). *A Primer of Infant Development.* San Francisco, CA: W. H. Freeman.

Bower, T. G. R. (1982). The origins of perception and cognition. Paper presented at the International Conference on Infant Studies, March, Austin, TX.

Bowlby, J. (1969). *Attachment.* New York: Basic Books.

Brazelton, T. B. (1973). *Neonatal Behavioral Assessment Scale.* Clinics in Developmental Medicine No. 50. London: William Heinemann Medical Books.

Brazelton, T. B., Koslowski, B., & Main, M. (1974). The origins of reciprocity: The early mother–infant interaction. In: *The Effect of the Infant on the Caregiver*, ed. M. Lewis & L. Rosenblum. New York: Wiley, pp. 49–76.

Brenner, C. (1974). On the nature and development of affects: A unified theory. *Psychoanalytic Quarterly*, 43: 532–566.

Brenner, C. (1980). Metapsychology and psychanalytic theory. *Psychoanalytic Quarterly*, 49: 189–214.

Broucek, F. (1979). Efficacy in infancy: A review of some experimental studies and their possible Implications for clinical theory. *International Journal of Psychoanalysis*, 60: 311–316.

Bruner, J. & Bruner, S. (1968). The growth and structure of skill. Paper presented at the CIBA conference, London, November.

Butler, R. A. & Harlow, H. F. (1957). Discrimination learning and learning sets to visual exploration incentives. *Journal of General Psychology*, 57: 257–264.

Cohn, J. & Tronick, E. (1988). Mother–infant face-to-face interaction: Influence is bidirectional and unrelated to periodic cycles in either partner's behavior. *Developmental Psychology*, 24(3): 386–392.

Compton, A. (1983a). The current state of the psychoanalytic theory of instinctual drives I: Drive concept, classification and development. *Psychoanalytic Quarterly*, 52: 364–402.

Compton, A. (1983b). The current state of the psychoanalytic theory of instinctual drives II: The relation of the drive concept to structures, regulatory principles and objects. *Psychoanalytic Quarterly*, 52: 402–426.

Damasio, A. R. (1994). *Decartes' Error.* New York: Putnam Press.

Darwin, C. (1872/1965). *The Expression of the Emotions in Man and Animals.* Chicago, IL: University of Chicago Press.

DeCasper, A. A. & Carstens, A. L. (1981). Contingencies of stimulation: Effects on learning and emotion in neonates. *Infant Behavior and Development*, 4: 19–35.

DeCasper, A. A. & Spense, M. (1986). Prenatal maternal speech influences newborns perceptions of speech sounds. *Infant Behavior and Development*, 9: 133–150.

Demos, E. V. (1982). Facial expressions of infants and toddlers: A descriptive analysis. In: *Emotion and Early Interaction*, ed. T. Field & A. Fogel. Hillsdale, NJ: Lawrence Erlbaum, pp. 105–112.

Demos, E. V. (1983). A perspective from infant research on affect and self-esteem. In: *The Development and Sustaining of Self-Esteem in Childhood*, ed. J. Mack & S. Ablon. New York: International Universities Press, pp. 45–78.

Demos, E. V. (1984). Empathy and affect: Reflections on infant experience. In: *Empathy*, vol. II, ed. J. Lichtenberg, M. Bornstein & D. Silver. Hillsdale, NJ: Analitic Press, pp. 9–34.

Demos, E. V. (1986). Crying in early infancy: An illustration of the motivational function of affect. In: *Affect and Early Infancy*, ed. T. B. Brazelton & M. W. Yogman. Norwood, NJ: Ablex, pp. 39–73.

Demos, E. V. (1988). Affect and the development of the self: A new frontier. In: *Progress in Self Psychology*, ed. A. Goldberg. Hillsdale, NJ: Analytic Press, pp. 27–53.
Demos, E. V. (1989). A prospective constructionist view of development. *Annual of Psychoanalysis*, 17: 287–308.
Demos, E. V. (1992). The early organization of the psyche. In: *Interface of Psychoanalysis and Psychology*, ed. J. W., Barron, M. N. Eagle & D. L. Wolitzky. Washington, DC: American Psychological Association, pp. 200–232.
Demos, E. V. (1993). Developmental foundations for the capacity for self-analysis: Parallels in the roles of care-giver and analyst. In: *Self-Analysis*, ed. J. W. Barron. Hillsdale, NJ: Analytic Press, pp. 5–27.
Demos, E. V. (ed.) (1995). *Exploring Affect: The Selected Writings of Silvan S. Tomkins*. Cambridge: Cambridge University Press.
Demos, E. V. (1998). Differentiating the repetition comopulsion from the trauma through the lens of Tomkins's scaript theory: A response to Russell. In: *Trauma, Repetition, and Affect Regulation: The Work of Paul Russell*, ed. J. G. Teicholz & D. Kriegman. New York: The Other Press.
Demos, E. V. (2001). Psychoanalysis and the human sciences: The limitation of cut-and-paste theorizing. *American Imago*, 58(3): 649–684.
Donaldson, M. (1977). *Children's Minds*. New York: W. W. Norton & Company.
Dunn, J. (1977). *Distress and Comfort*. Cambridge, MA: Harvard University Press.
Edelman, G. M. (1987). *Neural Darwinism*. New York: Basic Books.
Edelman, G. M. (1992). *Bright Air and Brilliant Fire: On the Matter of the Mind*. New York: Basic Books.
Edelman, G. M. (1998). Building a picture of the brain. *Daedalus*, 127: 37–70.
Erikson, E. (1950). *Childhood and Society*. New York: W. W. Norton & Company.
Erikson, E. (1964). Psychological reality and historical reality. In: *Insight and Responsibility*. New York: W.W. Norton & Company.
Ekman, P. (1972). Universal and cultural differences in expression of facial expression emotion. In: *Nebraska Symposium on Motivation*, vol. 19, ed. J. R. Cole. Lincoln, NE: University of Nebraska Press, pp. 207–283.
Ekman, P. (1990). Voluntary facial action generates emotion specific autonomic nervous system activity. *Psychophysiology*, 27: 363–383.
Ekman, P. & Frieson, W. V. (1975). *Unmasking the Face*. Englewood Cliffs, NJ: Prentice-Hall.
Ekman, P. & Frieson, W. V. (1978). *Manual for Facial Affect Coding System*. Palo Alto, CA: Consulting Psychologist Press.
Ekman, P., Levenson, R. W., & Frieson, W. V. (1983). Autonomic nervous system activity distinguishes among emotions. *Science*, 221: 1208–1210.
Elsner, R., Franklin, D. L., Van Citters, R. L., & Kenny, D. W. (1966). Cardiovascular defense against asphyxia. *Science*, 153: 941–949.
Fairbairn, W. R. D. (1952). *Psychoanalytic Studies of the Personality*. London: Routledge & Kegan Paul.
Field, T., Goldstein, S., & Guthertz, M. (1990). Behavior-state matching and synchrony in mother–infant interactions of depressed and nondepressed dyads. *Developmental Psychology*, 26: 7–14.
Field, T., Woodson, R., Greenberg, R., & Cohen, D. (1982). Discrimination and imitation of facial expressions by neonates. *Science*, 218: 179–181.

Fisher, K. W. & Pipp, S. L. (1984). Processes of cognitive development: Optimal level and skill acquisition. In: *Mechanisms of Cognitive Development*, ed. R. J. Sternberg. New York: Freeman Press, pp. 45–80.

Fogel, A. (1977). Temporal organization in mother–infant, face-to-face interactions. In: *Studies in Mother–Infant Interaction*, ed. R. Schaffer. London: Academic Press, pp. 119–151.

Fonagy, P. (1999). Points of contact and divergence between psychoanalytic and attachment theories: Is psychoanalytic theory truly different? *Psychoanalytic Inquiry*, 19: 448–480.

Fonagy, P. & Bateman, A. W. (2008). The development of borderline personality disorder: A metalizing model. *Journal of Personality Disorders*, 22: 4–21.

Fonagy, P. & Target, M. (2000). Playing with reality III: The persistence of dual psychic reality in borderline patients. *International Journal of Psychoanalysis*, 81: 853–873.

Fraiberg, S. (1982). Pathological defenses in infancy. *Psychoanalytic Quarterly*, 51: 612–635.

Freud, S. (1893/1966). *Some Points for a Comparative Study of Organic and Hysterical Motor Paralyses*, 2nd edition. London: Hogarth Press.

Freud, S. (1895/2001). Project for a scientific psychology. In: *The Standard Edition of the Complete Psychological Works of Sigmund Freud*, vol. 1, ed. J. Strachey. London: Vintage, pp. 283–387.

Freud, S. (1900/2001). The interpretation of dreams. In: *The Standard Edition of the Complete Psychological Works of Sigmund Freud*, vol. 5, ed. J. Strachey. part II. London: Vintage, pp. 339–622.

Freud, S. (1905/2001). Three essays on the theory of sexuality. In: *The Standard Edition of the Complete Psychological Works of Sigmund Freud*, vol. 7, ed. J. Strachey. London: Vintage, pp. 130–231.

Freud, S. (1915/2001). Instincts and their vicissitudes. In: *The Standard Edition of the Complete Psychological Works of Sigmund Freud*, vol. 14, ed. J. Strachey. London: Vintage, pp. 109–140.

Freud, S. (1920/2001). Beyond the pleasure principle. In: *The Standard Edition of the Complete Psychological Works of Sigmund Freud*, vol. 18, ed. J. Strachey. London: Vintage, pp. 1–64.

Freud, S. (1923/2001). The ego and the id. In: *The Standard Edition of the Complete Psychological Works of Sigmund Freud*, vol. 19, ed. J. Strachey. London: Vintage, pp. 12–59.

Freud, S. (1924/2001). The economic problem of masochism. In: *The Standard Edition of the Complete Psychological Works of Sigmund Freud*, vol. 19, ed. J. Strachey. London: Vintage, pp. 159–170.

Freud, S. (1926/2001). Inhibitions, symptoms and anxiety. In: *The Standard Edition of the Complete Psychological Works of Sigmund Freud*, vol. 20, ed. J. Strachey. London: Vintage, pp. 87–172.

Frodi, A. M. & Lamb, M. E. (1980). Child abusers' responses to infant smiles and cries. *Child Development*, 51: 238–241.

Galatzer-Levy, R. M. (2004). Chaotic possibilities. *International Journal of Psychoanalysis*, 85: 419–442.

Ghent, E. (2002). Wish, need, drive: Motive in the light of dynamic systems theory and Edelman's selectionist theory. *Psychoanalytic Dialogues*, 12: 763–808.

Gibson, E. J. (1969). *Principles of Perceptual Learning and Development.* New York: Appleton-Century-Crofts.

Gill, M. M. (1978). Freud's concepts of unconsciousness and the unconscious. In: *The Unconscious*, vol. 1, ed. A. S. Prangishvilli, A. E. Sherozia, & F. V. Bassin. Tbilisi: Metsniereba.

Gilligan, J. (2011). *Why Some Political Parties Are More Dangerous Than Others.* Cambridge: Polity Press.

Goldstein, J. (2007). Emergence and psychological morphogenesis. In: *Self-Organizing Complexity in Psychological Systems*, ed. C. Piers, J. P. Muller, & J. Brent. New York: Jason Aronson, pp. 111–133.

Goodwin, B. (1994). *How the Leopard Changes Its Spots: The Evolution of Complexity.* New York: Charles Scribner's Sons.

Green, A. (1977). Conceptions of affect. *International Journal of Psychoanalysis*, 58: 129–156.

Green, A. (1986). The dead mother. In: *On Private Experience.* London: Rebus, pp. 57–84.

Green, A. (1993). Two discussions of "The inner experience of the analyst" and a response from Theodore Jacobs. *International Journal of Psychoanalysis*, 74: 1131–1136.

Greenberg, J. (1991). *Oedipus and Beyond: A Clinical Theory.* Cambridge, MA: Harvard University Press.

Greenberg, J. & Cohen, R. L. (1982). Why justice? Normative and instrumental interpretations. In: *Equity and Justice in Social Behavior*, vol. 41. New York: Academic Press, pp. 437–469.

Grigsby, J. & Osuch, E. (2007). Neurodynamics, state, agency and psychological functioning. In: *Self-Organizing Complexity in Psychological Systems*, ed. C. Piers, J. P. Muller, & J. Brent. New York: Jason Aronson, pp. 37–81.

Gunner, M. (1992). Reactivity of the hypothalamic-pituitary-adrenocortical system to stressors in normal infants and children. *Pediatrics*, 90: 491–497.

Haith, M. M., Bergman, T. & Moore, M. K. (1977). Eye contact and face scanning in early infancy. *Science*, 198: 853–855.

Harlow, H. F. (1953). Mice, monkeys, men, and motives. *Psychological Review*, 60: 23–32.

Hartman, H. (1958). *Ego Psychology and the Problem of Adaptation.* Trans. David Rapaport, Monograph #1. New York: International Universities Press.

Hill, W. F. (1956). Activity as an autonomous drive. *Journal of Comparative and Physiological Psychology*, 49: 15–19.

Hillman, J. (1961). *Emotion: A Comprehensive Phenomenology of Theories and Their Meanings for Therapy.* Chicago, IL: Northwestern University Press.

Holt, R. R. (1976). Drive or wish? A reconsideration of the psychoanalytic theory of motivation. In: *Psychology versus Metapsychology: Psychoanalytic Essays in Memory of George S. Klein*, ed. M. M. Gill & P. S. Holzman. New York: International Universities Press, pp. 158–197.

Horn, D. & Waingrow, S. (1966, April). *Behavior and Attitudes Questionnaire.* Bethesda, MD: National Clearinghouse for Smoking and Health.

Izard, C. (1971). *The Face of Emotion.* New York: Appleton-Century-Crofts.

Kagan, J. (1981). *The Second Year: The Emergence of Self-Awareness.* Cambridge, MA: Harvard University Press.

Kagan, J. & Berkun, M. (1954). The reward value of running activity. *Journal of Comparative and Physiological Psychology*, 47: 108.

Kauffman, S. (1995). *At Home in the Universe: The Search for Laws of Self-Organization and Complexity*. New York: Oxford University Press.

Kelso, J. A. (1995). *Dynamic Patterns: The Self-Organization of Brain and Behavior*. Cambridge, MA: MIT Press.

Kernberg, O. (2009). The concept of the death drive: A clinical perspective. *International Journal of Psychoanalysis*, 90(1): 109–123.

Kernberg, O. (2011). *The Inseparable Nature of Love and Aggression: Clinical and Theoretical Perspectives*. Arlington, VA: American Psychiatric Press.

Klein, M. (1952/1975). Some theoretical conclusions regarding the emotional life of the infant. In: *The Writings of Melanie Klein*, vol. 3. London: Hogarth Press, pp. 61–93.

Kohut, H. (1971). *The Analysis of the Self*. New York: International University Press.

Kohut, H. (1977). *The Restoration of the Self*. New York: International University Press.

Kohut, H. (1984). *How Does Analysis Cure?* ed. A. Goldberg & P. Stepansky. Chicago, IL: University of Chicago Press.

Kohut, H. (1991). *The Search for Self*. Madison, CT: International University Press.

Kohut, H. (1996). *The Chicago Institute Lectures 1972–1976*, ed. M. Toupin & P. Toupin. Hillsdale, NJ: Analytic Press.

Lachmann, F. M. (2001). *Transforming Aggression: Psychotherapy with the Difficult-to-Treat Patient*. New York: Jason Aronson.

Lachmann, F. M. & Stolorow, R. S. (1980). The developmental significance of affective states: Implications for psychoanalytic treatment. *Annual of Psychoanalysis*, 8: 215–229.

Langsdorf, P., Izard, C. E., Rayias, M. & Hembee, E. A. (1983). Interest expression, visual fixation, and heart rate changes in 2- and 8-month-old infants. *Developmental Psychology*, 19: 373–386.

Langton, C. G. (1996). Artificial life. In: *The Philosophy of Artificial Life* ed. M. Boden. Oxford: Oxford University Press, pp. 39–94.

Lazar, R. & Erlich, S. (1996). Repetition compulsion: A reexamination of the concept and the phenomenon. *Psychoanalysis and Contemporary Thought*, 19(1): 29–55.

Lester, B. & Zeskind, P. (1982). A biological perspective on crying in early infancy. In: *Theory and Research in Behavioral Pediatrics*, vol. I, ed. H. E. Fitzgerald, B. M. Lester, & M. W. Yogman. New York: Plenum Press, pp. 133–180.

Leuba, C. (1955). Toward some integration of learning theories: The concept of optimal stimulation. *Psychological Reports*, 1: 27–33.

Levenson, R. S., Ekman, P., & Friesen, E. (1990). Voluntary facial action generates emotion-specific autonomic nervous system activity. *Psychophysiology*, 27: 363–384.

Levy, D. M. (1960). The infant's earliest memory of inoculation: A contribution to public health procedures. *Journal of Genetic Psychology*, 96: 3–46.

Lewis, M. & Brooks-Gunn, J. (1979). *Social Cognition and the Acquisition of Self*. New York: Plenum Press.

Lewkowicz, D. & Turkewitz, G. (1980). Cross-modal equivalence in early infancy: Audio-visual intensity matching. *Developmental Psychology*, 16: 597–607.

Leys, R. (2017). *The Ascent of Affect: Genealogy and Critique*. Chicago, IL: University of Chicago Press.

Lichtenberg, J. D. (1989). *Psychoanalysis and Motivation*. Hillsdale, NJ: Analytic Press.

Lichtenberg, J. D., Lachmann, F. M., & Fossage, J. L. (2011). *Psychoanalysis and Motivational Systems: A New Look*. New York: Routledge.

Lomax, A. (1968). *Folksong Style and Culture*. Washington, DC: American Association of the Advanced Sciences.

Mahler, M. S., Pine, F., & Bergman, A. (1975). *The Psychological Birth of the Human Infant*. New York: Basic Books.

Mandler, J. M. (1988). How to build a baby: On the development of an accessible representational system. *Cognitive Development*, 3: 113–136.

Martin, G. B. & Clark, R. D. (1982). Distress crying in neonates: Species and peer specificity. *Developmental Psychology*, 18(1): 3–9.

Melzoff, A. N. & Borton, W. (1979). Intermodal matching by human neonates. *Nature*, 282: 403–404.

Mitrani, A. L. (1995). Toward an understanding of unmentalized experience. *Psychoanalytic Quarterly*, 64(1): 68–112.

Modell, A. H. (2005). Emotional memory, metaphor and meaning. *Psychoanalytic Inquiry*, 25: 555–568.

Montgomery, K. C. (1954). The role of the exploratory drive in learning. *Journal of Comparative and Physiological Psychology*, 48: 132–136.

Moruzzi, G. & Magoun, H. W. (1949). Brain stem reticular formation and activation of the EEG. *Electroencephalography and Clinical Neurophysiology*, 1: 455–473.

Myers, A. K. & Miller, N. E. (1954). Failure to find a learned drive based on hunger: Evidence for learning motivated by "exploration." *Journal of Comparative and Physiological Psychology*, 47: 428–436.

Nesbitt, M. D. (1959). *Friendship, Love, and Values: A Technical Report* (Research Bulletin for Project on "Mathematical Techniques in Psychology"). Princeton, NJ: Princeton University and Educational Testing Service.

Noy, P. (1969). A revision of the psychoanalytic theory of the primary process. *International Journal of Psychoanalysis*, 50: 155–178.

Ornstein, A. (1974). Defense organizations, transference interpretations and reconstruction. *Annual of Psychoanalysis*, 2: 231–248.

Ornstein, A. (1991). Self–object transferences, intersubjectivity, and countertranference. *Progress in Self Psychology*, 7: 93–99.

Ornstein, A. (1998). Response to the discussants: The fate of narcissistic rage in psychotherapy. In: *Psychoanalytic Versions of the Human Condition*. New York: New York University Press, pp. 107–119.

Ornstein, P. H. (1985). *Self-Psychology and the Humanities*. New York: W. W. Norton & Company.

Ornstein, P. H. & Ornstein, A. (1993). Assertiveness, anger, rage, and destructive aggression: A perspective from the treatment process. *Rage, Power, and Aggression*, 2: 102.

Oster, H. (1978). Facial expression and affect development. In: *The Development of Affect*, ed. M. Lewis & L. A. Rosenblum. Hillsdale, NJ: Lawrence Erlbaum, pp. 43–75.

Little, W., Fowler, H. W., & Coulson, J. (1955). *Oxford English Universal Dictionary*, edition, ed. C. T. Onions. Oxford: Oxford University Press.

Panksepp, J. (1998). *Affective Neuroscience: The Foundations of Human and Animal Emotions*. New York: Oxford University Press.

Panksepp, J. (1999a). Emotions as viewed by psychoanalysis and neuroscience: An exercise in consilience. *Neuropsychoanalysis*, 1(1): 15–38.

Panksepp, J. (1999b). Drives, affects, id energies and the neuroscience of emotions: Response to commentaries. *Neuropsychoanalysis*, 1(1): 69–89.

Panksepp, J. (2001). The long-term psychobiological consequences of infant emotions: Prescriptions for the twenty-first century. *Neuropsychoanalysis*, 3(2): 149–178.

Papousek, H. & Papousek, M. (1975). Cognitive aspects of preverbal social interaction between human infants and adults. In: *Ciba Foundation Symposium in Patent–Infant Interaction*. New York: Association of Scientific Publishers.

Papousek, H. & Papousek, M. (1979). Early ontogeny of human social interaction: Its biological roots and social dimensions. In: *Human Ethology: Claims and Limits of a New Discipline*, ed. M. von Cranach, K. Foppa, W. Lepenies, & D. Ploog. Cambridge: Cambridge University Press, pp. 456–478.

Papousek, H., Papousek, M., & O'Connor. (1975b). *Parent–Infant Interaction*. New York: Associated Science.

Papousek, H., Papousek, M. & Koester, L. S. (1986). Sharing emotionality and sharing knowledge: A microanalytic approach to parent–infant communication. In: *Measuring Emotions in Infants and Children*, vol. 2, ed. C. Izard & P. Read. Cambridge: Cambridge University Press, pp. 93–123.

Parens, H. (1979). Developmental considerations of ambivalence: An exploration of the relations of instinctual drives and the symbiosis–separation–individuation process. *The Psychoanalytic Study of the Child*, 34: 385–420.

Penfield, W. (1975). *The Mystery of the Mind: A Critical Study of Consciousness and the Human Brain*. Princeton, NJ: Princeton University Press.

Penfield, W. & Jasper, H. (1954). *Epilepsy and the Functional Anatomy of the Human Brain*. Oxford: Little & Brown.

Piaget, J. (1967). The mental development of the child. In: *Six Psychological Studies*. New York: Random House, pp. 3–73.

Porges, S. W. (1992). Vagal tone: A physiological marker of stress vulnerability. *Pediatrics*, 90: 498–504.

Provence, S. & Lipton, R. C. (1962). *Infants in Institutions*. New York: International Universities Press.

Rangell, L. (1967). Psychoanalysis, affects, and the "human core." On the relationship of psychoanalysis to the behavioral sciences. *Pyschoanalytic Quarterly*, 36: 172–202.

Rapaport, D. (1960). On the psychoanalytic theory of motivation. In: *The Nebraska Symposium on Motivation*, ed. M. R. Jones. Lincoln, NE: University of Nebraska Press, pp. 173–247.

Sanday, P. R. (1981). *Female Power and Male Dominance*. Cambridge: Cambridge University Press.

Sander, L. (1965). Interactions of recognition and developmental processes of the second eighteen months of life. Paper presented at Tufts University Medical School, Boston, MA.

Sander, L. (1969). Regulation and organization in the early infant–caregiver system. In: *Brain and Early Behavior*, vol. 1, ed. R. J. Robinson. New York: Academic Press, pp. 311–332.

Sander, L. (1975). Infant and the caretaking environment: Investigation and conceptualization of adaptive behavior a system of increasing complexity. In: *Explorations in Child Psychiatry*, ed. E. J. Anthony. New York: Plenum Press, pp. 129–166.

Sander, L. (1982). The inner experience of the infant: A framework for inference relevant to development of the sense of self. Paper presented at the 13th Margaret Mahler Symposium, Philadelphia.

Sander, L. (1985). Toward a logic of organization in psychologic development. In: *Biologic Response Cycles: Clinical Implications*, ed. H. Klar & L. Siever. Washington, DC: American Psychiatric Press, pp. 19–37.

Sander, L. (1992). Recognition process: Organization and specificity in early development: A perspective on developmental process. Morton Levitt Memorial Lecture, University of California, Davis, April 21.

Sander, L. (1995). Identity and the experience of specificity in a process of recognition. *Psychoanalytic Dialogues*, 5(4): 579–593.

Schachter, S. & Singer, J. (1962). Cognitive, social, and physiological determinants of emotional state. *Psychological Review*, 69: 379–399.

Schaffer, H. R. & Emerson, P. E. (1964). The development of social attachment in infancy. *Monograph of the Society for Research in Child Development*, 29(3): 1–77.

Schwaber, E. A. (1981). Empathy: A mode of analytic listening. *Psychoanalytic Inquiry*, 1: 357–392.

Schwaber, E. A. (1992). Psychoanalytic theory and its relation to clinical work. *Journal of the American Psychoanalytic Association*, 40: 1039–1057.

Shapiro, D. (2000). *Dynamics of Character: Self-Regulation in Psychopathology*. New York: Basic Books.

Shay, J. (1994). *Achilles in Vietnam*. New York: Athenaeum Books/Simon & Schuster.

Shedler, J. (2010). The efficacy of psychodynamic psychotherapy. *American Psychologist*, 65(2): 98–109.

Shengold, L. (1989). *Soul Murder: The Effects of Child Abuse and Deprivation*. New Haven, CT: Hale University Press.

Smith, B. (1995). Introduction. In: *Exploring Affect: The Selected Writings of Silvan Tomkins*, ed. E. Virginia Demos. Cambridge: Cambridge University Press, pp. 1–12.

Solms, M. & Panksepp, J. (2010). Why depression feels so bad. In: *New Horizons in the Neurosciences of Consciousness*, ed. E. K. Perry, D. Collerton, F. E. N. LeBeau, & H. Ashton, Amsterdam: John Benjamins, pp. 169–178.

Solms, M. & Panksepp, J. (2012). The id knows more than the ego admits: Neuropsychoanalytic and primal consciousness perspectives on the interface between affective and cognitive neuroscience. *Brain Science*, 2: 147–175.

Spelke, E. (1976). Infants' intermodal perception of events. *Cognitive Psychology*, 8(4): 553–560.

Spelke, E. S. (1979). Perceiving bimodally specified events in infancy. *Developmental Psychology*, 15: 626–636.

Spelke, E. & Owsley, C. J. (1979). Intermodal exploration and knowledge in infancy. *Infant Behavior and Development*, 2: 13–27.

Sprague, J. M., Chambers, W. W., & Stellar, E. (1961). Attentive, affective and adaptive behavior in the cat. *Science*, 33: 165–173.

Stern, D. (1977). *The First Relationship*. Cambridge, MA: Harvard University Press.

Stern, D. (1983). The early development of schemas of self, other and "self with other". In: *Reflections on Self Psychology*, ed. J. Lichtenberg & S. Kaplan. Hillsdale, NJ: Analytic Press, pp. 49–84.

Stern, D. (1985). *The Interpersonal of the Infant*. New York: Basic Books.

Stern, D. (1988). Affect in the context of the infanat's lived experience: Some considerations. *International Journal of Psychoanalysis*, 69: 233–238.

Stolorow, R. D. & Atwood, G. E. (1992). *The Context of Being: The Intersubjective Foundations of Psychological Life*. Hillsdale, NJ: Analytic Press.
Stolorow, R. D. & Lachmann, F. M. (1980). *Psychoanalysis of Developmental Arrests*. Madison, CT: International University Press.
Sullivan, H. S. (1953). *The Interpersonal Theory of Psychiatry*. New York: Norton.
Thelen, E. (1984). Learning to walk: Ecological demands and phylogenetic constraints. In: *Advances in Infancy Research*, vol. 3, ed. L. P. Lipsett. Norwood, NJ: Ablex, pp. 213–250.
Thelen, E. (1986). Treadmill-elicited stepping in seven-month-old infants. *Child Development*, 54: 1498–1506.
Thelen, E., Corbetta, D., Kamm, K., Spencer, J. P., Schneider, K., & Zernicke, R. F. (1993). The transition to reaching: Mapping intention and intrinsic dynamics. *Child Development*, 64: 1058–1098.
Thelen, E. & Smith, L. B. (1994). *A Dynamic Systems Approach to the Development of Cognition and Action*. Cambridge, MA: MIT Press.
Thelen, E., Ulrich, B. & Niles, D. (1987). Bilateral co-ordination in human infants: Stepping on a splitbelt treadmill. *Journal of Experimental Psychology: Human Perception and Performance*, 13: 404–410.
Thomas, A. & Chess, S. (1977). *Temperament and Development*. New York: Brunner/Mazel.
Tomkins, S. S. (1962). *Affect, Imagery, Consciousness, Vol. I: The Positive Affects*. New York: Springer.
Tomkins, S. S. (1963a). *Affect, Imagery, Consciousness, Vol. II: The Negative Affects*. New York: Springer.
Tomkins, S. S. (1963b). The right and the left: A basic dimension of ideology and personality. In: *The Study of Lives*, ed. R. W. White. New York: Atherton, pp. 389–411.
Tomkins, S. S. (1966). Psychological model for smoking behavior. *American Journal of Public Health*, 56: 17–20.
Tomkins, S. S. (1967). The psychology of smoking. *Psychology Quarterly*, 2(3): 11–13.
Tomkins, S. S. (1968). Affects: Primary motives in man. *Humanities*, 3: 321–346.
Tomkins, S. S. (1978). Script theory: Differential magnification of affects. In: *Nebraska Symposium on Motivation*, vol. 26, ed. H. E. Howe, Jr. & R. A. Dienstbier. New York: Springer, pp. 201–236.
Tomkins, S. S. (1981). The quest for primary motives: Biography and autobiography of an idea. *Journal of Personality and Social Psychology*, 41(2): 306–329.
Tomkins, S. S. (1987). Script theory. In: *The Emergence of Personality*, ed. J. Arnoff, A. J. Rabin & R. A. Zucker. New York: Springer, pp. 147–236.
Tomkins, S. S. (1990). Inverse archaeology: Facial affect and the interfaces of script within and between persons. Plenary address given at the annual meeting of the International Society for Research on Emotions on July 15, 1990, Rutgers University.
Tomkins, S. S. (1991). *Affect, Imagery, Consciousness, Vol. III: The Negative Affects: Anger and Fear*. New York: Springer.
Tomkins, S. S. (1992). *Affect, Imagery, Consciousness, Vol. IV: Cognition: Duplication and Transformation of Information*. New York: Springer.
Tomkins, S. S. (1995). The socialization of affect and the resultant ideo-affective postures which evoke resonance to the ideological polarity. In: *Exploring Affect: The Selected*

Writings of Silvan S. Tomkins, ed. E. Virginia Demos. Cambridge: Cambridge University Press, pp. 168–195.

Tomkins, S. S. & McCarter R. (1964). What and where are the primary affects? Some evidence for a theory. *Perceptual and Motor Skills*, 18: 119–158.

Tomkins, S. S. & Minor, J. B. (1957). *The Tomkins–Horn Arrangement Test.* New York: Springer.

Tomkins, S. S. & Tomkins, E. J. (1946). *The Thematic Apperception Test.* New York: Grune.

Tronick, E. (1989). Emotions and emotional communication in infants. *American Psychologist*, 44: 112–119.

Vasquez, J. (1975). The face and ideology. Unpublished doctoral dissertation, Rutgers University.

Von Bertalanffy, L. (1952). *Problems of Life*. New York: Harpers.

Watson, J. S. (1966). The development and generalization of "contingency awareness" in early infancy: Some hypotheses. *Merrill-Palmer Quarterly of Behavior and Development*, 12: 123–135.

Watson, J. S. (1972). Smiling, cooing and "the game" *Merrill-Palmer Quarterly of Behavior and Development*, 18: 323–339.

Watson, J. S. (1994). Detection of self: The perfect algorithm. In: *Self-Awareness in Animals and Humans: Developmental Perspectives*. New York: Cambridge University Press, pp. 131–148.

Werner, H. (1957). *Comparative Psychology of Mental Development.* New York: International Universities Press.

Westen, D. (1979). Towards a clinically and empirically sound theory of motivation. *International Journal of Psycho-Analysis*, 78: 521–548.

White, R. W. (1959). Motivation reconsidered: The concept of competence. *Psychological Review*, 66(5): 297–333.

Wiener, N. (1960). Some moral and technical consequences of automation. *Science*, 131: 1355–1358.

Wiesenfeld, A. R., Malatesta, C. Z., & DeLoach, L. L. (1981). Differential parental response to familiar and unfamiliar infant distress signals. *Infant Behavior and Development*, 4: 281–295.

Wilson, A. & Malatesta, C. (1989). Affect and the compulsion to repeat: Freud's repetition compulsion revisited. *Psychoanalysis and Contemporary Thought*, 12(2): 265–312.

Winnicott, A. (1960/1965). Ego distortion in terms of false and true self. In: *Maturational Processes and the Facilitating Environment.* New York: International Universities Press, pp. 140–152.

Winnicott, D. (1965). *The Maturational Processes and the Facilitating Environment.* New York: International Universities Press.

Winnicott, D. (1966). Letter to Lili E. Peller, 15th April. In: *The Spontaneous Gesture: Selected Letters of D. W. Winnicott*, ed. F. R. Rodman. Cambridge, MA: Harvard University Press.

Winnicott, D. (1971). *Playing and Reality.* London: Tavistock.

Wolff, P. (1963). Observations on the early development of smiling. In: *Determinants of Infant Behavior*, vol. 2, ed. B. M. Foss. Methuen: London, pp. 113–134.

Wolff, P. (1965). The development of attention in young infants. *Annals of the New York Academy of Sciences*, 118: 815–830.

Wolff, P. (1969). The natural history of crying and other vocalizations in early infants. In: *Determinants of Infant Behavior*, vol. 2, ed. B. M. Foss. London: Methuen, pp. 81–109.

Wolff, P. (1973). Organization of behavior in the first three months of life. *Association for Research on Nervous and Mental Disorders*, 51: 132–153.

Wolff, P. (1987). *The Development of Behavioral States and the Expression of Emotions in Early Infancy: New Proposals for Investigation*. Chicago, IL: University of Chicago Press.

Yorke, C. (1999). Affects, psychoanalysis, and neuroscience. *Neuropsychoanalysis*, 1(1): 60–69.

Zimbardo, P. G. & Miller, N. E. (1958). Facilitation of exploration by hunger in rats. *Journal of Comparative and Physiological Psychology*, 51: 43–46.

Index

For Product Safety Concerns and Information please contact our EU
representative GPSR@taylorandfrancis.com
Taylor & Francis Verlag GmbH, Kaufingerstraße 24, 80331 München, Germany

www.ingramcontent.com/pod-product-compliance
Ingram Content Group UK Ltd.
Pitfield, Milton Keynes, MK11 3LW, UK
UKHW022218190926
475702UK00003B/426

9780415886499